Advance Praise

"Dr. Laurel Parnell played a massive role in helping me find my voice as an EMDR therapist, and I continue to be inspired by our early conversations on expanding the possibilities of EMDR-related interventions. In her latest offering, Parnell adds her perspective to a growing collection of EMDR-related interventions on a topic that is near and dear to my heart, addiction recovery. Clinicians and human services workers with a passion for healing the suffering caused by and connected to addiction receive plenty of new ideas for working with clients, especially in the area of resourcing. You can never have too many strategies for helping individuals struggling with chemical dependency, process addictions, and co-dependency issues. I am grateful to Parnell for offering her unique perspective on how to resource this work, which I know is near and dear to her heart as well."

—Jamie Marich, Ph.D., Founder, The Institute for Creative Mindfulness, coauthor of *EMDR Therapy and Mindfulness for Trauma-focused Care;* author of *EMDR Made Simple, Trauma and the Twelve Steps, Trauma Made Simple, Dancing Mindfulness*

"Dr. Laurel Parnell has written a landmark book which is a must-read for anyone struggling with substance abuse and/or addictive behaviors and for the people who support and counsel them. *Rewiring the Addicted Brain with EMDR-Based Treatment* provides a nuanced, compassionate and client-centered approach to treatment. Parnell focuses on enhancing resilience, healing attachment wounds, and trauma reprocessing. Her Resource Tapping techniques build new neural circuitry that supports resilience and an integrated shift towards health and wholeness."

—Kim Cookson, Psy.D., Director of Trauma and Resiliency Training and Services Southern California Counseling Center

"Since its introduction in 2013, I have used Parnell's Attachment-Focused EMDR in my work with persons, both inpatient and outpatient, who are stuck in life with destructive behaviors that are driven by addiction. In the complex addiction cases that I work with, Parnell's work has provided a clinical framework that functions to reprocess traumas that drive addictive behavior and help the individual stop their addictive behaviors by building stronger internal resources. These new internal resources allow the addicted individual to have more mature and healthy coping strategies in response to life stress, along with adaptive behavioral responses that help to rewire those dysfunctional neural circuitries that underlie and perpetuate their addictive behavior. In her latest work, *Rewiring the Addicted Brain with EMDR-Based Treatment*, Parnell shows how to use Resource Tapping, EMDR, and her new 'Connecting the Consequences' protocol to help addicted persons be successful in their efforts to develop a life free of addiction. Parnell's work is an invaluable resource for anyone who works with people who are impacted by addiction. For the professional clinician, this work provides the tool that will help you help your clients develop life changing internal capacities and skills, allowing them to live a life free of addiction. I recommend it highly."

—Roy A. Blankenship, M.A., LPC, LMFT, CSAT, CAADC, Chief Executive
Officer, HopeQuest Addiction Recovery Center, Woodstock, GA

"Dr. Parnell's work is at once brilliant and simple, deep yet accessible, validating of the destructive nature of trauma and hopeful of one's ability to completely heal. With compassion, attunement, and intelligence, Dr. Parnell guides therapists of all levels through reparative techniques that address many layers involved in healing; from core trauma to consequential addictive behaviors to enhancement of self-esteem, resilience, and reduction of shame. As an eating disorder specialist practicing for 26 years, I applaud Dr. Parnell's original and creative use of AF-EMDR, Resource Tapping, and the reparative, healing therapeutic relationship to effectively bring clients into full and joyous recovery!"

—Julie T. Anné, Ph.D., Licensed Psychologist and Eating Disorder
Specialist, A New Beginning / TheHealthyWeighOut

REWIRING THE ADDICTED BRAIN WITH EMDR-BASED TREATMENT

REWIRING THE ADDICTED BRAIN WITH EMDR-BASED TREATMENT

Laurel Parnell

W. W. NORTON & COMPANY
Independent Publishers Since 1923

For information about permission to reproduce selections from this book, write to Permissions, W. W. Norton & Company, Inc., 500 Fifth Avenue, New York, NY 10110

For information about special discounts for bulk purchases, please contact
W. W. Norton Special Sales at specialsales@wwnorton.com or 800-233-4830

Manufacturing by Lakeside Book Company
Production manager: Katelyn MacKenzie

ISBN: 978-0-393-71423-4 (pbk.)

W. W. Norton & Company, Inc., 500 Fifth Avenue, New York, NY 10110
www.wwnorton.com

W. W. Norton & Company Ltd., 15 Carlisle Street, London W1D 3BS

1 0 9 8 7 6 5 4 3

To all those who are struggling with addictions and addictive behaviors,

and to their family members and friends.

Contents

Introduction

Why do you stay in prison when the door is so wide open?
—RUMI

I have spent my 30-year career as a clinical psychologist working with people who have experienced trauma. I have worked in clinics serving low-income children, youth, and adults, as well as in private practice, treating clients with a range of presenting problems. I have trained thousands of therapists worldwide in the trauma therapy, Eye Movement Desensitization and Reprocessing (EMDR) and provided consultation on thousands of cases.

Through all my work with traumatized people, I have noted the co-occurrence of trauma and substance use and abuse and addictive disorders. I have seen how people who have experienced trauma from abuse, neglect, poverty, divorce, loss, and discrimination often turn to substances or behaviors to help manage unmanageable feelings. People raised in unstable families where parents or caregivers struggle with addiction or trauma may not have their early attachment needs met in a way that allows them to develop a secure sense of self and the capacity to soothe themselves when distressed. As they grow into adolescence or early adulthood and discover that substances or behaviors provide short-term symptom relief, they fall into addictive patterns.

Addiction can also develop in people without histories of trauma. They may have a genetic vulnerability or become addicted to a medication originally prescribed for pain or attention deficit disorder.

Effective treatment of addiction requires a holistic approach that takes into consideration its underlying causes and current behaviors and patterns. Techniques to aid in emotional regulation as well as attachment repair are required. Methods derived from what I call *Attachment-Focused EMDR* and *Resource*

Tapping can yield excellent results in a milieu that has proven very difficult to treat with more traditional approaches.

WHY THE NEED FOR THIS BOOK?

Most of us in the United States have friends or family members who struggle with addictions or addictive disorders. Some of us may struggle with such addictions ourselves. The pain and impact of these disorders is tremendous. Over the years, I have been frustrated with what I have observed to be a limited approach to the treatment of addictions that does not adequately take into consideration the complexity of each person's situation and the drivers for their behaviors. In my opinion, addiction treatment's one-size-fits-all approach has not kept up with what we know about addiction itself, or what we know about brain science, trauma, and disordered attachment.

Rewiring the Addicted Brain with EMDR-Based Treatment is my attempt to create a brain-wise, compassionate, resilience-supporting approach to the treatment of addictions that I wish my family members and all others struggling with addictions could access. Therapists and substance abuse counselors can use this as a guidebook to help them navigate the difficult and complex terrain of addiction treatment—one that recognizes and addresses trauma and integrates repair of attachment deficits. With this guidance, I believe many more people can be effectively helped and can then go on to live fuller, more fulfilled lives.

Because I wanted to reach as large a group of therapists as possible, I chose to write a book that is not primarily for EMDR-trained clinicians. This book was written for therapists, substance abuse counselors, and laypeople seeking user-friendly tools to help support themselves in recovery. It is full of EMDR-based techniques that can be easily integrated into all levels of addiction treatment.

Distinctions: EMDR and Resource Tapping

EMDR is a powerful trauma therapy that is only taught to licensed mental health practitioners. It can open up deep emotions and dissociated early memories for which clinical experience and advanced skills and training are required. Most of the counselors working in the field of substance abuse are not licensed mental health professionals and so would not qualify to be trained in EMDR.

Many EMDR-trained therapists have found that an EMDR-related technique called Resource Tapping can be helpful in the treatment of addictive disorders. These therapists who use Resource Tapping report reductions in their clients' craving for substances and their anxiety levels, in addition to an increase in self-esteem—even without the use of EMDR to reprocess the traumas. In many cases, the therapists never needed to employ the more intensive and demanding EMDR trauma-processing work, as the client's symptoms cleared with the use of Resource Tapping alone. I wrote *Tapping In* to support non-EMDR therapists and laypeople in using this simple technique.

Though this book focuses primarily on integrating Resource Tapping techniques into the treatment of addictions, I also include ways EMDR can be employed, and certain sections of the book will apply more to those trained in EMDR. For those without EMDR training, it will still be useful to help all readers understand how this therapy might be beneficial—where a referral to an EMDR therapist would make sense.

HOW THIS BOOK IS ORGANIZED

The emphasis in *Rewiring the Addicted Brain with EMDR-Based Treatment* is on the practical clinical application of principles and techniques helpful for addictions and addictive disorders. Case material is interwoven throughout the text; also included are chapters presenting in-depth cases that illustrate the techniques. These cases include history and background on the clients as well as actual sessions employing the interventions specific to rewiring the addicted brain. Also included in the case history chapters are details on the rationale for the interventions used, information about the effects of those interventions, and context around the overall course of treatment.

I have been teaching and presenting the material in this book for many years and use it in my clinical practice. The protocols and Resource Tapping techniques presented here evolved over several years, based on trial and error and feedback from therapists I have taught. I am always interested in what works, as well as in new ideas. I am deeply grateful to all of the talented clinicians who have shared with me their experiences with their clients so that I can share them with you.

Many people struggling with addictions know all they need to know about overcoming them. They've been to meetings and treatment. They've read self-help books. They know so much about it that they could teach a class or give someone else great advice, yet they have difficulty applying what they know to their own lives and addictions. This, of course, is not because they are in denial; rather, it is because the part of the brain that has all of this information is not linked up with the part that is driven by the urges. There is a lack of communication in the brain. They know, but part of them doesn't know. It's like a powerful race car that can't get into gear to move out of the garage and onto the road. The potential is there without the means to utilize it.

Therapists can help clients actualize this potential for change.

Rewiring the Addicted Brain with EMDR-Based Treatment is divided into five parts. You will find tools and techniques for supporting clients in addiction recovery in all five parts.

PART I: Treating Trauma and Supporting Resilience, is comprised of three chapters: Chapter 1, "Overview of the Rewiring the Addicted Brain Treatment Model," Chapter 2, "Getting to the Root of the Problem: Reprocessing Traumas with EMDR," and Chapter 3, "Resource Tapping for Addictions: Activating and Integrating Resilience." These chapters provide groundwork and rationale for specific techniques described in subsequent chapters.

PART II: Tools for Affect Regulation, has four chapters, each of which provides information and specific tools for managing difficult emotions associated with addictions. Chapter 4, "The Four Foundational Resources," explains what those foundational resources are, how they can be tapped in, and how they can be integrated into addiction treatment. Chapter 5, "Resource Tapping Tools for Managing Anxiety," provides resources that clients and therapists can use to decrease anxiety, which is a major contributor to relapse for clients in recovery. Chapter 6, "Repairing Developmental Deficits," provides resourcing ideas to aid repair of damage resulting from childhood abuse and neglect. Chapter 7, "Resources to Lift the Spirit: Antidotes for Depression and Inertia," offers helpful Resource Tapping techniques for clients who have an underlying depression fueling their addiction.

PART III: Rewiring the Motivation-Reward Circuits, provides Resource Tapping techniques to help shift neural circuitry away from patterns conducive to addictive behavior. Chapter 8, "Spiritual Resources," provides several ideas for helping clients discover, connect with, and reinforce a sense of something larger than themselves. Chapter 9, "Connecting to Inner Strength," provides Resource Tapping ideas for helping clients integrate and embody their own inner strength to support themselves in recovery. Chapter 10, "Resources for Restoring a Sense of Inner Goodness," aims to help heal the sense of shame felt by many people who have struggled with addiction. This chapter provides Resource Tapping protocols that support clients in bringing light to inner darkness and increasing motivation to stay the course of recovery. Chapter 11, "Resource Tapping to Enhance Motivation," provides several techniques to help clients focus on and remain motivated about goals.

PART IV: Change the Brain, Change the Behavior, provides protocols and techniques to help defuse and deactivate triggers for addiction and also to disrupt the reinforcement circuit that serves to maintain addictive patterns. This section has two chapters: Chapter 12, "Defusing and Deactivating Urges and Triggers," contains several Resource Tapping techniques that can be easily applied, as well as guidance on the use of the Bridging Technique to get to the root incidents that link to the trigger—at which point, these incidents can be reprocessed with EMDR. Chapter 13, "The Connecting the Consequences Protocol," introduces a new protocol for disconnecting the addiction-reward circuitry and rapidly reducing addictive behavior.

PART V: Putting It into Practice: Cases, shares the experiences of three talented therapists trained in Attachment-Focused EMDR and the addiction protocols described in the previous chapters. These case study chapters may be of special interest to therapists trained in EMDR as they demonstrate how EMDR, Resource Tapping, and other EMDR-oriented protocols can be used in the treatment of addictions. As these clinicians describe how they have used the tools and techniques with their clients, readers can see how the material introduced in this book might look in actual clinical practice. Chapter 14, by Elena Felder, LMFT, describes the use of the Bridging Technique to find triggers of a male alcoholic client with early attachment issues. Chapter 15, by Constance Kaplan, LMFT, describes a case in which Attachment-Focused EMDR and Resource Tapping techniques were used in the treatment of binge drinking. In Chapter 16, Julie Probus-Schad, LCSW, examines the use of Attachment-Focused EMDR, Resource Tapping, and the Connecting the Consequences Protocol in treating a woman's life-threatening diabulimia.

HOW TO USE THIS BOOK

This book does not need to be read chapter by chapter; think of it as a tool kit for supporting clients in addiction recovery. Search for the tool that might most help your client at a given time. For example, if your client is struggling with overwhelming anxiety, you might decide to begin with Chapter 5, "Resource Tapping Tools for Managing Anxiety."

Or imagine you have a client who is in recovery for alcohol addiction, is attending AA, and has completed a 30-day residential treatment program. She is emotionally fragile and struggling to stay sober. You might begin with tapping in her foundational resources (Chapter 4) and then add in resources to help strengthen and motivate her (Chapters 8 through 11). You might tap in inner strength and even a dream team of addiction-support figures (Chapter 10). You could ask her to imagine herself in a future where she is strong, healthy, and living a sober life, and then add BLS to better integrate that information.

You might have a client who grew up with parents who struggled with addiction and were unable to meet his basic attachment needs. Because of this, he feels empty inside and lacks the capacity for emotional regulation. This client may need to create and imagine parents who are able to provide him with stability and physical and emotional safety—who are capable of showing him love and meeting his developmental needs. The client can imagine growing up in a home with these ideal parents to help him heal his developmental deficits (Chapter 6).

You may have a client who was abused as a child and began to drink as a way to keep troubling memories from surfacing and to manage fear and anxiety. This client may need to tap in the four foundational resources. Then, when the client is ready, the therapist can use EMDR to reprocess the abuse memories that are activating the desire to drink. In all of these examples, we are assessing the needs of the individual clients to find out what they need first for support in recovery.

It may be that they need to begin with the foundational resources or to immediately use the Connecting the Consequences protocol to disrupt the trigger-addiction circuit. Some may need to use EMDR to address trauma early in treatment because the trauma is driving their addiction. In many cases, just beginning with the four foundational resources can make a big difference in decreasing distressing emotions and providing clients with something they can do to help themselves.

CONVENTIONS USED THROUGHOUT THIS BOOK

I have used fictitious names for clients throughout the book. (I prefer the term *client* to *patient*.) All identifying details of cases have been changed to protect clients' privacy. I have changed names, professions, family constellations, ethnicities, and specific life events. Some cases represent composites of more than one client. All clients are referred to by first names, which I feel creates a more personal feeling about the people whose lives I describe. Some case examples in the book are my clients; others are clients of my EMDR colleagues.

In sections about particular cases where EMDR sessions are being described, a device called the Tac/Audio Scan is used. The Tac/Audio Scan has small pulsers clients hold in their hands or place under their legs that vibrates alternately and also has headphones that emits a tone in either ear. Some clients prefer both the sound and tactile stimulation together synchronized, or choose either the sound or the vibrating pulsers. Some people prefer human contact, or to provide their own bilateral stimulation by alternate tapping on the sides of their legs or knees.

DEFINITION OF TERMS

Bilateral Stimulation (BLS)

BLS is the use of alternating right-left stimulation such as tapping on the knees, legs, or shoulders; tapping toes or feet on the floor; or alternating eye movements. Therapists also use a small portable device the size of a Walkman called the Tac/Audio Scan which produces auditory and tactile stimulation. BLS is used to activate and integrate information from the brain's two hemispheres.

Addiction

Addiction is a condition in which a behavior that can function both to produce pleasure and to reduce painful affects is employed in a pattern that is characterized by two key features (1) recurrent failure to control the behavior, and (2) continuation of the behavior despite significant harmful consequences.
—A GOODMAN, 2008[1]

Addictive Process

This is the term used to designate:

> [T]he underlying biopsychological process that addictive disorders are hypothesized to share. It can be defined operationally as an enduring, inordinately strong tendency to engage in some form of pleasure-producing behavior in a pattern that is characterized by impaired control and continuation despite significant harmful consequences. The class of addictive disorders includes psychoactive substance addiction, bulimia, pathological gambling, shopping or buying addiction, sexual addiction, and other enduring conditions in which a behavior that can function both to produce pleasure and to reduce painful affects is employed in a pattern that is characterized by two key features: (1) recurrent failure to control the behavior, and (2) continuation of the behavior despite significant harmful consequences.
>
> —AVIEL GOODMAN, 2008[2]

Eye-Movement Desensitization and Reprocessing (EMDR)

EMDR is a powerful and effective therapy for the treatment of trauma. It incorporates eye movements or other bilateral stimulation (BLS) into a comprehensive approach that processes and releases information trapped in the mind and body, freeing people from disturbing images and body sensations, debilitating emotions, and restrictive beliefs. This revolutionary therapy has helped millions of people of all ages recover from such traumas as war, accidents, assaults, disasters, and childhood abuse. EMDR has been extensively researched as a treatment for post-traumatic stress disorder (PTSD) and is considered to be an evidence-based therapy.

In addition to the treatment of PTSD, EMDR is also used to treat the psychological effects of smaller traumas that manifest in symptoms of depression, anxiety, phobias, low self-esteem, creativity blocks, and relationship difficulties. Not only does healing occur much more rapidly than in traditional therapy, but as a result of EMDR's clearing of emotional and physical blockages, many people also experience a sense of joy, openness, and deep connection with others. EMDR is a quantum leap in the human ability to heal trauma and maladaptive beliefs.

EMDR is based on the idea that negative thoughts, emotions, body sensations, and behaviors are the result of unprocessed memories. The treatment involves procedures that include focusing simultaneously on (1) spontaneous associations of traumatic images, thoughts, emotions, and bodily sensations and (2) BLS. Although EMDR therapy has been fully validated only for PTSD, numerous research studies are underway to evaluate its applications to a wide range of disorders. Excellent results have already been achieved with myriad diagnoses. In addition to the reduction of symptoms and the strengthening of adaptive beliefs, the client's experience of self and others typically shifts in ways that allow the person to respond in a healthier way to current and future life demands.

Attachment-Focused EMDR

Attachment-Focused EMDR (AF-EMDR) is an approach to EMDR therapy that I developed and described in my 2013 book, *Attachment-Focused EMDR: Healing Relational Trauma*. AF-EMDR is client-centered and emphasizes a reparative therapeutic relationship using a combination of (1) Resource Tapping to strengthen clients' resources and repair developmental deficits, (2) EMDR to process traumas, and (3) talk therapy to help integrate the information from EMDR sessions and to provide the healing derived from therapist-client interactions.

AF-EMDR extends the use and benefits of EMDR and BLS for use with clients who have been typically less responsive to traditional EMDR protocols due to acute or chronic relational trauma and attachment deficits. Those deficits include the effects of childhood physical or sexual abuse, neglect, early losses, birth trauma, medical trauma, parental substance abuse, lack of caregiver attunement, secondary trauma, and the cumulative effects of all of these factors. These clients often present in therapy as depressed, with relationship difficulties or problems at work. They don't feel fully alive. Childhood trauma has impacted their sense of safety and capacity to form close, emotional relationships in adulthood.

Attachment-Focused EMDR has five basic principles:

1. It emphasizes the importance of safety.

2. It is client centered.

3. The therapeutic relationship is fundamental.

4. A modified form of EMDR is used.

5. It employs Resource Tapping for ego strengthening, affect tolerance, and the repair of developmental deficits.

Resource Tapping

Resource Tapping is an EMDR-related technique that is effective and easy to use for ego strengthening, affect regulation, and stress reduction. Resource Tapping uses imagination to activate inner resources, which are then paired with bilateral stimulation to strengthen and integrate the resource. This technique can be used to help rebalance the nervous system, activate the parasympathetic restoration cycle, and teach self-regulation. This mind-body technique can be interwoven throughout the course of treatment and taught to clients to help with:

- anxiety and depression
- sleep problems
- triggers
- strong emotions such as fear, anger, shame, and sadness
- motivation
- addictive urges
- self-esteem

Resource Tapping can be used to prepare and strengthen clients prior to initiating emotionally intensive trauma-processing work such as EMDR, to help manage symptoms between EMDR sessions, to repair developmental deficits, and as a stand-alone technique with many applications. As previously mentioned, it can be used by therapists and counselors not trained in EMDR and can be taught to clients for self-use to regulate their emotions and help with symptoms. Resource Tapping can also be used with couples or in groups.

Resources

Resources are people, places, images, qualities, memories, and experiences—real or imagined—that we can draw upon to develop resilience. Resources may include inherent qualities such as love, wisdom, and joy.

Tapping

Tapping is the use of alternating BLS (right-left, right-left), which may include tapping on the knees, legs, arms, or shoulders, as well as alternating eye movements.

Tapping In Resources

Tapping in resources refers to the pairing of an activated resource with tapping or bilateral stimulation.. For instance, to tap in the resource of a Peaceful Place, imagine a place where you feel a sense of peace, such as a beach. When you can imagine the beach and feel peacefulness, alternately tap right-left, right-left for at least 6 to 12 sets. Tapping serves to strengthen and integrate the feeling of the resource so that it becomes more easily available.

REWIRING THE ADDICTED BRAIN WITH EMDR-BASED TREATMENT

PART I

TREATING TRAUMA
AND SUPPORTING RESILIENCE

CHAPTER 1

Overview of the Rewiring the Addicted Brain Treatment Model

What is addiction, really? It is a sign, a signal, a symptom of distress. It is a language that tells us about a plight that must be understood.

—ALICE MILLER

As a clinical psychologist specializing in the treatment of trauma, I have found that many people who have suffered the effects of trauma use addictive substances or behaviors in an effort to relieve their pain. We know from brain research that people with childhood trauma have difficulty with self-soothing, have more activated sympathetic nervous systems, and have lower pain tolerance. This helps explain why a large percentage of substance abusers are addicted to prescription medications that were initially prescribed for pain (which are, of course, highly addictive, but are more likely to become a problem for people with histories of childhood trauma).

Abusive, neglectful childhoods correlate with lower pain thresholds. Higher scores on the Adverse Childhood Experiences (ACEs) survey mean greater likelihood of chronic health conditions, which can then lead to prescribed pain medications with high risk of addiction. Clients from abusive backgrounds are also more prone to depression, which they may be self-medicating with their addictive substances or behaviors. Young people from violent households or communities struggling with systemic oppression or underresourced schools may turn to substances or behaviors that help them calm down or that give them a sense of power. Sometimes, a much-needed sense of community comes through being part of a group whose members share the same addiction. Clients who come from unstable childhood homes and have insecure attachment patterns may also turn to addictions as a way of managing anxiety and providing emotional regulation. Addiction may also be passed down from one generation to the next.

In some cases, the use of substances can keep traumatic memories from surfacing. Some of my early EMDR clients discovered this. When we began treatment, I asked an early client of mine to stop what I thought was intermittent drinking. (If at the time I had known what the client revealed to me later—that the drinking was actually daily—I would have referred them to a physician, as daily alcohol use can be dangerous.) The client did as I asked, but then began to have terrible nightmares. Drinking had served to keep nightmares and trauma memories from surfacing. Instead of waiting for a period of sobriety—which was the general rule at the time—we began to do EMDR on the nightmares and childhood trauma right away. As a result of our EMDR work, the client reported first a decrease and then a total elimination of the desire to drink. It became obvious to us that:

- drinking served as a means for repressing memories, and

- the urge to drink left when after reprocessing those memories with EMDR.

THE ADDICTIVE PROCESS: IMPAIRMENT IN THREE FUNCTIONAL SYSTEMS

According to research, the addictive process is an interaction of impairments in three functional systems: (1) affect regulation, (2) motivation reward, and (3) behavioral inhibition.[3] If we can focus our treatment on these three areas, using EMDR-related techniques to help increase affect regulation, support motivation, and increase control over dysfunctional behaviors, we may be better able to help our clients break the addiction cycle and support them in a life free of addictions. The approach outlined in this book addresses all three of these areas, integrating methods from *Attachment-Focused EMDR*,[4] Resource Tapping,[5] and a new technique, the Connecting the Consequences Protocol, all of which will be described in extensive detail later in this book.

REWIRING THE ADDICTED BRAIN

The techniques and protocols for addiction recovery support in *Rewiring the Addicted Brain with EMDR-Based Treatment* are derived from two areas: learning theory and brain science.

Learning Theory: Classical and Operant Conditioning and Social Learning Theory

Learning theory can help us understand how addictions might develop and perpetuate themselves. There are three types of conditioning and learning: (1) learning by paired association, called *classical conditioning*; (2) learning from the consequences of a behavioral choice, called *operant conditioning*; and (3) *social learning theory*, wherein an observation of behavior is followed by modeling. The three types of conditioning and learning and their relevance for rewiring the addicted brain will be briefly described next.

Classical conditioning. This type of learning occurs when a natural reflex responds to a stimulus. We are biologically wired so that a certain stimulus will produce a specific response. Classical conditioning was discovered by the Russian psychologist, Ivan Pavlov, who experimented with dogs. Every time he would bring out the dogs' food, causing the dogs to salivate, he would ring a bell. After doing this for a certain amount of time, Pavlov would ring the bell without presenting the food, and he observed that the dogs would salivate just from the sound of the bell. Classical conditioning regards this form of learning to be the same, whether in dogs or in humans. Repetition of stimulus-response habits strengthens those habits.

When the pleasure of addictive substances is paired with activities or environmental cues, addictive behavior may be perpetuated through classical conditioning. For example, suppose someone always drinks at a particular bar after work. The enjoyment of drinking forms a paired association with that bar. The time frame "after work" also forms a paired association. With repeated pairing of drinking after work and that particular bar, both the bar and the after-work time frame become cues to drink. These cues (getting off work, driving by the bar) may then create powerful cravings for alcohol.

Behaviorists would argue that the way to disconnect these associations would be to do something different after work, such as go to a gym and work out or meet a friend and engage in a pleasurable activity that does not involve drinking. Changing activities would help to form new associations. The power of the cue, in theory, is diminished over time as new behaviors are repeated. However, as we know, addictive patterns can be very deeply established, continuing to drive behaviors even when people know they should do something differently.

Operant conditioning. The theory of operant conditioning, developed by psychologist B. F. Skinner, posits that if a reward or reinforcement follows the response to a stimulus, the response becomes more probable in the future. A reward increases the likelihood of the behavior recurring; a punishment decreases its likelihood. Reward is more powerful in affecting behavior than punishment. You can see how this might apply to addictions. If the use of a substance is a rewarding experience, the person is more likely to continue with it. For example, if the man in the above example discovered as an adolescent that when he felt sad and then drank he felt better afterwards, he would experience reinforcement for drinking and be more likely to continue, especially when he was feeling low.

People may lack motivation to change their behaviors because they have not experienced negative consequences for those behaviors. However, many people continue with their addictions despite negative consequences. They have gotten DUIs, ruined their marriages, harmed their children, and lost their jobs; still, the addiction persists. How can this be? Why do people have to hit bottom and nearly die before they go for help? Why do some people never hit bottom, but keep using until they die? Is it denial, or perhaps something else? I believe the answer lies in neuroscience: the structure of the brain and the way our neural circuitry is shaped by classical and operant conditioning.

Social learning theory. Social learning theory, which was first posited by psychologist Albert Bandura in 1961, observes that we learn and make associations in a social context simply by observing and imitating the behaviors of others. When we observe others' behavior—especially those who are important to us growing up, such as parents, other close family members, and peers (but might also include a neighbor or teacher)—they model for us ways of behaving that also affect our thinking and emotional regulation. Social learning theory might explain in part why addiction is passed through generations, since watching parents and peers engage in addictive behavior can be a large part of how addictions form.

Take the example of a boy who grew up in a family where his father drank heavily when he was frustrated. This father became belligerent and disrespectful to his wife and children when drunk—very different from the mild-mannered man he was when sober. The boy looked up to his father, his role model for male behavior. When he grew up he, too, developed a drinking problem like his father.

As human beings, we have a powerful need for social interaction. Many addictions include a social aspect: alcohol is often a central feature of social interactions; some people smoke marijuana together to connect; even gambling casinos have a social element. The social circles of many people who abuse substances may be comprised almost entirely of others who share their addiction. In recovery, it is important to form relationships with healthier people while disengaging from people who are not creating healthy alternatives to the old networks. This is one of the reasons support groups like Alcoholics Anonymous and Refuge Recovery are helpful in addiction recovery: they provide social support and opportunities to observe and interact with healthier people.

BRAIN SCIENCE: HEBB'S LAW

Neurons that fire together, wire together. This phrase was first used in 1949 by Donald Hebb,[6] a Canadian neuropsychologist known for his work in the field of associative learning. According to Hebb, every experience, thought, feeling, and physical sensation triggers thousands of neurons (brain cells), which form a neural network. The more frequently these networks of neurons are activated together, the more likely they are to form neural circuits. This means that when neurons fire often in a particular pattern, they will tend to create a circuit of firing that will perpetuate itself. When a behavior is repeated, the neurons involved in that behavior will link up, and the behavior will repeat.

When a person behaves in a particular pattern over time, these patterns become more entrenched. The neural circuitry that supports the behavior *lights up* in a way that continues the pattern. If we apply this to someone with a drinking problem, it might look like this: a man drives past a familiar bar; it lights up memories of drinking there in the past, along with feelings of pleasure, and smells and tastes associated with the behavior. His body remembers the feeling he has when he drinks, and it activates a deep somatic craving. He stops to have a drink and then drinks too much. His body draws him into the familiar pattern, bypassing his best intentions. The pattern lights up like a circuit board. He acts automatically. This patterning is so strong that despite knowing better, he can't seem to change his behavior. Somatic reactions below the level of conscious thought create the great pull. It is as if a switch has been flipped; a pattern he can't seem to control is activated.

We now know that *the part of the brain where this pattern activates is not linked to the part of the brain that knows the consequence of the behavior*: that stopping at the bar will lead to loss of control. This part of the brain is not linked to the rest of the circuit.

When we think of addiction as neural circuitry firing in a particular pattern, we can begin to design ways to *change the circuitry*. How can we access, light up, and link in new ways to feel and behave? How can we link the part of the person that possesses plentiful health-promoting information and resources to the part that maintains patterns of addiction?

I believe the answer lies with:

1. *The use of Resource Tapping to link new, healthy resources and behavioral responses to the dysfunctional circuitry that perpetuates addictive patterns.* This modality is accessible to all treatment professionals, whether EMDR-trained or not, and can be used with groups and as a form of self-care for clients who learn it in therapeutic settings.

2. *The use of EMDR to reprocess the traumas that are driving the behavior.* Again, this is not necessary for all clients in addiction treatment, but it is vital for many whose addictive behaviors are driven by unresolved trauma.

3. *The use of the Connecting the Consequences Protocol to link the behavior with the consequence.* I believe that the addictive process is not about denial, but about dissociation—a lack of integration of information stored in different regions of the brain. This will be discussed in detail in subsequent chapters.

A HOLISTIC APPROACH TO ADDICTION TREATMENT

Over a period of many years, I have developed a holistic, integrative approach to the treatment of addictions and dysfunctional behaviors that is *compassionate, spiritual, brain-wise, resource-based, trauma-informed,* and *attachment-focused.*

There is no one-size-fits-all treatment for addictions. It is important that treatment professionals create a plan that fits best for each individual. We all want to be seen, known, and respected, not subjected to a cookie cutter "method." This approach allows for interindividual variation; it is compassionate and recognizes and aligns with the health, wholeness, and wisdom of each person while recognizing the power and destructive nature of addiction. We fit the treatment to the client rather than fitting the client into a proscriptive treatment. We work to strengthen resources, repair attachment deficits, reprocess traumas with EMDR, deactivate triggers, and connect actions to consequences. This is a tailor-made approach to treatment that works with both harm-reduction and abstinence-based approaches. The Rewiring the Addicted Brain Model emphasizes meeting clients where they are currently, using motivational interviewing to develop and work with clients' goals, and discovering what works best for them through all phases of treatment.

This book was written primarily for therapists and counselors who are working with clients struggling with substance abuse, eating disorders, self-harming, or dysfunctional addictive behaviors such as sex addiction, gambling, or compulsive shopping. Several of the techniques in this book can be used by nontherapists working in addiction treatment or by those who desire self-help ideas for overcoming addictions.

CHAPTER 2

Getting to the Root of the Problem: Reprocessing Traumas with EMDR

Not everything that is faced can be changed, but nothing can be changed until it is faced.

—JAMES BALDWIN

As a result of my work with clients who had both trauma and addiction, I came to see the importance of reprocessing traumas with EMDR as an integral part of addiction recovery. Over the years, I have found that the combination of addressing trauma through EMDR and strengthening and healing with Resource Tapping has worked well to heal addictions. During this time, I developed additional protocols useful in the treatment of addictive behavior, and I'll touch upon these in this chapter and chapters to come. A major discovery guiding the development of these protocols has been the recognition that addictions are not about purposeful denial, but about dissociation.

The unifying thread here is that trauma and substance abuse often coexist and that treating addiction without effectively treating underlying traumas is less likely to yield a successful outcome.

TRAUMA AND ADDICTIONS GO TOGETHER

Though not everyone who experiences trauma develops an addiction, research suggests a significant, undeniable link between trauma and substance abuse. Symptoms of PTSD— nightmares, flashbacks, anxiety, depression, frequent triggering by reminders of the traumatic event, hypervigilance, and hyperarousal—can be so painful to live with that people suffering from this disorder often use alcohol or drugs to try to ease their symptoms.

Several large scale epidemiological surveys have been conducted over the past two decades that show a high co-occurrence between PTSD and substance use disorders.[7] Research on veteran populations show that veterans are at increased risk for developing PTSD and substance abuse disorder and that high rates of PTSD and substance abuse disorder co-occur in these populations.[8] A diagnosis of PTSD correlates to increased risk of developing alcohol abuse.[9] Childhood sexual abuse survivors are at risk to develop a substance use disorder.[10]

Both research and clinical experience point especially to childhood trauma as a risk factor for substance use disorders, including abuse and dependence. In their 2010 study of 587 patients seeking care in urban primary care waiting rooms in Atlanta, Georgia, Lamya Khoury and her colleagues found strong links between childhood traumatization and substance use disorders.[11] They also found that the level of substance use, particularly cocaine, was strongly associated with levels of childhood physical, sexual, and emotional abuse, as well as current PTSD symptoms.

Researchers at the University of Texas studied 32 teenagers, 19 of whom had been abused during childhood but had not been diagnosed with a mental health disorder. The control group had no history of any major childhood trauma or psychiatric problems. For 3.5 years, all these teens were followed up every 6 months. The researchers found that *nearly half of the teens who had experienced trauma developed depression, an addiction, or both during the study.*[12] The comparison between the two groups showed that the rate of developing an addiction or mental health disorder in the abused teens was three times higher than in the control group.

We know from both clinical research and brain studies that childhood trauma impacts the development of the brain and that trauma at a young age can make a person vulnerable to several mental illnesses as well as to addiction. Recently, researchers have made advances into understanding exactly why this is—specifically, how trauma is linked to depression and addiction.

Childhood trauma gears the amygdala (the brain's threat detection center) to be on constant alert for threat, leading to chronic fear, anxiety, and feelings of vulnerability. Individuals who were abused or neglected in childhood are more likely to develop PTSD as adults. Childhood trauma also makes people more prone to depression and less able to calm or soothe themselves when distressed. Some research suggests that they may feel pain more acutely than other people.[13]

Trauma also interferes with the functioning of the hippocampus, the part of the brain responsible for the integrative processes that yield coherent memories. In the traumatized brain, images, emotions, sounds, smells, tastes, and somatosensory experiences from the traumatic event exist as fragments in the right side of the brain. Many describe it as puzzle pieces that are in disarray—no picture nor coherent narrative exists to make sense of the event. This is why, in response to any reminder of a trauma, people are activated into fight-flight-freeze—often, without knowing why. And because the right side of the brain does not record time chronologically, when triggered, the trauma survivor feels as though the traumatic experience is happening in the present. For many people with PTSD, memories get hung up in a loop of intrusive, disturbing, and uncomfortable recollections.

Childhood trauma disconnects neural networks between the cortex (the brain's center for executive control) and the parts of the brain having to do with survival-oriented instincts. In other words, the parts of the brain that activate the fight-or-flight response do not link up completely with the part that regulates logical thinking, as they would in a person without a history of childhood trauma. Even if traumatized people know—in the cortex, the thinking part of the brain—that they survived, that the traumatic event is past, and that they can now make healthy choices, they cannot connect to that part and make use of the information stored there when triggered into that fight-or-flight state.

For example, when a woman who was abused by her father as a child is triggered by her boss, a large, friendly man, she can't calm herself down by reminding herself that this man—unlike her father—is kind and will not hurt her. Her body has been hijacked by unintegrated memories from her traumatic childhood. As the fight-or-flight system takes over in its efforts to maintain safety and survival, she clicks into a reactive state and loses access to her higher brain functions. She becomes unable to distinguish her kind boss from her abusive father.

Young people who are abused or traumatized in childhood discover somewhere along the way that addictive substances or behaviors (including bingeing and purging) help them manage their PTSD symptoms. These substances or behaviors may help them to feel more optimistic and energetic and less anxious, at least for a short time. Maybe their addiction helps them sleep and keeps nightmares at bay, or it may help them survive the time they have to remain in a household that is chaotic or dangerous. The addiction brings temporary relief from feelings that feel unmanageable.

THE NEED FOR INTEGRATED TREATMENT

In individuals with addictions, we often find that trauma is the root cause of the addiction, and they use the addiction to self-treat the trauma symptoms—which, in turn, can create subsequent traumas. An integrative approach to treatment works best to support clients to be successful in recovery.

In a 2011 issue of the *Journal of Dual Diagnosis* focusing on co-occurring PTSD and substance use disorders,[14] guest editors Mark McGovern and Tracy Stecker note that a growing number of studies in the past decade have focused on treatment interventions that integrate treatment of PTSD and addictions. More recently, research has shown that if we try to treat addiction without treating the underlying trauma, clients will relapse. Early in recovery, clients who have trauma in their backgrounds are often unable to handle the emotions and memories that come up when they are no longer using drugs or alcohol or doing harmful behaviors.

According to Jamie Marich,[15] best practices for effective treatment of addictions are holistic. EMDR is highly effective for honoring the safety of the client, as the forging of a healthy therapeutic alliance is key to this modality. It is specifically designed to target core, unresolved emotional issues and lifestyle change issues. In particular, treatment for women's addictions is apt to be ineffective unless it acknowledges the reality that women experience a high prevalence of violence and other types of abuse.[16]

WHY EMDR?

EMDR works fast, is integrative, doesn't necessitate prolonged exposure (which can be re-traumatizing), and requires no homework. It activates natural processing capacities of the brain that are frozen and deactivated by trauma. It reestablishes disrupted communication between the brain regions impacted by traumatic experience and enables the traumatized brain to heal. Research by Hase, Schallmayer, and Sack[17] found EMDR to be helpful in reducing addiction craving and in preventing relapse. They concluded that "EMDR might be a useful approach for the treatment of addiction memory and associated symptoms of craving."

For individuals suffering from addiction who experienced long-term childhood abuse and neglect, no treatment—not even EMDR—can be brief. Healing from this kind of childhood experience requires a commitment to treatment, a strong bond with the therapist, and the capacity to handle strong and often uncomfortable emotions. They also need to be committed to their addiction recovery. Attachment-Focused EMDR is what I have seen work best for clients with early childhood abuse or neglect and addictive disorders. This approach recognizes the need for a dual approach for integrating repair of early developmental deficits and reprocessing of traumas.

USEFUL APPROACHES FOR BOTH EMDR-TRAINED AND NON-EMDR-TRAINED PRACTITIONERS

This book was written for individuals working in the field of addictions. My hope is that it will be useful for all therapists and counselors in this field, whether they are trained in EMDR or not.

For those who are EMDR-trained, the innovations provided here will expand your tool kit as you treat underlying traumas that give rise to addictive and compulsive behaviors in your clients.

For those who are not formally trained in EMDR, the EMDR-inspired protocols will help you to gain an increased understanding of how your EMDR-trained colleagues might integrate EMDR into collaborative treatment plans. My hope is that the concepts and protocols in this book will put your entire recovery team on the same page as you work together to heal your shared clients. Elements of resourcing and Resource Tapping described throughout are meant to be useful to both EMDR-trained and non-EMDR-trained addiction treatment professionals.

Because this book has been written for individuals working in the field of addictions, not necessarily trained in EMDR, I have provided recommendations for the *focus* of EMDR sessions without the details of the *mechanics* and *structure* of such sessions. This should enable all readers who work in addictions counseling to find useful information in each case study.

BEGINNING WORK WITH ADDICTED CLIENTS: EXPLORING CLIENT HISTORY

When working with people who suffer from addictions or addictive disorders, it is important to get to know the person with whom you are working. Take a history of their relationship to their addiction, as well as a thorough developmental history. It can be helpful to start with their family history around addiction.

Ask your clients to tell you the story of their relationship to their addiction: *When did you begin to use? Why did you begin to use? What purpose did the use fill for you? What was the age of first usage and what was happening around that time? What are the traumas linked to the desire to use, if any?*

Keep an open mind in exploring the history of your client's use or abuse. Losses, medical traumas, and learning difficulties due to disabilities and language barriers can all set the stage for addiction. For children and adolescents, the trauma can be rejection by friends, violence in their homes, or bullying from age mates. For some, there is no specific traumatic incident, but instead a general feeling of insecurity, of not being good enough, or of not fitting in. Also obtain a thorough developmental history: *"Tell me the story of your life, beginning with the circumstances around your conception and birth."*

As you gather this information, listen for key events, limiting self-beliefs, and themes that may link to the addiction. You can learn a lot from how they tell their story: Is it organized and coherent, or is it a jumble of random information that doesn't flow in chronological order? Are there large gaps, or do they remember things uniformly across the years? Do they recall disorder and chaos in their early childhood or safety and security? What traumas stand out for them? Did they experience family violence, parental substance abuse, neglect, divorce, frequent moves, or medical traumas? You don't have to solicit details of a person's history, as it may be too overwhelming for them; just start with a general overview and pace according to the ego strength of each client.

Don't forget to ask about the good things in your client's life, too. What were their favorite things? Who were the people they loved? What are their happiest memories? Did they have any spiritual experiences that have given them a sense of something larger than themselves, including a connection to nature? These positive resources from their past will provide material for Resource Tapping.

The gathering of information coincides with the development of rapport, which is essential to any healing of deeper psychological wounds. The relationship the client has with the therapist or counselor is central to the development of a template for healthy relationships based on trust, respect, and truth. Taking this kind of history can require several sessions. For the client, being able to tell their stories to someone who is empathic and nonjudgmental is part of healing; for the care provider, this time carefully spent building rapport and learning about the client is essential for developing a treatment plan that is client centered and tailored to the needs of the individual.

Addiction Assessment
by Elena Felder, LMFT

Many of the people I have worked with on recovery from addiction in a private practice setting do not bring up substance use or addictive behaviors when they initially come into therapy. They come in for trauma, anxiety, depression, or relational problems. The first part of my addiction assessment is determining whether their presenting issues are linked to an addiction to substances or behaviors that also need to be assessed. In my intake, I explicitly ask about use of drugs and alcohol, relationship with food, and any behaviors they are concerned about. I keep in mind that the client may underreport, both because they may minimize or dissociate and also because shame is often connected with addiction. I try to be aware throughout any assessment to communicate acceptance and that we will work toward the goals that they set. I also weave in questions regarding:

- Quantity and frequency of use or behavior that may represent addiction; I expect underreporting.
- Personal history with the substance or behavior.
- Relevant family history with the substance or behavior.
- How the substance or behavior has been and is helpful to them; the goal here is to truly understand and to help the client understand why they are doing what they are doing. This mitigates shame and is helpful in defining which internal and external resources might be most helpful.
- How the substance or behavior is affecting their health, moods, relationships, and work.
- Previous attempts to change the behavior: What worked and what didn't?
- What are their goals? Would they like to be abstinent, to cut down, to continue the behavior, or to use in a way that is less self-destructive?
- Are they taking any current action steps to achieve these goals?
- How, specifically, will we know if they have achieved their goals?
- What support they may need to achieve those goals: in addition to individual therapy, support can include medical supervision, absti-

nence-based or harm-reduction support groups, intensive outpatient programs, or residential treatment.

If there is an addiction to drugs or alcohol, I will ask the client to check in with a doctor before making any changes in their behavior. Withdrawal can be dangerous. I also request medical supervision for clients who are struggling with bulimia or restricting food.

PREPARING ADDICTED CLIENTS FOR EMDR

Ideally, before using EMDR, clients have detoxed from their substance(s), are motivated for treatment, and have the ego strength and affect tolerance to handle the intensity of reprocessing of traumas. For those clients who are not able to detox from substances or stop behaviors before beginning treatment with you, you might use Resource Tapping to strengthen them and help get them prepared for recovery. You might also refer them for a physical or medication evaluation to help address some of the somatic drivers for the addiction that cannot be ameliorated sufficiently with therapy.

There is no rule for how long it may take to sufficiently stabilize clients before they are ready for EMDR. Some people have been so locked into their addictions that direct targeting and processing of traumas with EMDR is the only thing that can give them relief. This was the case for some of my clients. When the root traumas were reprocessed with EMDR, the desire to drink vanished.

For many people from unstable, violent childhoods during which they were abused or neglected, the healing journey can stir memories their addiction kept buried. A residential setting can provide the support they need to continue the work without relapsing in response to the distress these memories can bring. Safe, supportive residential settings can be ideal for doing this deeper trauma work with EMDR.

DEFINING TARGETS FOR PROCESSING

In EMDR therapy, we talk about *targets* as focus points of EMDR sessions. Targets are typically key incidents or events that link to the client's symptoms. When we make these key incidents or events a session's focus, processing them with bilateral stimulation (BLS), the emotional charge is reduced. The client comes to feel as if the incidents are in the past and gains insight and understanding from a broader perspective.

Typically, when these incidents are reprocessed to completion with EMDR, the symptoms associated with them also diminish. Where substance abuse has been used to relieve the pain of emotions associated with traumatic incidents, the craving or need for that substance naturally diminishes with reprocessing. For example, if the client began drinking after being continually bullied in secondary school, and one of the key bullying incidents is targeted and reprocessed with EMDR, the incident itself will feel as if it is in the past by the end of the session. The emotional charge is reduced; a new sense of empowerment replaces the feeling of powerlessness. With these shifts, the association to alcohol begins to reduce. For most clients, many other such incidents have occurred, and more EMDR sessions are needed.

Potential EMDR Targets for Addicted Clients

These are described here to set the stage for addiction treatment with EMDR, but they should not be addressed in treatment until clients have been stabilized and have their resources well established. Targets should not be worked with directly until sufficient safety has been created through resourcing, which will be the central subject of the next several chapters.

Look for the most direct links to the addiction. What in the past is most directly linked to the present addiction or behavior? From information gathered in the history, the EMDR therapist can develop hypotheses about the reasons for the addiction. For example, if the drinking began after a sexual assault, you might begin EMDR targeting that incident. If the client began use after a car accident, target the car accident. If the client began using drugs after deployments in Iraq, what happened there that the drugs are managing? If there are no simple answers—perhaps the client describes general anxiety about a time in life when they didn't feel okay about themselves—then look for incidents that represent that time, such as a rejection from a friend or not being invited to a social event.

Process big "T" traumas, targeting childhood traumas chronologically. If you believe your client is using an addiction to manage symptoms from early childhood trauma, target these traumas chronologically, beginning with the earliest experiences. These so-called big "T" traumas can include physical or sexual abuse, early loss, divorce, medical traumas, witnessed domestic violence, and accidents.

If the client came from a violent home and there was a long history of abuse, try to get a time line of incidents (if the client knows them) and then target and reprocess the incidents *chronologically*, beginning with the earliest one. You don't have to target each trauma; you can group them by time and place. For example, target abuse by the father that occurred in the client's bedroom, then abuse by a babysitter later. You can use a representational incident or a composite of many incidents, with the aim being a treatment effect that generalizes to many such experiences.

Many people use substances to manage symptoms of traumas that occurred in both childhood and adulthood. Many of my EMDR colleagues working with veterans have found that the earliest origins of their clients' symptoms were not the battlefield, but their violent family homes. These men and women often turn out to have joined the armed forces in part as a defense against the powerlessness they felt as children living in unstable homes. The terrible experiences many of these men and women had in war zones served to reinforce the powerlessness they felt in early childhood. To most effectively help these clients, these practitioners saw that they needed to begin EMDR with the traumas from childhood before working on the traumas from war.

Beginning with early experiences seems to generalize more thoroughly through the memory networks. The decisions made at 10 years old may be based on experiences from earlier years—for example, the decisions that arise from a belief that it isn't safe to tell when an adult harms them. When faced in their present with a moment that recalls those moments in childhood, their body freezes. They feel powerless even when in the current moment they are not. The past is overlaid on the present, leading to patterns of response that may no longer serve.

When we target these early experiences, clients often bring their own insight and understanding to their behaviors and self-concepts. There is a clearing of the old patterns that can generalize to memories that link through many stages of their life. This approach can help build self-compassion as well as understanding about why they were drawn to their addiction.

Target adult "big T" traumas. Sometimes, early traumas prove less significant to the client than later life traumas. There may be incidents by which they are *haunted*, that plague their dreams or affect how they view themselves and the world. It may make more sense to begin with one of these traumas. If clients report that their addiction began after a trauma that occurred in their adulthood, EMDR sessions might begin with this target. Such traumas can include accidents, sexual assaults, witnessed violence, domestic violence, war, terror attacks, medical trauma, or traumatic loss.

Process "small t" traumas. Some people do not have large, significant traumas in their histories but still try to manage an intense hurt with addictive behaviors. This hurt is connected to seemingly small things. Perhaps they felt invisible at home because their single mother was working all the time and had no time to spend with them when they struggled with their homework. Perhaps, when they lagged behind other students in school because they lacked the support they needed to learn, other children called them stupid and teachers mocked them. As a result, they began to view themselves as stupid and damaged. Then, as adolescents, they discovered that marijuana would relieve some of their anxiety. They could smoke with friends and feel a sense of belonging. But instead of it helping, it led to more problems learning and to riskier behavior both to help engender a feeling of belonging and to manage anxiety around school performance.

Many such examples of patterns of behavior and addiction are established due to multiple "small t" traumas linked to low self-esteem, anxiety, and depression. Self-beliefs such as "I'm worthless," "I'm not good enough," and "I'm unlovable" can have multiple origins and can be reinforced over time by subsequent life experiences. Seek to discover what in the client's past is linked to these self-beliefs. What are the early linkages? These incidents, even if minor, can be targeted and reprocessed.

For example, I remember working with a high school teacher in her fifties who had a history of addictions and unsatisfactory relationships with men. She believed deeply that she was not good enough for a healthy relationship—that she was somehow unlovable. When we explored the origins of this belief, she linked it to a rejection by a high school boyfriend who stood her up for the prom. He broke her heart and damaged her sense of self-worth as a desirable woman. During the reprocessing of this trauma, she realized that she had based her self-esteem on the actions of an awkward, pimple-faced boy who didn't know what to do with a girl. She laughed out loud and was immediately relieved of the frozen view of herself. She was okay, and so was the boy. They were just awkward adolescents.

Other large and small traumas can be targeted with EMDR to help with addictions:

Regret. What do they feel most regretful for doing? What are the things they did during the time of their use or behavior that they feel bad about? Perhaps their regret is also triggering a desire to use. The EMDR therapist can target things like DUIs, domestic violence, fights, accidents, criminal behavior, prostitution, behavior that runs counter to their moral code, or other things they regret doing, and support them in reprocessing and repairing. Allow them to imagine making different choices. They can also imagine doing something different in the future.

School traumas. School traumas can include those linked to learning difficulties, bullying, and teachers who were not attuned to their needs.

Grief and loss. Were they drawn to their addiction due to a loss or losses that were too large to process? These can include childhood losses of close family members due to death, divorce, or moving; the loss of a beloved pet; or the loss of one's country due to immigration or dislocation. Perhaps it was a loss they experienced in their adult life that they couldn't manage, such as the loss of a child or partner.

The addiction itself. Some clients need to process the loss of the addiction itself with EMDR. Many people *bond* with the addictive substance or behavior and grieve when they give it up. This, too, can be processed with EMDR. Some of my clients have needed to process the loss of friends with whom they drank. In order to maintain sobriety, they had to cut off contact with their social circle. This can leave a painful emptiness inside until new connections with sober friends and community members can be established. EMDR may also help them process the loss of a lifestyle; although a dysfunctional one, it is familiar, and may also be associated with family.

Pain management. Many people become addicted to substances to manage physical pain. If clients have had an accident or a medical procedure that caused pain and they become addicted as a result, it is important to help them find a healthier way to manage the pain after the initial cause has been resolved. This seems especially relevant in light of the opioid crisis that has developed through the overprescribing of opioid drugs for pain.

Sometimes, targeting and reprocessing the initial trauma associated with the pain—a car accident, for example—can help. The work of Mark Grant, whose focus is on reducing the impact of pain, reinforces the effectiveness of targeting memories of the pain, future imaginations of the pain, and the experienced pain in the present.[18] Using Resource Tapping can also help with pain management.[19]

USING THE BRIDGING TECHNIQUE TO LOCATE LINKS TO TRIGGERS

In Chapter 12, I explain several ways to work with triggers and urges to use. One of the ways to deactivate triggers is to locate the internal or external trigger for use and then trace it back in time to discover what in the past is linked to this. The Bridging Technique is a method derived from the affect bridge[20] in hypnotherapy; it is used to find early links to symptoms or behaviors. I explain how to use the Bridging Technique in two of my EMDR books (*A Therapist's Guide to EMDR*[21] and *Attachment-Focused EMDR*).

Again, the aim here is to locate what in the past is linked to the desire to use in the present. More often than not, the client doesn't know what this is. When the bridge is used to find the incident, it can then be targeted for EMDR processing. After processing the early root experience associated with the trigger, the therapist can then direct the client to return to the trigger and check it. If the client reports a reduction in the feelings and urges associated with the trigger, the therapist adds BLS. Finally, if they feel good and strong—no longer triggered—the therapist asks them to imagine a future scenario and add BLS.

For example, if the client is triggered when in a social situation because he feels anxious, and then drinks to overcome his anxiety, the therapist can bridge him back from a recent time when he found himself doing this. You want to find what was happening *right before* he had the desire to take the drink. When you find that moment—which may include feelings of anxiety, somatic sensations of butterflies in the stomach, sweating, flushed face, and thoughts like, "I'm an idiot"—the therapist then asks him to *"trace it back in time. Go back as far as you can without censoring it."*

He might land in a memory of a high school dance where he felt anxious and insecure. Perhaps he remembers that friends offered him some whiskey, and in that moment, he felt as if he belonged, and his anxiety vanished. This would become the first target for EMDR, which would be processed with BLS until it is no longer charged. After that, the therapist would return to the recent scene bridged from and ask what he experiences. If he says he feels good, he doesn't need a drink, add BLS. Finally ask him to imagine a future social situation and see how he feels. If he says he feels good, he no longer feels the need to drink, ask him to imagine that, and add BLS.

Lastly, in some cases, because of the reinforcement of the habit pattern over time, it can be helpful to target the trigger directly with EMDR. This may aid in disrupting the old pattern and reducing the association between trigger and behavior.

CHAPTER 3

Resource Tapping for Addictions: Activating and Integrating Resilience

Remember, the entrance door to the sanctuary is inside you.
—RUMI

Many people abuse substances to manage anxiety or trauma symptoms. If this coping method is withdrawn and no substitute is provided for support and pain management, relapse is more likely. This is especially true if substance abuse is managing PTSD symptoms and keeping trauma memories at bay.

Before undergoing surgery, patients are strengthened, and their pain is managed. This compassionate, sensible approach promotes faster healing. In much the same way, as we ask our addicted clients to abstain from the drugs or behavior that has helped them to cope with their lives, we must give them something to strengthen them—to build their resilience, reduce their pain, and better enable them to heal. Resource Tapping, an EMDR-related technique, combines imagination and bilateral stimulation (BLS) to activate and integrate positive resources and strengthen resilience.

RESOURCE TAPPING: AN INTRODUCTION

Resource Tapping involves guiding clients to use their imagination to focus on a positive resource—such as a peaceful or comfortable place—and then adding short sets of BLS. There is considerable research support for the effectiveness of imagination alone for peak performance and healing; however, the combination of imagery with BLS works better than imagery alone to generate calm and increase self-esteem and self-efficacy.

To guide others in Resource Tapping, EMDR training can be helpful, but is certainly not needed. Resource Tapping can also be taught to clients for self-use. Resource Tapping helps clients access and develop ego strength, build affect tolerance, and repair developmental deficits.[22] It helps reduce anxiety, enhances coping with trauma and illnesses, facilitates sleep, and increases confidence.

The Difference Between EMDR and Resource Tapping

With EMDR, the therapist focuses on the trauma memory, adds BLS—often using two small pulsers, one held in each hand, using devices such as the Tac/Audio Scan or the Theratapper—and allows free-associative processing within the frame of a structured protocol. In contrast, when we *tap in resources*, we focus on positive resources and use a shorter set of BLS.

When I refer to *tapping* here, I mean tapping alternately, right-left, right-left—softly drumming on the knees, thighs, or sides of the legs, or crossing the arms across the chest and tapping each shoulder alternately. This latter form of tapping is called the *butterfly hug* because of the hugging posture of the arms. Tapping can also include bilateral eye movements.

Some practitioners confuse Resource Tapping with other tapping techniques from energy psychology, such as Thought Field Therapy and Emotional Freedom Technique (EFT). EFT and others work through physical tapping on acupressure points that helps to open blocked energy. Resource Tapping uses BLS to activate the body-mind's natural information-processing systems to help integrate neural networks and strengthen positive resources.

As I have written in my other books, I believe it is helpful to tap in four basic resources or their variants prior to beginning an EMDR session: Peaceful Place, Nurturing Figures, Protector Figures, and Wise or Spiritual Figures. Tapping in these places and figures creates a safety net that provides the client with support for trauma work and in recovery from addictions. Resource Tapping helps clients access and develop ego strength, build affect tolerance, and repair developmental deficits.[23] Besides the four resources listed above, others can be tapped in for the treatment of addictions; much more will be said about this in later chapters.

Throughout this book, I will use the terms *tapping into* and *tapping in* resources. We *tap into* resources by locating the best ones and then using imagination to activate these resources. Tapping in means that the resource is being activated through imagination and that we are strengthening and integrating the resource more fully into the nervous system with BLS. It is important to understand that with Resource Tapping, we are not taking something from outside and putting it in; rather, we are enhancing resources that are already inside.

RESOURCE TAPPING: BASIC PRINCIPLES

The following basic principles form the foundation upon which Resource Tapping is built. Understanding and experiencing these principles will enable you to use Resource Tapping creatively in any number of ways. These evolved out of my own clinical experience using EMDR and Resource Tapping, Buddhist and non–dual spiritual philosophy, and perspective and insight I have developed from over 45 years of spiritual practice.

THE SIX BASIC PRINCIPLES OF RESOURCE TAPPING

1. **We are essentially whole and complete just as we are. This wholeness is our true nature.** It remains in the ever-present background of being and is unchanged by the events of our lives. Wisdom, compassion, equanimity, power, and joy are expressions of this wholeness.

2. **Within each of us is the potential to realize this wholeness.** Indeed, this wholeness wants to be realized and impels us to realize it.

3. **We also have within us a reservoir of positive, stored experiences.** These can include experiences of loving and being loved and of feeling comforted, competent, powerful, happy, joyful, peaceful, and calm.

4. **We become unhappy and feel disconnected and fragmented when we are unable to access our wholeness** or our reservoir of positive experiences, or when we are out of balance.

5. **We have a natural healing system** that, when accessed and activated using BLS (tapping), can restore us to balance.

6. **We can assess, strengthen, and integrate our wholeness** and reservoir of resources through Resource Tapping.

PRINCIPLE 1: We are essentially whole. Wholeness is our true nature. There is an abiding presence or consciousness that is never touched by the events of our lives. Like the sun obscured by clouds, it remains, shining in the background. Stressful life experiences and our interpretations of these experiences are like the clouds that obstruct our connection to our wholeness—our True Nature.

Every person has moments in life when we are able to express ourselves freely, where there is a natural flow of expression that springs from our deepest selves, our place of wholeness. We manifest this expression of wholeness when words of wisdom we didn't know we had issue forth from our mouths.

In those moments of full expression and wisdom, we feel empowered, because we are coming from the ground of our being. When we are in our fullness, we feel an expansion in our bodies. Our hearts are open. We feel joyful. This experience is innately available to every human being.

PRINCIPLE 2: Within each of us is the potential to realize this wholeness. This drive toward health, wholeness, and freedom comes from our highest source; one might call it our Higher Power. Deep within us is the desire to be free from the constraints of identification with the false self. The false self is comprised of negative experiences that have been stored as memories, with associated body sensations and negative self-referencing beliefs. These networks of associations pass themselves off as being "who we are," but are only neural circuits firing in a familiar pattern that we call "me." All that isn't the true self is experienced as contractions in the mind and body.

People caught in addictive behaviors feel cut off from their wholeness. They feel small; bad; contracted. They may say mean things to themselves, thus increasing this feeling of badness and unhappiness.

We naturally know and recognize freedom. We are drawn to it. When we are blessed with glimpses of our true nature, we crave more. Any client who has had a spiritual experience—which could also be described as a direct experience of wholeness—recognizes its significance. Despite addiction and addictive behavior, wholeness abides in the background, ready to be rediscovered.

PRINCIPLE 3: We also have within us a reservoir of positive stored experiences. Everyone has stored memories and experiences that are positive. Even when hidden in dark, forgotten corners of the mind, they remain—awaiting discovery and recovery, to be brought out like treasured gems. These positive experiences can include memories of feeling safe, loved, comforted, healthy, happy, joyful, awed, inspired, powerful, courageous, and peaceful.

Even where a person had a terrible childhood, there were times not fraught with trauma. Stored in their warehouse of experiences are simple pleasures like playing with a puppy, feeling the warmth of the sun, or enjoying a good meal. Every person possesses a memory of at least one person from childhood who was kind, such as a neighbor, teacher, or grandparent.

These positive memories are stored in memory networks. From these key life experiences, webs of associations radiate. The strands that make up these webs can include images, emotions, body sensations, sounds, smells, tastes, and beliefs. An example of a positive resource memory could be an experience of fishing with your grandfather as a child. You have the *image* of yourself as a child with your grandfather in the rowboat out on the lake. You *smell* the lake and the fishy smell of the bait. You *feel* the rocking of the boat, the sun on your face, and the light breeze. You *hear* the sound of the oars as they hit the side of the boat, the splash of the sinker as it hits the water, and the wind in the trees. You *feel* comforted, happy, and loved. Later in life, when you think of fishing with your grandfather, you feel warm inside. The smell of a lake makes you happy because it lights up the memory network where these pleasant memories of being connected and loved reside.

The problem is, we don't pay as much attention to these positive experiences as we do the negative ones. We tend to focus on what is lacking rather than what is working well. Likewise, we may focus on what we see as flaws in ourselves rather than appreciating our strengths. In spite of the tendency to focus on problems, our good experiences remain inside us as potential resources that can be accessed and integrated into our broader view of ourselves and our world through Resource Tapping.

PRINCIPLE 4: We become unhappy when we are not able to access our wholeness or our reservoir of positive experiences or when we are out of balance. Life events and our interpretation of those events can throw us off balance and trigger feelings of fear, anxiety, and depression. We can get down on ourselves for not feeling or doing better. Of course, this makes us feel worse. Unpleasant experiences and our interpretations of these experiences can create life-limiting memory networks that dramatically affect how we view ourselves and our world in the present.

Over time, we create a sense of self from our interpretations of experiences. For example, if you were shamed as a child for difficulty with learning in school, you may have come to fear learning in school. If your parents and teachers told you that you were bad and stupid when you didn't do your homework, you may have believed them. You came to believe you were stupid and couldn't learn. You avoided school, failed to complete your education, and were left with a diminished sense of self. Because your body holds the memory of this humiliation, you may have anxiety when learning something new without having any conscious idea why. The experience may be over, but your story about it continues to run your life. This negative view of yourself may then be reinforced throughout your life when you experience other humiliations.

PRINCIPLE 5: We have a natural healing system that, when accessed and activated using BLS (tapping), can restore us to balance. For many people (and even some animals), using BLS in whatever form is most comfortable and convenient will calm the nervous system and bring some stress relief. When we experience anxiety, tapping alternately, right-left, right-left, on the knees or shoulders can help to calm us down. Even taking a walk—a very simple form of right-left, right-left stimulation—helps relieve stress.

PRINCIPLE 6: We can access, strengthen, and integrate our pure potential and reservoir of resources by tapping into our imaginations. Many forms of therapy utilize techniques involving imagination and visualization to heal physical and psychological problems. Brain research has shown that when we *imagine* doing something, neurons in the brain are activated as if we are actually doing it. For example, if you imagine moving your right arm, the region of your brain responsible for moving that arm is activated—just as if you were actually moving it. Clinical experience has shown that alternate tapping strengthens the effects of visualization even more.

Many of the resources explored in this book are accessed with the imagination. In order to help clients develop their resources, you'll want to have them imagine a resource that they want to cultivate. They can do this by bringing to mind a memory of how they experienced it, an image that evokes it, or someone or something that represents it for them. Activating the imagination by bringing in as many of the senses as possible helps to bring the image more alive for the client.

Let's say your client is anxious and unsettled, and you want to help her feel calmer and more peaceful. You might begin by asking her to close her eyes and go inside, then bring to mind a time when she felt calm and peaceful. She might remember a time at the beach when she was a girl. You ask her to imagine herself there, bringing in her senses as much as she can. What does she see, hear, smell, and feel? She tells you the sun is warm and the waves gentle, and the air carries a salty scent. She recalls the feeling of the sand soft on her feet. If it serves to increase her positive feelings, you can ask her to enhance the memory with more sensory information. You know that the desired memory network has been activated once the client actually feels a sense of peacefulness. She has used her imagination to locate stored positive information. When her resource has been activated, and she has a strong feeling for it, you add BLS. The client can tap herself; or, if it *feels* safe and comfortable to her, the therapist can tap on her hands or knees. Tap for only a short time—6 to 12 times, right-left, right-left. The tapping helps the person to *feel* the resource more fully in every way. Using the imagination brings it up, but the tapping makes the resource experience more embodied.

With this understanding of the six basic principles, we can begin to identify, cultivate, and enhance the most beneficial resources for our clients who need support in recovery.

How Does Bilateral Stimulation (BLS) Work?

Despite all the empirical evidence of the power of BLS to help people in the ways I'm describing here, we don't have a definitive explanation for how it works. A few theories can shed some light on the mechanism.

Psychiatrist and researcher Bruce D. Perry has posited a theory for the mechanism of action of BLS. He theorizes that the rhythmicity of stimulation creates a calming effect on the nervous system. The calming effect rhythm has on us may simply be hardwired into the human nervous system. For thousands of years, cultures all over the world have used drumming and dancing to process traumatic experiences. When most people are in their mother's womb, they experience a safe, calm environment and hear the rhythm of their mother's heart. Perhaps the sound of her heartbeat then becomes linked to a feeling of calm in the developing baby's brain. Rhythm may reconnect us to this feeling.

Some brain researchers believe that the processing effect of EMDR's alternating BLS has to do with the client's constant shifting of attention across the midline of the body. This process mimics the neurological effect of REM or dream sleep—specifically, the activation of memories and their integration into a broader contextual understanding. Brain scans have demonstrated that activating both sides of the brain helps facilitate the processing of information. The alternating aspect of Resource Tapping and EMDR is important, too: research[24] has also shown

> us that alternating bilateral stimulation is more effective than stimulation on both sides simultaneously.
>
> Rhythm and BLS do seem to be inherently soothing to the nervous system. We instinctively rock and pat a baby to soothe it when it cries; when we are upset and go for a walk, we almost always feel better afterwards. Should we attribute these calming effects to the bilateral nature of the stimulation, or to the rhythm of rocking, patting, or walking? We don't know. It's likely that they have complementary, additive effects.

RESOURCE TAPPING: BASIC INSTRUCTIONS FOR ALL PRACTITIONERS

Tapping in resources seems to help assimilate them, making the resources more accessible. Resource Tapping seems to *integrate memory networks*. When we tap right-left, right-left, we help the brain process and integrate information that is stored in different compartments.

I like to use a metaphor borrowed from the poet, Rumi: imagine a large house with many rooms. Only a few rooms are used on a daily basis, many of the best rooms are rarely used, and some are entirely forgotten. When focus is brought to resources we wish to cultivate and then tap into, the doors to the forgotten rooms seem to open. These closed-off rooms are then made accessible to the rest of the house.

The basic instructions for Resource Tapping are very simple:

1. Begin by asking clients to imagine the resource, evoking as much sensory information as they can in order to feel the desired qualities. (For instance, as I'll describe in the next chapter, they can imagine their Peaceful Place.)

2. When they feel their resource well activated, begin BLS. Adding BLS strengthens and integrates the activated image, feeling, and sensory information.

3. After establishing a Peaceful Place, you might then ask the client to think of Nurturing Figures and tap each one in, then Protectors and Wise Figures, tapping each one in consecutively.

4. Continue in this way with all the resources you wish to collect, giving your client a basic resource tool kit. You will know what your client's resources are and will be able to activate and tap them in with them when they are needed

in treatment. The client will also be able to use these resources themselves between sessions.

When tapping in a resource, it is important for clients to use their imaginations to enhance their sensory experience of the resource. The client has to *feel* the resource in the body—just thinking about it is not enough. I ask my clients to close their eyes and go inside, and then imagine their resource. Some clients do not feel safe with eyes closed; I instruct them to go through the process with eyes open, which can be more difficult. After imagining the resource, instruct them to notice what they are seeing, hearing, feeling, and perhaps even smelling. Activating more of the sensory experience helps activate the network where the resource is stored. I have found that many people think that they must visualize the resource, and this proves difficult for them. I've begun to use the words "imagine" or "think of" to lead them into their resourcing process. Visual imagery is not required for this to work. We are seeking to access whatever sensory networks are associated with the desired resource.

When people are skeptical about the use of imagination—some clients will say it's "silly"—I point out how the use of imagination in athletics has been proven to promote peak performance. I remember watching Bode Miller, the Olympic medal–winning skier, before a downhill race on the top of a run. His eyes were closed and he moved his body as he reviewed and imagined the course before launching himself down the slope. He was rehearsing his performance in his mind so that he could more easily accomplish his goal. I explain that we all use our imaginations all the time without realizing it. We are hardly ever in the present; our minds are constantly busy projecting backward and forward, thinking about the past, worrying about the future, and creating pictures in our minds and feelings in our bodies. I point out to clients struggling with addictive behavior how often they imagine using or engaging in the problematic behavior and how strongly they react to that imagining.

I help clients come to feel the power of imagination as a tool for their own healing when used skillfully. I point out that its most common use is to reinforce negative loops (reviewing mistakes and the things we have done wrong or thinking about all that could go wrong in the future). Instead, we can choose to imagine and tap in positive resources to improve our state of mind and emotional state. When we choose positive uses for our imagination, we give the brain an alternative pathway—a new way of thinking and feeling.

Tapping Methods

Tapping in resources can include many forms of alternating BLS. You can tap on your client's legs or knees, or use vibrating pulsers from equipment developed for EMDR, such as the Tac/Audio Scan. Directed eye movements can also be used.

Whatever the modality, it is important to use *alternating* BLS to stimulate each side of the brain. The alternating pattern can start on either the left or the right. Exploring the type of BLS that feels best for clients helps to enhance a feeling of safety with the therapist. The therapist and client can also discover together what tempo of BLS feels right for the client. Some people prefer very slow BLS for resourcing; others prefer a faster speed. Most of my clients set the speed initially for both Resource Tapping and EMDR. It is always best to explore with individual clients what feels and works best for them.

Therapist or client taps the client's legs. When using any form of touch in therapy, the therapist must ask the client's permission and be aware of the significance of touch for this client. Many of our clients struggling with or in recovery from addictions were sexually abused in childhood. Even suggesting that you tap on their knees may feel unsafe to them, thus damaging trust in the therapeutic relationship. If I even suspect that the suggestion of physical touch would be uncomfortable or triggering for a client, I won't suggest it.

Client taps the sides or tops of their own legs. Placing one hand on either thigh, the client alternately taps right-left or left-right.

Client uses the "butterfly hug." This variation is especially helpful when a client wants to feel comforted. Ask the client to cross their arms across their chest and tap the shoulders, right-left or left-right.

Therapist provides pulsers. These small plastic buzzers are connected by cords that attach to a manual controller that the therapist holds. The speed and intensity of the vibratory stimulation can be adjusted according the client's preference. Clients can place pulsers under their legs or in their pockets or can hold them in their hands.

Resource Tapping can be done in group settings. More will be said about this in Chapter 4.

STAY FOCUSED ON THE POSITIVE

The idea with Resource Tapping is to keep it focused on the positive; this is why we suggest doing short sets of BLS initially. For others, longer sets of BLS feel right and help them delve deeper into webs of positive associations.

Some people may quickly have painful memories come up once this stimulation begins. A rule of thumb is if it's going positively, keep going. If it goes negative, stop. With clients who are tapping themselves, instruct them to stop tapping immediately if the resource becomes negative in some way. Let the client inform you when they feel that they have tapped in their resource sufficiently.

These steps outline the most basic approach to tapping in resources. In the course of this book, we will discuss many variations on this technique, but this method serves as the starting point and foundation of this practice.

Other General Guidelines for Resource Tapping

Instruct clients to:

Close their eyes and go inside. "Bring to mind the resource you have chosen to work with. It can be a positive memory, an inherent quality, an experience, a spiritual figure, or an important person or animal."

Imagine the resource as well as they can. "Open your senses. Notice what you are seeing. Notice what you are hearing. Notice what you are smelling. What sensations do you feel on your skin? What do you feel? Take the time you need to elicit this information and fill out the resource."

When they have a strong sense of the resource, when they can feel its quality, have them begin tapping their knees. right-left, right-left. or they can do the butterfly hug, crossing the arms in front of their chest and tapping alternately on either shoulder. Whatever tapping mode is used, have the client tap 6 to 12 times, then stop and check in with themselves. If it feels good and the resource is strengthening, have them tap some more. Ask your client to begin to tap at a slow, rhythmic pace and then find the pace that feels best to them. While they tap, ask them to focus on the whole feeling the resource evokes in them and allow the feeling to increase and expand.

Tap as long as it feels positive. If other memories or resources come to mind that feel good, you can tap them in also. If the resource should flip to the negative or become contaminated in some way—for example, if the Peaceful Place evokes a sad memory—stop BLS. Many people can only do a few right-left taps before they begin to commence free-associative processing that can take them far afield. It is best to do short sets and see how the client is feeling. With practice, you will learn what works best for each client.

If a resource becomes contaminated in some way from unpleasant associations, stop BLS. Explore with your client what came up. This will help you devise next best steps.

As mentioned earlier, tapping can cause your client's mind to connect to and light up all kinds of old memories, including ones that are distressing. If your client has a lot of trauma in their background, be very careful with the tapping in of resources. Do very short rounds of tapping; then stop and check in with the client before continuing to tap.

If You Stop BLS Because of Unpleasant Associations

Here are a few things you can try; see what works best for the client:

After tapping stops, see if they can think of another, different resource that is fully positive. *It is important that the resource feel completely positive.* If they can find another one, tap it in, tapping for a shorter duration this time.

If a distressing memory has arisen, you can ask them to imagine placing it in a container that can hold it for them. This container can be made of anything they can imagine that can safely hold the material that has come up: a safe, a treasure chest with a good lock, or a vault. It is important that the container have a strong lid. This imagery can help the client consciously compartmentalize information that is too much to integrate. It is a skillful way to handle material that does not feel manageable. When you feel the memory has been sufficiently contained, ask the client to return to the resource they began with, or to bring up another one that has only positive feelings and associations. This time, have them tap very briefly.

One way to support clients whose resources are easily corrupted by negative associations is to give homework assignments to find visual representations (pictures from magazines, online, or elsewhere) of their resources. They can compose collages with the pictures they find that represent the different resources you wish to develop. When they have found what feels like strong representations of the desired resource, ask them to close their eyes, go inside, and bring to mind the pictures they have compiled of the resource. When they have a strong sense of this resource, add BLS. In this way you are helping them to more fully develop the resources they need for their healing.

Resource Tapping can be a powerful tool and, as such, should be used with care and caution. Although the natural healing resources we are accessing are trustworthy, as I will go into later, tapping can elicit a free-associative processing of information that can be overwhelming and in some cases even traumatizing. For the applications I'm describing in this book, using this technique can be entirely safe and very beneficial, but must be done responsibly. For work with larger traumatic experiences or childhood trauma, I recommend seeing a certified EMDR therapist.

PART II

TOOLS FOR AFFECT REGULATION

CHAPTER 4
The Four Foundational Resources

Be wise. Treat yourself, your mind, sympathetically,
with loving kindness. If you are gentle with
yourself, you will become gentle with others.

—LAMA THUBTEN YESHE

This chapter will introduce you to the four foundational resources: Peaceful Place, Nurturing Figures, Protector Figures, and Wise Figures. I have found that identifying and tapping in these foundational resources creates an internal structure that helps clients feel more secure and stable. They help clients help themselves to cope with their anxiety and difficult feelings through accessing and tapping in resources for themselves. This process supports clients in discovering an internal treasure trove of resources that can be used both to calm, comfort, and protect, and to provide useful guidance.

STRENGTHENING THROUGH RESOURCE TAPPING

Many people who struggle with addictions feel powerless over their lives, emotions, and anxieties. They tend to look outside themselves for something that will help them cope. When we teach our clients that the resources they need to help them with their problems are carried within themselves and that they can reliably access and make use of those resources, they come to feel more empowered and confident.

Many EMDR therapists have found that simply beginning with the four foundational resources (or others that are strengthening and empowering) can start to give clients more control over their feelings and their addictions. As I said earlier, in some cases, clients benefit so much from the resourcing work that they don't need to do the EMDR trauma processing to become free of the symptoms that drove the addictions.

Where EMDR is called for, clients must be stable enough to handle strong emotions that can come up as they process traumatic memories and strong enough to allow themselves to drop into the flow of free-associative processing. Addicts tend to have chaotic lives. They are overwhelmed by and avoidant of strong feelings; they may be fearful of losing control and feeling all the feelings they have worked to bury. Experiencing these feelings may trigger intense urges to use or to engage in addictive behavior. It may take time for them to build the stability to process the intense affects that may come up with EMDR trauma-processing work. Resourcing allows for time and the building up of the strength, trust, and stability required for this deeper psychotherapeutic work.

FINDING EFFECTIVE RESOURCES

We gain a lot of valuable information about our clients by working with them to identify resources. Can they easily identify them, or is it a struggle? Which ones are easier for them to find, and which present more of a challenge? Clients who can't seem to find any figure who is nurturing or compassionate more than likely did not have a connection to such figures growing up. Through searching out such figures, I may discover that the client had no one in their childhood that they could depend on. I may see a link between their adult anxiety and insecurity and this lack of secure attachment in childhood. This may also be why the client was drawn to substance use as a way to manage anxiety. If they have difficulty coming up with protectors, it may be because no one ever protected them.

I believe that resources can nearly always be found. Within each person lies the capacity to use their imagination or tap into their life experience to find these resources. It may not be easy, but with a playful attitude of mutual exploration and discovery, it can be done in virtually every case.

Resources don't have to be drawn from real life. Encourage clients to access their imaginations and explore digital or print media to find resources if necessary. To find a Nurturing Figure, for example, they can search magazines or the internet for images of nurturing in animals or in humans, or they can look at photos or watch YouTube videos of healthy nurturing interactions. Have the client draw from movies, books, inspiring works of art, or television shows that include nurturing characters. The therapist or counselor can make a fun home-work assignment of looking for images that represent these figures. In choosing Nurturing Figures, the client does not have to imagine being nurtured or pro-tected by the figure. Clients simply need to be able to *imagine* the figure and have a *feeling* of it—a *felt* sense of what the figure represents. Using the imagination is the stimulus for the activation of the neural circuit.

For example, if the client imagines a mother grizzly bear as a protector, he doesn't have to imagine himself being protected by her. When he imagines that mother bear manifesting her protective quality, he feels that energy in himself. With the BLS, this feeling that he has lit up in his circuitry will be linked to his overall wiring. BLS links the circuits together.

Sometimes, I am surprised to learn that a client who was severely abused in childhood and who has struggled with substance abuse can readily locate resources to tap in. This is a wonderful discovery for both the client and therapist, as they now have access to a previously unrecognized wellspring of resilience. I remember being particularly inspired by the case of a man whose severe heroin addiction had destroyed his health to the point where both of his legs had been amputated. He lived in a residential medical setting, where his addiction and medical needs could be addressed. Despite the extent of his trauma history and the serious life issues he was facing, he was able to tap in resources. He easily imagined a Peaceful Place and quickly got a sense of it. Tapping the sides of his thighs, he reported that his body relaxed, and he felt comfort for the first time in many years. He was then able to utilize this resource when he desired comfort, simply by bringing it to mind and tapping the sides of his thighs.

Some people think they need to be able to visualize the resource. They do not. They simply need to think of it, or imagine it, and activate a feeling state. Most people can access these resources and report an embodiment of them when BLS is added. Some find that they can imagine resources but cannot feel them. The feeling is the most important part, but it can be more difficult to access when clients have a reduced capacity for imagining—for example, if they were not allowed to play as children. More work may need to be done with them to help develop this capacity. For those that can imagine, but not feel the resource, I have often found that clinical depression is blocking access to feeling. They report being able to *imagine* but not *feel*, as though an invisible wall separates them from the felt sense they are seeking. In cases like these, I may refer the client to a specialist for treatment of depression through either medication or through non-pharmacological means (e.g., diet, supplements). Depression is common for people raised in families where there was addiction, abuse, or neglect. Clients may use addictive substances or behaviors—self-medicate—to try to treat their depression. The addiction then serves to exacerbate their depression at a biochemical level, creating havoc in their lives and relationships and reinforcing negative beliefs they may have about being weak or bad. Proper treatment for depression may be an integral part of treating addiction.

TAPPING IN FOUNDATIONAL RESOURCES

- Provides information to the therapist or counselor about clients' resilience and strengths, as well as areas that need more strengthening.
- Provides a kind of safety net for trauma-processing work, helping to hold it within a structure and foundation.
- Strengthens and empowers clients.
- Rewires the nervous system, linking up resources with clients' neural circuitry so they have access to them.
- Broadens clients' sense of themselves and their capacities.
- Heals attachment trauma by linking in Nurturing and Protector Figures who can help heal these early wounds.
- Increases self-esteem by helping clients discover the good, healthy parts of themselves.
- Provides a self-help technique for managing emotions, calming anxiety, and facilitating sleep.

THE TAPPING-IN PROCESS: AN OVERVIEW

I recommend tapping in all of the following resources at least once: Peaceful Place, Nurturing Figures, Protector Figures, and Wise Figures. I typically begin with the Peaceful Place, activate it (have the client confirm that a felt sense of the resource is present for them), and then add BLS. I then ask the client for Nurturing Figures. We make a list of them and tap each one in. We then move on to the Protector Figures, make a list, and then tap them in. Finally, we name the Wise Figures and tap them in, too. We might also bring all the figures together as a team of inner support and tap in the team.

When foundational resources have been tapped in, they can be easily summoned for many kinds of problems or situations. For example, if the client is feeling anxious about an upcoming work situation, he can close his eyes, imagine his Peaceful Place, and tap on his knees. A client who has trouble falling asleep at night might imagine all her resources surrounding her and providing comfort and protection, and then tap the sides of her legs or tap her arms in the butterfly hug so that she can let go into sleep.

PEACEFUL PLACE

This resource will support clients in finding imagery that will serve to calm them down and create an internal, always-present refuge from their active minds and agitated bodies. For clients struggling with addictions, the Peaceful Place can help calm down an activated nervous system—a state of being that has, in the past, been linked to the client's urge for the substance or behavior used as a remedy. Whether the therapist or counselor calls this place "calm," "sacred," or "happy," it should produce the same desired effect. (In my own practice, I have stopped using the term "safe place." I've found that the word "safe" can trigger associations of its opposite in people with trauma histories.)

The Peaceful Place can be a real place they know or a place they create in their imaginations. Work with the client to create a place of self-nourishment and comfort where they can relax or can feel a sense of sanctuary where they can contact their wisdom and creativity. Clients can imagine going to their Peaceful Place as a means of self-soothing. Suggest that they can access this place just before going to sleep at night. The Peaceful Place can also serve as a gathering spot for their allies when extra safety and support are needed. This will be described in more detail later in this chapter.

Peaceful Place imagery has been widely described and used. Simply imagining a place that is peaceful and comfortable can be powerful in and of itself. Combining imagination and BLS serves to strengthen the imagery more fully, integrating it into the nervous system and making it more accessible and useful. I have heard many stories of people creating a feeling of calm during times of duress by tapping and imagining their Peaceful Place. People in countries all over the world, rich and poor, young and old, have used this resource. Children can be taught to tap in their Peaceful Place, too.

Adapt the Peaceful Place instructions for each client's unique needs. What is important to achieve? Do you want to create a place of peace and calm where the person can turn off the outside world and the triggers to emotional upset? Do you want this to be a place where the person can access their inner resources? Many people choose a place in nature, such as a beautiful beach or mountain lake; others reach for more symbolic imagery—for example, feeling themselves nestled in the arms of an angel. The therapeutic relationship and therapist's office can also be used as the place if no other place can be found. They also don't have to imagine being alone in this place; if they like, they can imagine their friends, family, or other support people in their Peaceful Place with them.

Art can be used to create or enhance the Peaceful Place. The client can draw the place and then tap it in with BLS. For very fearful, traumatized clients who are afraid that bad things will happen if they relax or that a bad person will invade their space, I suggest that they make their place extra safe by putting up a protective barrier around it, made of anything they wish. I ask, "*Would you like to imagine a protective barrier around your place? It can be made of whatever you think will most safely secure it.*" Variations I've heard in my practice include a protective shield like the one from *Star Trek* or fierce protectors positioned to guard the perimeters of the Peaceful Place.

Some clients might choose a place they escaped to in their childhood. For some, this is a place in nature that provided them solace and comfort, away from the drama of the family home; for others, it's a place where there were happy times. Try to ensure that the place the client chooses does not bring up pain from the past.

Some people can drop in easily to contact an image and feeling of a Peaceful Place; others may need more help and preparation. The time necessary for relaxation depends on the emotional and body state of the client. It can be helpful to engage the client in relaxation exercises before beginning the Peaceful Place experience. If the client has their own way to relax, encourage them to take that path into a relaxed state.

Typically, I begin with simple instructions, asking the client to close their eyes and go inside.

What If a Client Doesn't Want to Close Their Eyes While Tapping?

I generally ask clients to close their eyes while tapping in resources to facilitate contact with their inner experience. Some people don't feel safe closing their eyes, however, and I don't insist that the client do so if it triggers a sense of vulnerability and lack of safety; instead, I let them connect with resources with eyes open.

I say something like this to begin Resource Tapping: *"Imagine a place that is peaceful. A place where you feel comfortable and at ease. It can be a place from your past or present. It can be a real place, or a place you create in your imagination. Let me know when you have found a place and have a sense of it."*

Often, with eyes closed, they will nod their heads. Then, I say: *"I'm going to start the bilateral stimulation for a little bit to strengthen this."* (I use the type of BLS chosen by the client before we begin the exercise.) As we begin BLS, I look for any signs of relaxation: a deep breath, a release in the shoulders, eyes settling down. Often, I don't see a shift; if this is the case, I stop the BLS after several seconds and check in with my client, asking, *"How was that for you?"*

If they tell me it was good, that they could feel and connect with the resource and felt a shift into a more relaxed state, then I know they have responded to the resourcing. If they tell me they couldn't connect with it—perhaps that it was too vague, or they couldn't feel anything—then I work to facilitate them entering a more relaxed state prior to summoning the resource again. We may also add more sensory information to better activate the resource network.

I might then ask them again to close their eyes and go inside. *"Imagine a Peaceful Place, a place where you can relax and be at ease. What do you see? What do you smell? What do you hear? What do you feel?"* I'll ask the client, *"Do you have a good sense of it now?"* or say, *"Let me know when you can really feel your Peaceful Place."* When the client signals "yes" with a nod of their head, I again begin a short sequence of BLS. I might ask, *"Is it getting stronger?"* If they respond affirmatively, I might go a little longer with the BLS.

I watch my client for signs of deepening relaxation or increased agitation. If I see their breathing increase, I will stop immediately and ask them what is happening. While BLS works quite well to increase the feeling and imagery of the Peaceful Place for many clients, it may open up processing of traumatic material for others.

Some clients respond very quickly to BLS by beginning to open up trauma memories, or their Peaceful Place may become contaminated in some other way. If you see distress or agitation in your client during this process, stop BLS and explore with them what they are experiencing. You may need to develop another Peaceful Place using imagery only or use only very short sets of BLS. Stay closely attuned to your client and accommodate to their needs.

TAPPING IN THE PEACEFUL PLACE

The following is a guided imagery script to the Peaceful Place. It can be recorded for the client to use later:

"Find a comfortable way to sit so that your back is straight but relaxed and your feet are uncrossed and resting on the floor. You may also sit cross-legged if you wish. Close your eyes and be aware of how your body feels. Notice the places of contact . . . your bottom on the seat and your feet on the floor. Be aware of your breathing. Where do you feel it? What is its rhythm?

"Now imagine as you inhale a deep, full breath, that you are taking the air from deep within the earth. This breath comes up through your legs and fills your belly . . . then your chest . . . and now your throat. When you feel the breath in your throat, hold it a moment, then exhale, letting the air leave the throat . . . then the chest . . . and now the belly . . . releasing the air back down into the earth. When the need arises to take another breath, again breathe in from the earth, filling the belly, chest, and throat . . . pause . . . and then, again slowly exhale: throat, chest, belly, back down into the earth. Let the air fill your body. Let the inhalation and exhalation be gentle and smooth. Be aware of the sensations in the body. If your mind wanders away, gently bring it back to the breathing. Smooth and gentle. Be present. The goal is attained moment to moment.

"Now imagine yourself in a peaceful, relaxing place. This place can be real or imaginary. It might be somewhere you've been before, from a dream or fantasy you have had; somewhere from a movie or book; or somewhere you have heard about. Let the image of the place come to you . . . this place that is peaceful, calm and serene . . . a special inner place for you . . . some place where you feel at ease . . . a place where you feel safe and secure. It can be a sanctuary . . . somewhere to go to be quiet and reflective . . . somewhere special and healing for you.

"When you have found your Peaceful Place, let yourself explore and experience this place as if you were there now. Notice what you see there. Notice what sounds you hear. What do you smell? Notice what it feels like to be there. Allow yourself to absorb the feelings of peacefulness . . . of being secure and at ease. Immerse yourself in serenity.

"When you can sense and feel the peacefulness of this place, nod your head, and I will begin the BLS."

Watch to see how your client is doing. If they seem to be relaxing, keep going, if they seem agitated or distressed, stop the BLS. If all goes well with this first round of tapping, stop the BLS after a few seconds and check in with the client. Ask *"How is that for you?"* If they tell you that they were just getting into it when you stopped, ask them to tell you when it feels well established and integrated. They can signal "stop" with their hand or nod their head.

If they are enjoying this and have positive associations, you can continue longer with the BLS. *"Good! Keep going. Let me know when it feels complete to you."* In this way, you are more fully lighting up and integrating healthy, positive networks.

When they feel complete—when the Peaceful Place is well established—tell them, *"You can return to this place anytime you wish. This special place of relaxation and serenity is always available to you."*

SACRED PLACE

A variant on the Peaceful Place resource is the Sacred Place. Instead of focusing on the sense of peacefulness, the emphasis is on the feeling of sacredness—a spiritual sense. The Sacred Place can be a place clients have been to or a place they can imagine. In this place, they feel peaceful, but also have a sense of something larger than themselves. Examples of sacred places are the Notre Dame Cathedral, Delphi, Machu Picchu, Bodh Gaya, Mt. Kailash, Sedona, the Great Pyramid, the Taj Mahal, and Jerusalem. Many places in nature evoke a feeling of the sacred: consider the Grand Canyon, a grove of redwoods, or Mount Denali.

TAPPING IN THE SACRED PLACE

Instruct the Client: *"Close your eyes and go inside. Spend a few moments bringing yourself to the present. Feel yourself sitting. Now take some deep, full breaths. Allow yourself to relax and let go as you slowly exhale. When you feel relaxed, imagine yourself in a Sacred Place. It can be a place you have been before, a place you have read about, or a place that you create in your imagination. It can be a physical structure or a place in nature. Maybe you have visited this place in a dream.*

"In this place, you feel peaceful and sense a beautiful spiritual vibration. It is your sanctuary. You can invite Spiritual Figures to be there with

you, or you can be there by yourself. Create it however you like. Feel a
sense of profound peace in this special place. Here, you can contact your
higher wisdom and source of creativity. Your sanctuary can open you to
a broader perspective on your life.

"When you have found your Sacred Place, notice what you see
there. Look around. What do you hear? What do you smell? What does
your body feel?

"When you have a strong feeling of your Sacred Place, begin to tap.
Tap right-left, 6 to 12 times. If the feeling gets stronger, tap longer.

"Spend as much time as you would like in your sanctuary. Remember
that this special place is always here for you whenever you need it."

Alternatives to the Peaceful or Sacred Place

Some clients do not feel comfortable with a Peaceful Place or a Sacred Place. Being calm and peaceful may not appeal to many young people—especially young men, who might think it too boring. Some people with PTSD may not feel safe letting their guard down. Relaxing may actually make them feel unsafe. What might appeal more to these clients might be imagining doing a grounding and empowering activity that they enjoy—something healthy and enlivening. It could be participating in a sport, listening to music with friends, playing music, running, or creating art.

"Can you think of an activity that you enjoy? It can be something you have done in the past that makes you feel healthy and strong, or something you have done more recently. It can be listening to music with friends, enjoying a great meal, walking in nature, playing with children, or playing catch with a football. It can be anything you can think of as long as it is a healthy activity not associated with your addiction."

When they can imagine the activity, add BLS.

NURTURING FIGURES

Nurturing Figures are real or imaginary figures who have a compassionate, nurturing quality. The feeling state we desire to activate is one of a soothing, comforting presence. For clients who had chaotic, unsafe childhoods and a lack of people who provided steady comfort they could rely on, these figures are very helpful to tap in. Many people struggling with addictions have dysregulated nervous systems, in part because they lacked a stable, healthy home life growing up. They use addictive substances and behaviors to calm anxiety and regulate their nervous systems. Tapping in Nurturing Figures can help with emotional regulation and with repair of some of this early damage.

Helping clients imagine compassionate and comforting figures supports them in accessing these networks within themselves. With BLS, they can integrate them more fully, so they can feel this nurturing sense as part of themselves.

Tapping in Nurturing Figures can help with ego strengthening and stabilization prior to doing trauma work such as EMDR, but it also provides therapeutic value specifically for addiction recovery. If a client can feel soothed by recalling and tapping in a loving mother figure, an angel, or their grandmother, they can experience relief from anxiety and distress that drives them toward substance use. When we are very young and distressed, we don't reach for alcohol to comfort ourselves; our innate systems for seeking comfort involve reaching out to other human beings. Nurturing Figures, which can include real or imaginary figures from the present or past, inner guides, or animals with nurturing qualities, can begin to return the client to that healthier innate system for calming and comforting one's self.

When we imagine something, we activate the nervous system in a particular pattern. Tapping in any resource figure is meant to activate these nurturing qualities in the client's own nervous system. When my client can imagine a loving mother, for example, she feels those qualities in herself. It's as if that loving mother is within her—which she is, because it is her imagination that has created her. We aren't taking an outside mother figure and putting her into our client; rather, we are inviting the client to activate qualities of a loving mother into her own nervous system through imagination and BLS. When we add BLS to these imagined figures, we integrate this healing imagery more fully into her neural networks.

To begin establishing a Nurturing Figure, while taking an initial history ask the client about loving, safe, nurturing people in their lives. There may be a grandparent, nanny, aunt or uncle, teacher, coach, counselor, friend's parent, or neighbor who was an important source of caring for the client. Sometimes, the nurturing experience may be a one-time experience of being seen and understood by someone—and it has made such an impression that when it is recalled, connecting to the kindness of the person is easy.

If clients choose their mother or father, I want to be sure they are appropriate figures who were not chosen because of dissociation or wishful thinking. If I suspect the parent was neglectful or abusive, I will suggest that the client choose a different figure who is fully trustworthy as a nurturer.

There may be people from clients' current lives who are important resources for them, such as a current spouse, partner, lover, or friends. They can also use figures from movies, television, or books, historical figures, or people from popular culture. Some of my clients have chosen the African American nanny, Aibileen, from the book and movie *The Help* as a nurturing figure. Spiritual Figures can also be used as nurturers: a few examples are Quan Yin, Tara, Mary, Jesus, a Native American elder, or an angel. The same figure can be used as Nurturing Figure, Protector Figure, and Wise Figure.

For clients with significant attachment trauma from neglect or abuse, or who never had secure attachment to a compassionate caregiver, I will work with them to create and tap in an Ideal Mother. This is the mother they wish they had—a mother who "fits" them and can love and care for them in a consistent, healthy way. They can also tap in the Universal Good Mother. This mother figure goes beyond the failings of a human mother and encompasses universal qualities of love, tenderness, and compassion.[25]

The adult self can be used as a nurturer, too. I ask clients to think of a time when they gave love and care to someone or something—to their own children or to a pet, for example. When they have located the memory, I tell them, "*This is your nurturing adult self. This is the part of you that is caring and compassionate toward others.*" After locating this part of themselves, I ask them to connect with it, and then we add BLS.

Where clients have always taken care of themselves and have never had anyone take care of them, I try to find another nurturing figure in addition to their adult self. It can be anyone or anything that has nurturing qualities.

Animals can be valuable resources, too. These can be pets from the client's present or past—for example, a loving dog—or animals for which the client has a special affinity. A special dog from the client's past who was an ally and comfort can be very helpful and calming. A cat who snuggled with them when they were distressed as a child can be used as a Nurturing Figure. Other animals that the client has a special connection to or affinity with can also be used, such as a mother bear caring for her cub or a mother elephant sheltering her baby.

I typically try to find more than one figure, as each one has a different feeling and fills a different need. I work with my client to compile a list of Nurturing Figures; then we tap them in, one at a time. I will begin with the first one, asking the client to close their eyes and bring up the image as strongly as they can. "*See your friend Julie in her nurturing aspect,*" I will say. "*When you can feel that, let me know.*" At that point, I begin the BLS. I might ask them to tell me when it feels complete—when they feel it more deeply. I then move on to the next one on the list and ask them to imagine their cat in its nurturing aspect. When they have a good sense of that, I add BLS.

For clients who have been neglected, coming up with Nurturing Figures can be a challenge. They may need more help finding someone or something with a nurturing quality. I offer suggestions and brainstorm with them, throwing out ideas. I remind them that they don't have to imagine the figure nurturing or caring for them. *"Just think of someone or something you have seen providing caring or nurturing. Have you seen a mother cat with her kittens? A mother duck with her ducklings?"* Encourage the client to look for pictures in magazines or to search online, either with you or as homework. Another homework assignment that can support this process is to create a collage of nurturing relationship images from pictures cut out of magazines. Make this fun, not a chore. I let them know that they can do it—they can find the resources they need to heal. They are all around us; we just need to take them in.

TAPPING IN NURTURING FIGURES

Have your client first spend a few moments going inside and quieting their mind.

"Think of a figure or figures from your present or past that you associate with nurturing. This can be a person or animal, real or imagined; a Spiritual Figure; or even someone from a book or movie. When you imagine the figure, feel the nurturing quality in your body.

"After finding your Nurturing Figure, enhance the image as strongly as you can. What do you see? What do you hear? What do you smell? What do you feel in your body?

"When you have a strong sense of the nurturing quality of the figure, let me know. Now I'll begin the BLS." Use BLS for 6 to 12 right-lefts. Then stop and check in with your Client: *"How was that for you? How do you feel?"*

If the nurturing quality continues to strengthen, do more BLS if you wish. Continue with BLS as long as your client feels the figure and the nurturing quality strengthening and integrating. If there is more than one resource, they can bring the next Nurturing Figure to mind and then tap it in also. Repeat this process for each nurturing figure, tapping in one resource at a time.

When the client is through, they might want to imagine being held by the Nurturing Figure or Figures. As they imagine this, add more BLS to strengthen and deepen the feeling of being nurtured.

PROTECTOR FIGURES

Protectors are real or imaginary figures who have a protective quality. Protectors can help make what feels like an intolerable vulnerability manageable, mitigating the need for "liquid courage" or whatever other substance clients have been using to boost themselves up.

When these figures are imagined, clients feel stronger. The power of these imagined resources is activated within themselves. Protector Figures are helpful allies for clients who have not felt protected and who need a team of support to "watch their back." These allies can be summoned in your clients' imagination to give them strength and to help them to feel protected during times of vulnerability. Survivors of abuse carry childhood feelings of being helpless and unprotected as children in their adult nervous systems; protectors are important resources for these clients.

For clients who would not feel comfortable feeling vulnerable tapping in Nurturing Figures first, begin instead with Protector Figures. Meet clients where they feel most comfortable and where you can connect with them most easily. Many people who struggle with addiction feel safer connecting with strength and power in the beginning of treatment.

As with Nurturing Figures, Protector Figures can include people or animals or imaginary figures from books, movies, television, or dreams. Clients can use people from their childhood or from their present lives, or even their protective adult selves, as Protector Figures. Who would they like to summon that is strong, powerful, and protective?

I ask clients, *"Can you imagine a Protector Figure? It can be real or imaginary, as long as it has a protective quality. It can be someone you know from any time in your life, or someone from a movie or a book. It can be an animal or a Spiritual Figure that represents protection for you."* It is most important that, when they think of their Protector Figures, the client can *feel* their protective quality.

Action figures can make good Protector Figures. Many such figures can be found in movies or television shows. The client's spouse or partner can also be called up as a Protector Figure. As with Nurturing Figures, clients don't have to imagine the figure protecting them. For instance, a lioness with teeth and claws bared, vividly imagined protecting her cubs, is a strong protector. The client doesn't have to imagine her keeping him safe; it is sufficient to imagine this mother keeping her cubs safe and to feel her energy and power.

Many clients choose large animals as Protector Figures, including bears, tigers, lions, panthers, wolves, and elephants. Spiritual figures from many traditions can be used, including protective angels and deities. Other examples of Protector

Figures include grandparents, friends, partners, spouses, dogs, the protective adult self, or figures from movies and television such as James Bond, Spider-Man, Superman, Wonder Woman, the Hulk, Iron Man, Xena, and Rambo. Figures from myth like Hercules, Thor, and the goddess Athena also have come up as Protector Figures in my work with clients. You might find that the figure your client uses for nurturing also serves as a protector, but with the protective manifestation of the figure emphasized. Actual memories from life of positive interactions with Protector Figures can be tapped in: for example, a memory of a friend stepping in to protect them from being bullied in grade school.

I ask clients with abuse histories who were powerless as children to tap in strong, powerful Protector Figures. In this way, I help advocate for and protect my clients and help them access the neural circuitry associated with power in their own bodies. For example, if the client imagines the lioness as a Protector Figure, she can feel the power of her body, the strength in her legs, her size, and her capacity to defend and protect her young. She has, in a sense, embodied the lioness, who becomes a powerful and effective Protector Figure for her. This resource can then become available to her in daily life. If she feels anxious or fearful in a situation, she can imagine her lioness, feel her power, and even imagine that when she taps her own legs she is tapping the powerful legs of her lioness protector.

As in the case of Nurturing Figures, I like to gather more than one Protector Figure for my clients. We work together to create a list of Protector Figure resources that feel powerful and resonant. After we have the list, we go through and tap each one in; following each tapping in, I check in with them—*"How was that for you?"*—and then bring up the next one on the list. We go through all the Protector Figures the client has named; if others come to mind, we tap them in, too. Making drawings of these Protector Figures can help to strengthen the client's felt sense of them.

TAPPING IN PROTECTOR FIGURES

Ask your client to think of someone or something that has a protective quality. It can be real or imaginary. *"It can be someone you know from the present or past, an animal, or even a figure from a movie, book, or television. It can be a spiritual figure that is protective. It can be your adult protective self. It can be helpful to have more than one."*

Write down the client's list of Protector Figures, then go through and install them one by one: *"Close your eyes and go inside. Bring up an image of* [the first Protector Figure on the list]. *Feel the protective qual-*

ity. When you have a good sense of it, let me know. Good, now I'll begin the BLS." Remember: it is most important that the client have a body sense of the figure's protective quality.

Keep BLS going, 6 to 12 times, right-left, then stop and check in with your client. Ask how he or she feels. If it is getting stronger, or they want to go longer, continue with BLS, as long as it remains positive. Stop BLS when the client feels their protector resource strong inside them.

Then bring up the next Protector Figure. Be sure the client experiences its protective quality. *"Let me know when you have it. Good."* Repeat the imagination and tapping of protectors for as long as you feel it is being a positive experience.

The adult self can also be a Protector Figure. This is the part of us that can be contacted to protect ourselves or those we care for. Help clients find this adult protective self by guiding them to get in touch with a number of skills and traits that they already have inside and to then use BLS to strengthen and integrate these qualities.

FINDING AND TAPPING IN THE PROTECTIVE ADULT SELF

Tell your client to close their eyes and go inside, to take some deep breaths and slowly let them out. *"Relax and release with your exhalation. Bring yourself to the present moment. When you feel yourself present, see if you can find a time when you were protective. Can you think of a time when you defended someone you cared about? Be aware of whatever memory or image comes to mind."*

Allow the client some time to find the memory. *"When you find the memory, notice what you see. What are you hearing? What do you notice in your body? When you have the image and can feel the quality of protectiveness, let me know."* Once the client affirms that the image and quality are present and felt, have them do a short set of BLS.

"How are you feeling? Can you feel the sense of protectiveness? If you wish, we can add BLS again as long as it remains positive and the feeling of protectiveness strengthens." Allow more time if indicated.

"Now think of a time when you were courageous. What picture comes to mind? As you bring up the picture, notice what you feel. Notice

what you hear, smell, and sense. What do you feel in your body? When you have the image and the feeling of courage strongly activated, let me know." Begin BLS, 6 to 12 times, or do more if the client wishes and tolerates it well. Then stop BLS and check in with the Client: *"How do you feel?"* If you want the client to go longer to continue to strengthen the quality of courage, have them tap some more. *"What other qualities are associated with protectiveness? Strength, confidence, grounded-ness? Others? Continue to think of times when you felt these qualities."* Add BLS to strengthen and deepen the resource. *"After you have felt all these qualities within yourself, bring them together into a single sense of self."* Add BLS to strengthen and integrate.

"You might have an image that arises that represents the protective adult self. Let any image arise that feels as if it captures all the qualities of protectiveness that you have tapped. It is important that you have a bodily sense of the resource."

CIRCLE OF PROTECTION

Your clients can increase the feeling of protection by imagining a Circle of Protection comprised of all their Protector Figures. This can be used during times when clients feel vulnerable and afraid and wish to feel their protectors more fully. This Circle can also be called in when they want to protect themselves from their own urges to relapse—their own internal relapse prevention team.

TAPPING IN THE CIRCLE OF PROTECTION[26]

Have your client close their eyes and go inside. *"Take some deep breaths in and slowly let them go. Relax with the exhalation. Bring yourself to a quiet place inside.*

"When you are more relaxed, imagine yourself surrounded by your Protector Figures. Look around the circle. Look at each protector, one at a time. Feel their protection of you. If you would like to, you can enhance the details of the imagery and sense of protection. It is important that you feel the sense of them. Begin to tap. Tap 6 to 12 times. Stop and check in; if it is getting stronger, continue to tap, taking in the feeling of

being surrounded by protection. Take in their strength; let in their courage. Receive their determination to protect you."

Tell the client that making a drawing of their Circle of Protection can help reinforce the feeling of being protected. Have them take the time to draw themselves surrounded by their Protector Figures; have them view it when they need comfort. They can also tap as they look at their drawing.

Using Protector Figures to Handle a Challenging Family Situation That Threatened Relapse

Melinda always had a difficult time with the holidays, especially when visiting her family—a prospect she dreaded. Throughout her childhood, her father had drunk heavily and would explode verbally with little warning. Everyone in the family tried to avoid setting him off, and when it happened despite their best efforts, it would leave them all shattered. No one in her family had ever confronted Melinda's father about his behavior.

Melinda was new in her sobriety and feared relapse if she were to be surrounded by readily available alcohol and her father chose to level his scathing, drunken criticism at her. She was afraid that she would end up drinking as a defense against the powerlessness she felt in that situation. To decrease her anxiety and help her feel more protected, we decided to tap in Protector Figures. After exploring who might be good protectors for her, Melinda compiled a list that included her husband, her best friend, Joanna, her childhood German Shepherd, Riley, and Iron Man.

The first one she brought up was her husband. As she imagined him in his protector aspect, she felt the quality of protectiveness in him. She could feel that he would protect her in a time of need. When she could see him and feel that quality in him, she tapped on her knees for a short time, then stopped as soon as she could feel the feelings well established. She then brought her friend, Joanna, to mind, thought of the protective quality in her, and tapped to strengthen it.

Next, she thought of her dog, Riley. But when Melinda thought of Riley and tapped, she began to feel sad. She missed her steadfast childhood companion. The tapping was bringing up memories of the loss. Because of these feelings, she was not able to use him as a protector resource at that time. She put aside the upsetting memories of her dog and focused her attention again on the protective qualities of her husband and friend. When she could feel their protection again, she tapped for a short time to strengthen it. Finally, she brought up the image of Iron Man. She saw him in her mind's eye, full of confidence, intelligence, and power. She tapped to strengthen that image and feeling. When she had tapped in all her Protector Figures, she felt much better. She even thought of others who might serve. She no longer felt all alone with her difficulties.

To prepare for her visit home, she imagined getting triggered and upset by her father. Then she imagined leaving the scene and going to the bathroom where she could collect herself, go inward, and summon her Protector Figures. She played this dress rehearsal in her mind with BLS, feeling increasingly confident that she would be able to get through her visit without relapsing. She now had a strategy besides drinking for emotionally managing a potentially triggering situation.

WISE FIGURES

When we ask a client, "When you think of a wise being, what comes up for you?" their response reveals their Wise Figures. Such Wise Figures can include people they have known personally, such as family members with whom they are close or people from their family they have never met but heard about; spiritual figures; figures from movies or television; literary characters; or historical figures. They can include a sponsor, a mentor, or someone who has overcome addictions and can serve as a good role model. Some people have used Aslan, the sage, majestic lion from the *Chronicles of Narnia* or Yoda from the *Star Wars* movies. Other Wise Figures to use as resources could include spiritual teachers like Jesus or Buddha.

For some clients, the easiest way to find a wise resource is to simply ask them to compile a list of Wise Figures they would like as resources. They provide me a list of Wise Figures, and we tap each of them in, one at a time. For example, a client might choose Jesus, his grandfather, and his sponsor as Wise Figures. I would ask him to close his eyes, go inside, and bring up the image of the figure, along with the sense of the wise quality. When he indicates he has a sense of it, I begin the BLS. I do a short set, then check in with him. If he tells me it is getting stronger, I do more BLS until he tells me if it feels complete to him. I then ask him to bring up the next figure, imagine it, get the sense of its wisdom quality, and use the BLS again. I repeat this process with each of the figures he has chosen.

Multiple figures work best for most clients; I find that each figure has a different quality that is evoked with the installation. The wisdom called forth by these figures then serves as the resource wherever a client needs help or advice.

Inner Wisdom Figures

Another way to develop Wise Figures is to use guided imagery and to then invite an Inner Wisdom Figure to arise in the place being imagined—a process described in four of my previous books.[27]

I have found developing and tapping in an Inner Wisdom Figure to be particularly powerful and helpful, as it arises directly from the client's unconscious mind. Everyone has within themselves wisdom that they can tap into; discovering a wise voice that originates inside themselves is inspiring and empowering. Inner Wisdom Figures can be very valuable allies who—once they have been tapped in—can be called on in times of difficulty as a source of support and comfort.

If clients have a question or problem or don't know what direction to turn, they can take a moment to go inside themselves, call to mind their Inner Wisdom Figure, and ask the Inner Wisdom Figure for guidance while tapping. They will learn to become still and listen for their Inner Wisdom Figure's advice and to then tap more to take in that advice. In this way, these figures can provide guidance and support for them during times of difficulty in the recovery process.

More than one Inner Wisdom Figure can be tapped in; they may change each time they do the exercise. They may discover that different Inner Wisdom Figures serve best in different situations.

TAPPING IN INNER WISDOM FIGURES

Tell your client to close their eyes, go inside, and take a deep breath, filling their belly, chest, and throat. *"Hold it a moment, then exhale slowly from your throat, your chest, and your belly. Relax; let go with the exhalation. Now take another breath. Take your breath in from deep in the earth, filling your belly, chest, and throat. Hold it a few moments. Now exhale, releasing from your throat . . . chest . . . and belly. Relax. Let go. Let yourself settle into the present moment.*

"When you feel yourself relaxed, imagine going to your Peaceful Place. This is your special place where you are at peace, where you feel at ease. Take as much time as you need to find this special place.

When you are there, notice what you see. Look around. What sounds are you hearing? What are you smelling? What bodily sensations do you notice? Go inside yourself. How are you feeling in this special place?"

Allow the client to go inward and to answer your questions.

"As you relax in your Peaceful Place or sanctuary, invite your Inner

Wisdom Figure to join you in this special place. Just allow an image to form that represents your Inner Wisdom Figure, a wise, kind, loving figure who knows you well. Let it appear in any way that comes, and accept it as it is. It may come in many forms—man, woman, animal, friend, someone you know, or a character from a movie or book.

"Accept your Inner Wisdom Figure as it appears, as long as it seems wise, kind, loving, and compassionate. You will be able to sense its caring for you and its wisdom. Invite it to be comfortable there with you and ask it its name. Accept what comes. When you have found your Inner Wisdom Figure, begin to tap. Tap a few times and see how you feel. If it feels good, continue tapping. If it feels bad in any way, stop tapping and return to your Peaceful Place."

Follow your client's lead as they go inward and tap.

"You may end here, or you may continue this conversation with your Inner Wisdom Figure. Tell the figure about your problem; ask any questions you have concerning this situation, and then listen for the answers that come. Listen carefully for the figure's response. You may imagine your figure talking with you, or you may simply have a direct sense of its message in some other way. Allow it to communicate in whatever way seems natural. If you are uncertain about the meaning of the advice, or if there are other questions you want to ask, continue the conversation until you feel you have learned all you can at this time."

Let the client share or allow them to move through this process silently.

"As you consider what your Inner Wisdom Figure has told you, imagine what your life would be like if you took the advice you have received. If you have more questions, continue the conversation. When it seems right, thank your Inner Wisdom Figure for meeting with you, and ask it to tell you the easiest, surest method for getting back in touch with it. Realize that you can call another meeting whenever you feel the need for some advice or support. Say goodbye for now, in whatever way seems appropriate, and allow yourself to come back to the room."

INNER SUPPORT TEAM

When foundational resources have been tapped in, you can ask your clients if they would like to imagine all the figures together as a team. Some people will love this idea and immediately imagine all their resource figures assembled in a circle around them or behind them as a strong support. Others will not be able to imagine the figures but have a sense of them together without a visual impression of what it might look like.

Some people don't respond to the idea of the team at all. They can't imagine their grandmother nurturer and the grizzly bear protector together. Some people will want to add more figures to their team. Welcome as many resource figures as they would like to their team. Who or what else would they like to add to their resource team? They can add spiritual figures who will remind them of their higher values, or friends or family who have overcome addictions or obstacles in the past. You might even create a recovery support dream team, a resource I describe more in Chapter 10.

Now that you have tapped in and assembled the client's foundational resources, you will find that they can be used in many different ways. The chapters that follow will provide even more examples of how these resources can be integrated into support for addiction recovery.

RESOURCE TAPPING IN GROUPS

Many addiction therapists have used Resource Tapping in group settings with excellent results. Consider this option as you learn about the additional resources described in chapters to come.

In the group setting, each group member taps in their resources for themselves. Offer group members options for tapping in: they may choose to use the butterfly hug, where they cross their arms and tap either arm or shoulder; or they may alternately tap the sides of their thighs or their knees; or alternately tap their feet on the floor. After determining the form of BLS each wishes to use, the therapist can guide the group in the resources that they choose. Be prepared to thoroughly explain and demonstrate the resourcing and tapping processes. Allow time for group members to ask clarifying questions before beginning the exercise, and practice it yourself as part of the group.

You might begin by asking the members to think of a Peaceful Place. Invite them to bring in their senses as much as possible to allow the resource to strengthen. *"Notice what you see, what you hear, what you feel, what you smell."* Then tell them that when they have a strong sense of the place, and they can feel it inside, begin the BLS or tapping. They might begin by tapping to 6 to 12 times, keeping their internal attention only on positive feelings and associations.

Instruct them to stop tapping immediately if the resource becomes negative or if distressing associations or memories should arise. When they feel they have the resource sufficiently developed, they can stop.

When the group has stopped tapping, ask if individuals would like to share their experiences. How was it for them? If they have questions, this is the time to answer them. It can be helpful for group members to share their places and experiences. In this way, they can inspire one another and get more ideas. They can also be advised that they can tap in their resources whenever they wish to activate the experience the resource provided for them: if they feel anxious, for example, and want a way to calm down, they can imagine their Peaceful Place and tap their legs.

This same instruction can be used in a group setting for all of the resources in this book, including the other foundational resources—Nurturing Figures, Protector Figures, and Wise Figures. Art can be integrated as well: have group members draw their resources, close their eyes while holding the picture inside with the feelings evoked, and add BLS. These pictures create a visual record of their resources that they can keep with them as a reminder of their resilience and can be shared with the group. Clients who take part in a group might even create a booklet of their resources that can be kept with them.

Many addiction therapists have used these resources in group settings with excellent results. It is especially supportive in pretreatment.

CHAPTER 5

Resource Tapping Tools for Managing Anxiety

*So still were the big woods where I sat,
sound might not yet have been born.*

—EMILY CARR

Many people with anxiety disorders turn to alcohol, benzodiazepines, food, or other substances for relief of their symptoms. People with anxiety disorders are two to three times more likely than the general population to have an alcohol or other substance abuse disorder at some point in their lives.

Anxiety impacts self-confidence, self-esteem, and sense of self-efficacy. Helping clients with addiction issues to pay attention to how they feel, discover what they need, and learn what might help them—besides the addictive substance or behavior—is essential to their successful recovery.

ANXIETY AND ANXIETY DISORDERS: PREVALENCE AND CAUSES

About 20% of Americans with an anxiety or other mood disorder, such as depression, also have an alcohol or other substance use disorder. About 20% of those with an alcohol or substance use disorder also have an anxiety or mood disorder.[28] Many adolescents begin to abuse alcohol as a way of managing social anxiety, especially when this anxiety becomes severe enough to lead to unhealthy isolation.

People who come from unstable families and lacked secure attachment may experience generalized anxiety. Not having felt safe and secure as children, they have a more difficult time with self-soothing and emotional regulation as adults.

This is where using imagery to rewire the nervous system can be useful in providing support and decreasing the experience of general anxiety—and then, in turn, reducing the urge to use or abuse alcohol or other substances.

Another major source of anxiety is trauma. Many clients suffering from post-traumatic stress disorder (PTSD) experience major anxiety and have a difficult time regulating their sympathetic nervous system responses. Panic and anxiety can be activated when people are triggered by a reminder of the traumatic experience. They feel a loss of control, as though their nervous system has been hijacked: heart racing, sweating profusely, or a feeling that they may die.

In PTSD, the traumas involved may be traumas the client experienced as an adult, such as traumas from war, disasters, or violence; or they may originate in childhood, from abuse or medical traumas. Someone who has been sexually assaulted may become so fearful and anxious she becomes unable to leave her house to go to work. Sometimes, as in the case of dissociated early abuse memories, clients may not even remember the original traumatic event. It is essential that traumas linked to PTSD are addressed and reprocessed with EMDR or other trauma therapies when the client has the ego strength and affect tolerance to do so.[29]

Research indicates that there is a genetic predisposition to anxiety; some of our nervous systems are more prone to anxiety than others. According to the National Institute of Mental Health, nearly 40 million people in the United States have suffered from some kind of anxiety disorder, including panic attacks and phobias. Anxiety disorders are the number one mental health problem among American women and the second most prevalent among men. One of the reasons clients relapse is that they cannot cope with anxiety. We cannot remove the substance or behavior they have used to manage their distress without providing them with something to replace it. They simply can't handle how uncomfortable they feel in their bodies as anxiety arises. If anxiety is not proactively addressed, clients will resort to what they have used in the past to manage it—their addiction. Over years of use, they may have lost their capacity to handle even small amounts of anxiety. They'll go for the quick relief of substance use right away.

Resource Tapping can be used to help manage anxiety, but underlying causes should also be addressed with medications and trauma therapy such as EMDR.

RESOURCING FOR CLIENTS WITH ANXIETY

It is important to help clients learn to understand themselves, their triggers for anxiety, and the general means to manage anxiety levels. Educating them about what anxiety is, what it feels like, and its causes can be helpful to normalize what they are experiencing. Ask them about their family history. Do others in their family have anxiety? How long have they felt this uneasiness in their bodies? When did they have their first panic attack, and what set it off? Informing them about PTSD can also be helpful in relieving some of the stigma attached to the symptoms they experience and will help them understand why talking about it may not be helpful in reducing their symptoms.

You might tell them, *"Anxiety resides in the part of the brain not connected to your thinking. When you get triggered, it sets off your body response, even if you try to talk yourself out of it. This is why we need to use methods that reach where your emotions are stored and can help to calm them down."*

Educating clients about triggers—things that send their nervous systems into fight-flight-freeze responses—is helpful. If they can begin to recognize and name the things that trigger them, they can begin to explore what might be linked to those triggers. Once they are identified, triggers can be deactivated by tapping in the resources that would be most helpful to their particular situation.

Tapping in resources is a simple, easy, self-care strategy for reducing anxiety, especially when clients take time regularly—morning and evening, for example—to tap in their resources. Positive, calming memories can help begin to rewire nervous systems and support adequate sleep. Evoking and tapping in a resource team can bring calm and give an overworked nervous system a rest. Taking time to access resources and tap them in can help decrease general stress levels. Anxious clients can be encouraged to imagine their Peaceful Place before going to sleep at night or when they wake up in the morning. When feeling stressed at work, they can take a break, imagine their special place at the beach, and tap it in. By paying attention to their general stress levels and tapping in resources, clients can begin to feel better without getting high or drunk.

All the foundational resources described in Chapter 4 can be used to reduce anxiety. For many clients, these resources are sufficient. In this chapter, I will provide a number of other resource ideas that can be tapped in to reduce anxiety. Clients can tap in comfort memories, memories of being peaceful and calm, memories of calm and peaceful people, images from nature, food memories, or a *body safe place*—a location in the person's body that feels safe and comfortable to them.

Clients who suffer from anxiety can activate and tap in these resources during sessions and can use them for self-regulation when they feel anxious or depressed or want to calm themselves down. In this chapter, we'll also look at how music and sound can serve as resources for soothing the nervous system. Even tapping without imagery can be useful, and we'll touch upon this in the current chapter as well.

I will provide a protocol for putting these resources to work, including ways they might be used to help with sleep. In subsequent chapters, you will find more resources and resource ideas that might also help with anxiety, including love resources and resources for inner strength. Think of these resources as a menu of possible choices for helping with anxiety. Together with your clients, you will discover what works best for them; everyone will respond to some resources better than others.

RESOURCES FOR MANAGING ANXIETY

- Foundational resources: Peaceful Place, Nurturing Figures, Protector Figures, and Wise Figures
- Comfort memories
- Memories of being peaceful and calm
- Calm and peaceful person
- Images from nature
- Food memories
- Body safe place
- Music and sound
- Tapping without imagery

MEMORIES OF COMFORT

Any comforting memory that evokes feelings of comfort and well-being can be useful for resourcing. Memories from childhood or adulthood can be used; the important element is their evocation of completely positive feelings. Memories of being held by a beloved grandparent, playing fetch with the family dog, sharing a meal with a good friend, holding their son or daughter in their arms, snuggling in bed with their partner, or listening to or playing a favorite piece of music are all examples of comforting memories. Other possibilities include times spent engaged in an activity that gave them a feeling of well-being: fishing, swimming, hiking, watching a good movie, or going for a drive. Any memory that includes the addiction is off limits, however. We are trying to create new circuits, not reinforce the old ones linked to addictive behaviors.

Give clients a homework assignment to create a list of comfort memories. When they come in to session, you can talk about them and then go through them and tap them in. Clients can be instructed to call up these comfort memories when they need to calm themselves and change their state. Some clients may find it helpful to call up a comfort memory before going to sleep at night: for example, they can recall their grandmother singing them a lullaby as she rocked them and then tap themselves right-left, right-left, on the sides of their legs until they drift off to sleep. The tapping in of comfort memories helps with anxiety in the moment and also begins to alter neural circuitry around the addiction pattern. By recalling and tapping in times when they experienced comfort and ease of being *without the addiction*, they are helping their brains remember healthier ways of being.

Let's imagine that your client identifies a comfort memory of baking Christmas cookies with her grandmother as a child. In the memory, she describes her grandmother's kitchen, the animal-shaped cookie cutters, Christmas trees, snowmen, and ornaments. Her grandmother is kind and patient and a lot of fun. The client recalls the taste of the dough and of her grandmother patiently showing her how to roll the dough and cut the shapes. Together, they spend time decorating the cookies with sprinkles and candy pieces. She recalls the lovely aroma of the baking cookies and how pretty they looked coming out of the oven. As she recalls these memories, she feels happy, at ease, and relaxed. This memory is an island of comfort in what was a stormy home life. As such, she can take it out like a treasure, recall it, and tap in its gifts.

TAPPING IN COMFORT MEMORIES

Ask your client to identify a comfort memory: "*Think of a time when you felt comforted, a time when you had a sense of well-being. What picture comes to mind when you think of your comfort memory that evokes completely positive feelings?*"

Now bring in the senses associated with this memory. "*What are you seeing? What are you hearing? What are you smelling? What does your body feel?*"

Ask the client to let you know when they have the memory well established, eliciting only positive feelings; at that point, have them begin to tap right-left, right-left, 6 to 12 times. Have them continue to tap for longer, as long as it remains positive.

They can locate another comfort memory and repeat this process. Tell the client that they can tap in as many comfort memories as they would like.

Your client can practice using this technique to manage distressing emotions. "You can bring up comforting images and cue words before going to sleep or at times when you feel anxious; tap to elicit the positive feelings associated with them."

In the example above, the client could use the memory of baking cookies with her grandmother as one of her comfort memory resources. As she imagines a special or representational time with her grandmother baking, she brings in all the senses associated with the scene. When she feels a relaxed sense of comfort and well-being, the therapist instructs her to tap on her knees. As she taps, she feels the scene more fully. She takes in the love that was there for her then and that she continues to carry inside her.

CONTAINING NEGATIVE MEMORIES DURING TAPPING SESSIONS

Let's use this example to describe how a client can be guided to contain troubling or difficult memories that come up while tapping, then redirect to another positive resource not associated with these kinds of memories. If the client should begin to feel sad, remembering that her grandmother has passed away, the therapist might advise her to stop tapping, then ask her if she would like to put the sad feelings in a container with a good lid on it so that she can focus on the positive feelings only: *"If memories or feelings begin to arise that are not positive, see if you can put the disturbance in a container of some kind. The container can be made of anything you would like with a good lid that allows you to close off and contain the unpleasant feelings or memories. If you cannot do this, then find another memory and associated image."* The client imagines a strong box with a firm lid where she places the sadness. The therapist then asks how that feels, and whether she can return to the memory of baking cookies with her grandmother. *"How is that now?"* When the client can feel the comfort feelings again, the therapist directs her to resume tapping. If it feels right and is not too overwhelming for the client, the therapist might also have her imagine being held and comforted in her sadness by her Nurturing Figure or Figures as the therapist uses bilateral stimulation (BLS) to help her process through a tough emotion and get to the other side. Part of working with people with addiction is giving them a felt experience of being able to move through emotions without using their addiction crutch. Providing support as the client feels the sadness and allowing the BLS to help her move through the feelings in a safe way can build reparative neural networks and an increased capacity to feel emotions and process through them in a healthy way.

CHOOSING A CUE WORD OR PHRASE TO BRING BACK POSITIVE MEMORIES

Clients can find a cue word associated with a positive memory or image. Repeating this cue word to themselves as they hold the image and tap can help them bring back the relaxation and sense of peace associated with that memory.

Let's use the example of the client with the comforting memory about baking cookies with her grandmother. With tapping, the client's body relaxes and she feels her heart soften. While she is in this space, the therapist asks her if she would like to choose a cue word or phrase to associate with this memory to help with its recall at other times. She chooses "Grandma cookie baking."

As the client repeats to herself, "Grandma cookie baking," the therapist has her tap on her knees, still imagining the scene in her grandmother's kitchen. The memory and the cue phrase become linked together in the client's mind; the circuits are linking up. The therapist lets the client know that if she feels anxious or distressed about something, she can bring up the image of baking cookies with her grandmother by saying to herself, "Grandma cookie baking," and tap on her knees to bring back that same feeling of comfort and relaxation.

MEMORIES OF FEELING PEACEFUL

Memories of feeling peaceful and calm can also be powerful resources for Resource Tapping. Remember, our clients have been looping in circuits that are activating anxiety and fight-or-flight responses. We want to help them link in memory circuits that contain images and body memories of peace and calm that can then be linked into their larger circuitry. These memories can include time spent listening to music, taking a bath, lying down in a grassy field and gazing at the clouds floating by, petting their cat, singing with a group, walking their dog, floating in warm water, napping in a hammock, sitting in a favorite rocking chair drifting to sleep, riding their bike—anything they've done that created a peaceful, calm feeling.

Ask your clients to spend a few moments thinking of some of these times and write them down. Ask them to tell you how they feel when they think of them. They can call each one to mind, feel the feelings associated with it, and then add BLS. These memories can be called up and tapped in when they need to contact a feeling of peace and relaxation.

CALM AND PEACEFUL RESOURCE PERSON

Ask your client to think of someone who is calm and peaceful. Can they bring to mind a person who displays a sense of balance and equanimity? This can be someone they know or someone they have heard about. Is there a character from a movie or book, someone from history, or a spiritual figure they can think of that gives them a feeling of peace and calm? They might remember a neighbor they knew growing up who was a calming presence. It could be an archetypical figure such as the Universal Good Mother. It could even be a person they met one time, but who has left an impression on them that they can call up, feel, and remember well. It is most important that they feel the quality of peace and calm the image of the person evokes.

> ### TAPPING IN A RESOURCE PERSON WHO EVOKES FEELINGS OF PEACE AND CALM
>
> Ask your client to close their eyes and take a deep breath. *"Slowly let it out. Take another deep breath. As you exhale, let yourself relax and let go, coming to the present moment.*
>
> *"When you feel yourself here, bring to mind a person you associate with peace and calm. This can be someone you know or a person from a movie or book. It can be a historical, religious, or spiritual person. It can be a real person or someone from your imagination. What is most important is that when you bring this person to mind, he or she evokes a sense of peace, calm, balance, and equanimity."*
>
> When the client finds the resource person, ask them what they see. *"What do they look like? What expression do they have on their face? Where are their hands? Bring in as much visual detail as you can. As you imagine the resource person, notice how you feel."*

When the client feels a sense of peace, calm, and equanimity, have them begin to tap. "After tapping 6 to 12 times, stop tapping and see how you are feeling. If you are feeling good, and the image and good sensations are strengthening, you can tap some more. Tap as long as it feels good and continues to strengthen and integrate."

Your clients can also imagine taking their calm and peaceful resource person into a present situation that requires the qualities they manifest or represent to them.

LINKING THE CALM AND PEACEFUL RESOURCES TO A PRESENT-DAY STRESSOR

Ask your client to think of the situation they are currently in that makes them anxious and requires peace, calm, and equanimity. *"What scene or image comes to your mind when you think of this situation? What is the most disturbing part of it?"*

Have the client bring to mind a memory of their having qualities of peace, calm, and equanimity, or imagine one of the resource figures they have tapped in exhibiting these qualities. As they bring to mind the resource, have them tap 6 to 12 times to activate and strengthen it. *"Feel the qualities within yourself as you tap. If you would like, bring in another memory of having the quality or other resource figures. Tap those in as well to further activate and strengthen these qualities."*

Once the client has a strong sense of peace, calm, and equanimity, have them return to the scene or image they began with. When they bring that up now, what do they experience? If the scene feels more peaceful, have them tap a few times to further strengthen and integrate that feeling. If it helps and feels right, they can even imagine their resource figures there with them, in the scene.

AN EXAMPLE: USING PEACEFUL RESOURCES

George was anxious about meeting new people. He avoided social situations, especially those where there was alcohol. His tendency was to drink to overcome his anxiety, and he then would lose control. Anticipation around an unavoidable work-related social gathering was bringing up considerable anxiety for him.

The therapist asked George, *"Can you bring to mind an image that represents your current anxiety or stress? What is the current trigger for the most anxiety you feel? Can you find a recent time when this came up for you?"*

"Yes. It's my boss telling me that we have this social gathering coming up and that I am obligated to attend," he answered.

"As you imagine this, what do you feel?"

"I feel anxious and fearful. I feel light-headed."

"Can you think of a memory of when you felt calm and peaceful? Or, can you bring to mind one of the peaceful and calm resource people you have tapped in?"

George called to mind Yoda from *Star Wars*, a resource who was calm, peaceful, and balanced. He imagined him with wise eyes and kind smile, untroubled by the ups and downs of life. As he envisaged Yoda and felt his peaceful quality, George tapped on his knees for a while and felt his sense of peace increase. He stopped tapping when he felt it was well established.

The therapist continued, *"Now let's return to the image you began with, of your boss telling you about the social event. What do you notice now?"*

"It feels different. I don't feel so agitated. I feel calmer."

"Would you like to bring in another calm and peaceful resource? It could be a memory of being peaceful or other resource figures."

"Yes. I want to remember a time when I was completely at ease. When I was a boy, I had a group of friends, and we used to go down to the field and play ball. It was easy and fun."

"Bring up that memory as strongly as you can with your senses engaged. Let me know when you have it, and then tap your knees again."

After a little while the client stopped tapping and opened his eyes.

"How was that?" asked the therapist.

"That felt good. I was remembering other fun times with my friends as a boy."

"Let's go back to the image of your boss again telling you about the social event. What do you notice now?"

"I feel calm. I feel okay. It doesn't feel like a problem."

"Great. Would you like to imagine taking these feelings and resources with you into the future? Imagine the scene with your boss, and then move forward into the social event."

"I think I can do it," the client answered.

"Good. Then imagine doing that with the feelings of calm and your resources as you tap your knees. Keep tapping as long as it feels good and is helpful to you."

George tapped on his knees for a few minutes, as he imagined taking feelings of peace with him into the future with his boss and into the social event. When he stopped tapping and opened his eyes, he reported feeling more relaxed and better able to handle future social situations.

IMAGES FROM NATURE

Nature can inspire a sense of deep peace and be a generous source for positive resource images. Ask clients whether they can recall any memories or experiences in nature that brought them a feeling of well-being. They might imagine a lake in the country surrounded by conifers giving off their piney scent in the soft summer breeze and lake water that reflects the green of the trees and invites a swim to the raft where people sunbathe. Perhaps they recall the view from a high mountain peak with vistas of green valleys and distant snow-capped mountains.

Does this memory open up their chests, expand their lungs, bring up a feeling of inner space and freedom? Do they remember a lush mountain meadow with vibrant patches of wildflowers, where a gentle deer grazes peacefully and the gurgling of a brook teeming with silvery trout can be heard over the rustling of grasses blown by the breeze? Or perhaps they imagine a circle of giant redwood trees in a fragrant forest, with wisps of mist floating through the upper branches that reach for the sky. Standing in the center of this "fairy ring" would certainly create the feeling of a peaceful sanctuary.

Maybe they can picture themselves walking along the seashore, feeling the sand and the warmth of the sun and watching pelicans glide effortlessly over the water in synchronous formation, their bellies inches from the waves. All of these experiences conjure up feelings of calm that can be tapped in to bring up a remembered ease of being. Images in nature are also powerful because they remind us that we are part of something beautiful, balanced, and far bigger than ourselves.

Ask clients about their favorite places from nature that bring them a sense of peace. These can be places they have been to or places that they create in their imagination. When they tell you what they are, make a written list. Each of these places can be activated in their imagination and tapped in. They can tap them in during sessions or on their own at home as a way to calm themselves and reduce anxiety. Here are a few additional suggestions along these lines:

- Suggest that clients visually represent these natural places by drawing or painting them, looking for photographs, or making collages from magazine pictures. These pictures or collages can be displayed as reminders of ease of being.

- If possible, invite clients to visit places in nature. For some—if they have lived a rough urban life, cut off from the natural world—this might be a new experience or one that they have neglected for a while because of the life they have been living under the effects of their addiction. Just getting out into nature can begin to connect one to a peace beyond the disturbance of mind chatter, whether in an urban park that has flowers, trees, and grass or a wilder spot, such as a state or national park.

- Remind clients to open their senses next time they are in a natural setting, to notice what they smell, sense, and hear. Have them take note: What does their body feel in these settings?

- While in the setting, if they feel a sense of peace and well-being, they can tap it in for themselves. As they tap right-left, right-left, they strengthen and integrate the image and sensations, so they can more readily access them later. Getting into nature is a wonderful way to create a feeling of calm and peace.

I've introduced clients who were new in recovery from alcohol abuse to one of my favorite places for peace and ease, Limantour Beach at Point Reyes National Seashore. These clients often live a narrow, limited life, in large part due to the childhood trauma and the abuse of alcohol for coping with symptoms. Clients may have difficulty creating a Peaceful Place. This beach can be a meaningful experience, one that opens clients to nature in ways they've never known. Some delighted in how light reflected on the water; how the shore birds scurried along the water's edge; and how the harbor seals swam close to shore, peeking their glistening, black heads out of the water to look at them.

A natural place can become an important calming resource. It can also inspire clients to expand into exploring other places in nature, which can also serve as resources. As clients venture into new places, absorbing the beauty and peace of the natural world, their view of themselves and their potential for a life full of possibilities enlarge. Walks in nature, along with enthusiasm for integrating these resources into the nervous system, can help provide support during the years spent reprocessing trauma memories with EMDR and can help provide support for her recovery from alcohol abuse.

TAPPING IN IMAGES FROM NATURE THAT EVOKE PEACEFUL FEELINGS

Ask your client to close their eyes and go inside. *"Feel yourself sitting: the contact with the seat, your feet on the floor. Be aware of your breathing. You might even take some deep, relaxing breaths to settle down."*

Have them bring to mind a place in nature that makes them feel peaceful and calm. It can be a place they've been to, or an image from a movie, book, or magazine. *"You can use any of the resources you developed earlier or something else that comes to mind.*

"Now notice what you see there. Look around. Notice the details of the picture. Pay attention to colors, shapes, and textures. What do you hear? What sounds would you hear if you were there? What do you smell? What do you feel on your skin? What temperature would it be? How does your body feel as you imagine this scene?"

When they feel a sense of calm and peace, have them begin to tap, 6 to 12 times, right-left, right-left. Then, have them stop and see how they feel. *"If you feel good and wish to continue tapping, you can do so. Tap as long as it feels positive. If for any reason it feels bad, stop tapping and either return to the nature resource you began with, or think of another one and begin the steps again."*

You can have the client add a cue word to their nature resource. For example, if their image was a clear mountain lake, they could say to themselves "mountain lake" as they tap the image. This will help them evoke the feeling of calm associated with the image by saying the cue word and tapping.

Let the client know that they can bring up other nature resources and tap them in if they would like.

FOOD MEMORIES

Memories of favorite meals can be tapped in to bring comfort. My German friend and colleague Christa Diegelmann finds that this resource helps bring comfort to many people she works with who suffer from anxiety and are experiencing great stress in their lives. Recalling meals they have enjoyed can bring clients a sense of pleasure and relaxation. (I would not use this with someone who had a food addiction or with someone who might switch addictions—i.e., from alcohol to food.)

Opening the senses to recall tastes and aromas along with related feelings of pleasure and enjoyment can be light-hearted and fun. You can brainstorm with clients to come up with foods they have loved. They might want to include memories of special shared meals with friends and family.

TAPPING IN FOOD MEMORIES

Ask your client to think of one of the best meals they have ever had. Have them activate their sense memory of the meal. *"What are you seeing? Where is the meal being served? What does the setting look like? How does the food appear? Notice the colors and textures. What aromas do you smell? Take your time and really smell them. What are you hearing? Who is with you? Are you engaged in conversation as you eat? How does your body feel as you eat the food? Pay attention to the sensations in your mouth."*

Tell the client to begin to tap once they feel comfort and pleasure. Begin by tapping 6 to 12 times. *"If it continues to feel good, you can continue tapping. If it feels complete, you can stop tapping and savor the experience."*

Once that tapping in is complete, invite the client to repeat these steps if they would like to think of another wonderful meal.

CREATING A BODY SAFE PLACE

The body safe place is a comforting location in the body that is free from disturbance or conflict. This can be a part of your client's body that feels uncontaminated by trauma or pain, or a place where they feel relative expansion or openness. Even a neutral place, such as their elbow or little finger, can suffice. When your client can locate a safe place, add BLS. They can return to this resource when they are feeling distressed and want to rest. For clients dealing with issues of chronic pain, locating a place in the body that is pain free and tapping it in can begin to change pain circuits and provide some relief.

TAPPING IN THE BODY SAFE PLACE

Ask your client to close their eyes and go inside. *"Spend a few moments quieting your mind and settling your body. Take some deep breaths in, and then slowly let them out. Relax with the exhalation. Let the stress melt from your body.*

"When you feel relaxed and present, find a place in your body that is free from trauma and pain. This is a place that has no particular meaning or feeling attached to it. It can be a kind of neutral, conflict-free part of your body. Spend a few moments inside yourself, scanning for a place in your body that is slightly more comfortable than the rest of you.

"When you identify the place, bring your attention there and begin to tap. Tap 6 to 12 times, then stop. See how you are feeling. If you would like to tap longer, you can. Tap only as long as it feels positive."

MUSIC AND SOUND AS RESOURCES

Music or other sounds such as prayers or mantras can be used as resources to bring comfort and ease. Sound can be a powerful healer. It can bring calm and a feeling of great peace. The resonance of different vibrations can powerfully affect the nervous system. What appeals to your clients will be very individualized; it is important to discover what feels good and meaningful to each person.

Are there pieces of music, prayers, or mantras that inspire your clients—that soothe their souls? When they wish to be comforted, what music comes to mind? Is there a lullaby they remember that warms their heart? Many people are drawn to the resonance of Gregorian chants or singing Tibetan bowls. For some, the Gospel spiritual, "Amazing Grace," brings ease. Others find spiritual inspiration in pieces of country music, classical music, or jazz. As for me, I am moved to a deep inner state by the Gayatri mantra, the world's oldest known mantra for purification and healing, in two versions: the one sung by Deva

Premal on her beautiful CD *Essence,* and the one sung by Andrea Bocelli on his CD *Romanza.*

For some clients, recalling prayers appeals to them and touches their hearts. They can recite a meaningful prayer and, as they feel it, they can tap to strengthen it. For example, the Serenity Prayer used in 12-step programs can be recited, felt, and tapped. Clients might wish to pray for peace, love, or healing and tap as they pray.

Therapists can ask their clients for music, prayers, mantras, or sounds that inspire them or create feelings of calm and ease. If you know of music you think your clients might like, you can see how they respond to it. As they listen to a piece of music that they associate with peace and well-being, ask them to notice how they feel as they hear it. If they feel good and experience a sense of peace, add BLS; the therapist can do the BLS, or clients can tap themselves. Clients can be instructed to tap as long as they like, as long as it feels good to them. You might tell them, *"Let the feeling permeate your whole being. Allow yourself to resonate with this feeling."*

USING RESOURCES FOR ANXIETY IN SPECIFIC SITUATIONS

Clients can tap in resources to manage their anxiety in specific situations. For example, if they are anxious about returning to work after being in rehab, they can call up in their imagination their foundational resources and tap them in or find and tap in resources that more specifically fit the situation:

CLIENT: I'm feeling anxious about returning to work. I'm worried about what other people are going to think of me, and it was stress at work that made me want to drink.

THERAPIST: *When you imagine going back to work, what picture do you have in your mind about that? What might that look like?*

CLIENT: I imagine walking in the door and everyone staring at me and then looking away. I'll go to my desk and want to hide. I'd want to drink to feel better.

THERAPIST: *When you imagine that scene, what would help you feel less anxious? What would you need? You can call up any of your resources or think of something else.*

CLIENT: I'd want to feel calm and relaxed.

THERAPIST: *Can you think of a time when you felt calm and relaxed? Would one or more of your resources help you?*

CLIENT: Yes. I want to remember fishing with my grandfather by the lake when I was a boy. I felt happy and at ease.

THERAPIST: *Okay. Bring up a memory of doing that, as strongly as you can, with the feeling of calm. When you have a good sense of it, let me know.*

The client signals that he has it, and the therapist begins BLS.

THERAPIST: *How was that? What did you notice?*

CLIENT: I felt better. More relaxed.

THERAPIST: *Okay. Now imagine walking into work again. What do you notice?*

CLIENT: I feel better, but still somewhat anxious.

THERAPIST: *Can you think of another memory or resource that would help you?*

CLIENT: Yes. I want to remember all my support. I have a great team of support from my recovery program.

THERAPIST: *Great. Bring up all the supportive people you can think of. Bring up each one and really take in the support they provide you. Feel your support team with you as you return to work. Can you do that?*

CLIENT: Yes.

The therapist begins BLS and continues until the client signals to stop with a nod of his head.

THERAPIST: *How was that for you?*

CLIENT: That felt good. I feel more self-confident, much less anxious.

THERAPIST: *When you imagine returning to work, how does that feel now?*

CLIENT: I can do it. I feel calm and confident.

THERAPIST: *Great. Now imagine going to work tomorrow feeling calm and confident.*

The therapist adds BLS and continues until the client nods to stop.

CLIENT: I can do it. I feel much better.

AN EXAMPLE: TAPPING IN RESOURCES TO MANAGE SOCIAL ANXIETY

Sam had suffered from social anxiety for as long as he could remember. He said it probably began in adolescence, when he was gawky and insecure. That was about the time he discovered that alcohol could take the edge off, enabling him to feel bolder and more confident with groups of kids his age. His wife was tired of staying at home on weekends and wanted to socialize more. Sam was anxious about even attempting to attend a social gathering without a drink in his hand. He wanted to get over this problem and socialize without anxiety and even enjoy himself at a gathering while sober.

Treatment for Sam began by tapping in the foundational resources. For his Peaceful Place, he imagined a crystal-clear lake in the Sierra Nevada mountains, surrounded by granite outcroppings on which he could sit. When he imagined this place, he felt a sense of peace and relaxation. The therapist instructed him to tap on the sides of his legs to strengthen it. As Sam tapped and imagined, the therapist could see his face relaxing. After a while, he took a deep, releasing breath and reported that it felt good. He had managed to relax. The therapist asked if he would like to tap longer and let him know that he could continue to imagine this place and tap for as long as it felt good. Sam liked doing this, and he found that it worked well for him. Sam's therapist told him he could practice doing this whenever he felt anxious or wished to calm himself down.

Sam had reported often feeling anxious in the morning, anticipating awkward conversations with other parents at his kids' school during drop-off. The week after this resourcing session, he reported that he had been successful at calming himself down before taking his kids to school. Before leaving, he had imagined his Peaceful Place and tapped. He also began to feel some hope that he might be able to get some control over his anxiety without alcohol and without avoidance of social situations.

The following week, the therapist continued to tap in the rest of the foundational resources. He responded especially well to the Nurturing and Protective Figures. He tapped in his wife and himself as Nurturing Figures, and his AA sponsor as a Protector Figure, and he also tapped in a very strong inner-support team. This team was particularly helpful for him in increasing confidence.

TAPPING ALONE CAN CALM

Many of my clients will arrive in session wound up from the week, stressed out, and disconnected from themselves. Some will ask right away for the Tac/Audio Scan pulsers, which they place under their legs as I turn on the machine. After a few minutes of BLS, they take a breath, visibly relax, and focus. They learn that they can do this for themselves, too, by tapping the sides of their legs until they feel calm.

BLS without imagery helps many people calm down quickly and easily. It won't work for everyone; it depends upon the person. Try this in session with your client to see how they respond. Be careful that your clients do not begin free associating into their trauma networks.

If a client comes into session anxious and activated, you can direct them to feel themselves sitting, feel their feet on the floor, take a few deep relaxing breaths, and then gently tap on the sides of their legs for a few moments to see if this calms them down. It sometimes helps to repeat comforting words, like "It's okay. You're okay." Sometimes, imagining being held by one of their Nurturing Figures as they tap themselves can bring calm.

Outside of sessions, if clients feel anxious about speaking in front of a group, or performing in some way, or are triggered by something that has gotten their heart racing, or are just stressed out, they can be taught to tap to calm down. As they tap, they can repeat encouraging words to themselves, such as "I'm going to be okay. I can relax. I can let go"—whatever helps them.

You can instruct your clients to continue to tap, right-left, right-left, right-left alternately, for as long as it helps. If, for any reason, they begin to associate to something distressing, or if they feel more upset, instruct them to stop tapping and bring themselves back to the present moment. Tell them to find their breath; then have them take some deep, relaxing breaths and exhale slowly.

If tapping alone is not helpful for clients, instruct them that they might want to use the resources they have tapped in before—that at any time, they can call them up and tap them in.

TAPPING WITHOUT IMAGERY

Ask your client to bring their attention to a still place inside. *"Take some deep, relaxing breaths and slowly let them tot, Begin to tap alternately, right-left, right-left, on your knees or the sides of your legs, or cross your arms in front of your chest and tap either shoulder. As you tap, you can say comforting words to yourself."*

Have the client tap 6 to 12 times; then have them check in and see how they are feeling. If they are relaxing and feeling better, have them continue to tap for as long as it feels good to them.

HELPING WITH SLEEP

Nearly 30% of adults suffer from insomnia, and sleep disturbances are common in people with addictions.[30] People with dysregulated nervous systems often have difficulty sleeping. A common reason people use substances is to help them sleep, but these same substances can interfere with sleep. Being sleep-deprived can intensify pain and decrease impulse control, both of which leave us more susceptible to addictive behavior.

Whether sleep issues are characterized by difficulty falling asleep, difficulty staying asleep, or PTSD-related nightmares that cause trauma survivors to dread going to sleep, Resource Tapping can help clients get the 7 to 8 hours of sleep they need each night. It can be used to help calm a client's mind and body so that they can fall asleep and can also be used to help them fall back asleep if they should wake up.

TAPPING TO HELP WITH SLEEP

Suggest to clients with sleep challenges that they avoid caffeine, the nightly news, the computer, or anything else that will stimulate the mind and body in the hour or so before bed. Advise them to take a bath, meditate, pray, do some yoga or gentle stretches, or listen to relaxing music— to prepare to let go and relax completely. You might make a recording of this relaxation exercise for your client to listen to while going to sleep. Clients can also be guided to listen to comforting music at bedtime; they can tap as they listen.

Have them take some deep relaxing breaths after climbing into bed. *"Breathe up from the soles of your feet, filling your abdomen, chest, and throat with air. Hold the inhalation for a few moments and then slowly release it, letting go from your throat, chest, and abdomen, deflating like a balloon. Take several of these deep, relaxing breaths.*

"When you feel calmer, bring to mind imagery that will relax you, with as much detail as possible. You might imagine your Peaceful Place, Sacred Place, Nurturing Figures, Spiritual Figures, or a pleasant memory. You may want to evoke resources that are comforting, calming, or spiritual. You can create an imaginary scene that will relax and comfort you, such as being wrapped in the arms of a loving, nurturing figure, or in the wings of an angel.

"*You can bring to mind images or memories of letting go, expanding, or opening. For example, you might imagine flying like an eagle, wings spread, soaring and free. Feel yourself letting go and expanding with the imagery. When you have the resource well activated, tap it in. You can cross your arms over your chest and tap your shoulders in a hug, or tap the sides of your legs. Tap as long as it feels good and you feel relaxed.*"

While they tap, they can add in more sensory detail, as long as it remains completely positive. For example, they can feel the softness of their Nurturing Figure's arms, feel themselves cuddling into her warmth, and hear the beating of her heart. Tell the client, "*As you tap, you can also say calming words to yourself such as, 'I can let go, I can relax, I'm done with my work, I can drift off to sleep.'*"

They can even bring to mind a lullaby. "*What lullabies touch your heart and soothe you? Are there lullabies from childhood that come to mind or perhaps something you have heard more recently that touches you? Tap until you let go into sleep. If you should wake up in the night, tell yourself it's okay, bring up your comforting images, and tap. Tap until you relax into sleep.*"

USING IMAGES FROM NATURE TO HELP WITH SLEEP

If your clients are having difficulty sleeping, they can use their nature resources to help them. You might make an audio recording for them to play as they go to bed at night.

Guide your client to close their eyes and go inside. "*Take some deep, slow, relaxing breaths. Relax your body as you exhale. Take several more slow, deep inhalations and exhalations.*

"*When you feel some relaxation, bring to mind an image from nature that evokes calm and peaceful feelings. Bring in as much visual detail as you can. Next, imagine what you would hear. Bring in as much visual detail as you can. Next, imagine what you would hear. Bring to mind what you would smell. What sensations would you feel? Take in the feeling and information from all your senses as much as you can.*

"*As you take all of this in, you feel peaceful and calm. When you can feel it strongly, you tap on the sides of your legs, right-left, right-left, taking in the feeling of peace from this place. Tap until you begin to drift to sleep. Then let go into sleep.*"

All the resources I have described in this chapter and in others can be imagined and tapped in during sessions and kept as tools in a client's anxiety management tool kit. Different clients will respond to some resources better than others. What is important is that together, you and your clients discover what works best for them and that after discovering this, they can learn to use these tools when they need them.

If clients tell you they had a bad week and are feeling anxious, work together to find the resources that would help soothe them. You might explore with them what is causing the anxiety. When you find the cause, you might be better able to find a remedy. What do they need to feel less anxious? What resource or resources would help them? Which of the resources you have tapped in might be most useful for this situation?

Below, find a list of resources useful for clients in managing anxiety. Some of these resources have already been described; others will be covered in later chapters.

RESOURCE TOOLBOX FOR ANXIETY

Foundational Resources: Peaceful Place, Nurturing Figures, Protector Figures, Wise Figures (Chapter 4)

Ideal Mother (Chapter 6)

Ideal Father (Chapter 6)

Inner Sponsor (Chapter 5)

Inner Support Team (Chapter 4)

Spiritual Figures (Chapter 8)

Calm and Peaceful Resource Person (Chapter 5)

Sacred Place (Chapter 4)

Comfort Memories (Chapter 5)

Food Memories (Chapter 5)

Music and Sound (Chapter 5)

Love Resources: Circle of Love, Memories of Loving and Being Loved, Loving-Kindness Meditation (Chapter 10)

Images from Nature (Chapter 5)

Memories of Being Peaceful (Chapter 5)

Body Safe Place (Chapter 5)

Empowerment Resources (Chapter 4)

Protector Figures

Circle of Protection

Inner Strength

Courage

Music or Sounwwd

Tapping Without Imagery, with Encouraging, Supportive Words

CHAPTER 6

Repairing Developmental Deficits

*The great gift of human beings is that we
have the power of empathy; we can all sense
a mysterious connection to each other.*
—MERYL STREEP

Clients with addiction often report histories of parental substance abuse, chaotic home life, general neglect, physical or sexual abuse, mentally ill parents, or lack of stability growing up. Addictive behaviors represent the client's efforts to cope with the developmental deficits that come from lack of safe, stable parenting. Many clients with addiction turn to their substance or behavior of choice to manage general anxiety and depression associated with insecure childhood attachment. Their nervous systems are fragile. They have a hard time with self-soothing and are easily triggered.

Without early foundations of secure parenting, clients with addictions may feel incapable of managing their depression, anxiety, and fear without using addictive substances or behaviors to help them feel better. Clients from backgrounds where basic needs for a sense of physical safety and emotional connection were not met also report an inner emptiness they find intolerable, which they seek to fill with food, drugs, sex, or alcohol. When the substance or behavior they have been using to manage these feelings is removed, they often cannot handle the terrible emptiness they feel, and relapse is the result.

Along with the foundational and other resources I have described, I have found that such clients benefit from additional resources to repair developmental deficits. Two of the resources most helpful for the repair of developmental deficits are the *Ideal Mother* and *Ideal Father*, as well as other family constellations that, for them, were better suited to either their identity or their needs. I have written extensively about how to create and use them;[31] here, I'll describe some ways you might use Resource Tapping to aid this repair.

DEVELOPING AND TAPPING IN AN IDEAL MOTHER

The Ideal Mother is the mother the client wishes they'd had; the mother who would have met their needs in a way that was safe and felt good. This mother was healthy and whole, secure in herself, strong, and happy. She can now be developed as a resource figure and tapped in to help repair early childhood attachment deficits.

In supporting the client in tapping in the Ideal Mother, we begin to create a healthy alternative to an unhealthy childhood attachment pattern. Through the power of imagination, the client creates an alternate reality that serves to build new neural pathways; this, in turn, changes the way they feel about themselves and how they relate to others. We are supporting the client in building a new, healthy template for human relationships.

I recognize a need for the Ideal Mother when, through the content of a client's history (neglect, abuse, parental substance abuse, parental mental illness) or through *how* the client relates the story of their life, I assess that the client lacks a foundation—an inner structure for the development of a secure, cohesive self.

Some clients' stories have gaping holes, gaps in time they cannot recall; others float away into dissociation or try to distract me with entertaining exploits. These kinds of signs indicate to me that the client lacks the ego strength or internal structure to tolerate challenging emotions and maintain sobriety.

In many cases, clients do not hold an emotional charge related to neglect they experienced growing up; it was simply "the way it was" for them. They may need help to see a need for an ideal parent. Before creating an Ideal Mother, I explain to the client why I think this is important to do. I explain that they didn't have the kind of stable upbringing and healthy mother needed for development of an inner sense of security. I tell them that not having had this as a child may have created a kind of emptiness and insecurity—and that they can remedy this by rewiring their nervous systems through imagination and bilateral stimulation (BLS). *"We can't change what happened to you in your childhood,"* I tell the client, *"but we can change how you feel inside."*

Creating the Ideal Mother

In creating an Ideal Mother, I want to keep in mind the kinds of qualities that activate the right hemisphere, where early attachment takes place. These include eye contact, tone of voice, smell, touch, and qualities such as calmness, stability, compassion, love, confidence, and happiness. If the client's mother was an alcoholic or drug addict, the Ideal Mother will be sober. If the real mother was depressed, bipolar, or psychotic, the Ideal Mother will be mentally healthy and stable.

I will typically ask my clients, *"Can you imagine an Ideal Mother? You can create the mother you wish you had. She can be any way you would like her to be. You can construct her from someone you know, from aspects of people you know, from neighbors or friends, from your actual mother, or from characters from books or movies."*

The client can also draw on qualities they themselves possess: *"You can take aspects of your own nurturing self to construct this mother."* If the client has difficulty, and you know they have children they have loved and nurtured, ask the client to remember nurturing and loving their own children.

Clients don't have to have an *image* of the Ideal Mother; a sense of her will suffice. I might direct the client to look into her eyes and see the love she has for them. All they might be able to imagine is the look in her eyes, but this is adequate to have a felt sense of that loving, safe mother. This feeling state will begin to develop right-brain pathways of comfort and security.

For clients who have a difficult time finding an image, compile a list of all the qualities of the mother they wish to have. Then, with their eyes closed and BLS going, I read the list back to them, telling them to take in the feeling of the qualities. I tell them that if an image appears spontaneously, to notice that and take it in, too.

When the client has imagined the Ideal Mother and has a strong felt sense of her, add BLS to tap her in. If clients really get into this, continue to elaborate on the imagery and feelings. Let them go on for as long as it remains positive. If it should turn negative, stop and return to only positive imagery and feelings. What is most important here is to construct this Ideal Mother and develop a strong felt sense of her nurturing quality.

Using the Ideal Mother to Repair Developmental Deficits

When the Ideal Mother has been created and tapped in, she can be used to repair aspects of the client's childhood.

"Would you like to imagine redoing your life beginning with conception with this

new mother? You can begin by imagining being in this loving mother's womb. Imagine a safe, warm womb in a mother who is secure and happy to be pregnant. You can create the situation in whatever way you would like. You might want to imagine being conceived in love and wanted from the beginning."

When the client indicates that they are in the scene, I begin BLS. After a few minutes, I check in and ask the client what is happening. If they report feeling happy and good in the womb, I might ask them if they want to stay there a while, or if they would like to get bigger and imagine being born. If they say yes, I say, *"Imagine that"* and add BLS.

We then move forward with the birth, imagining it in an ideal way with love, tenderness, welcoming, skin-on-skin contact, and a loving period of gazing into each other's eyes. The therapist can seed information helpful for more fully activating the client's imagination and repairing attachment wounds. For example, you might say, *"Notice how your mother gazes at you with love; how it feels to feel warmth and security in her arms."* Some clients prefer continuous BLS as they immerse themselves in their imaginations, whereas others prefer dipping in and out with shorter sets. Follow your client's lead, adjusting what you do according to what feels best to them.

After they are born, you might then ask if they would like to go home with their mother. If they say yes, ask them to imagine it in a way that feels best to them, and add BLS. Then, ask if they want to imagine themselves as a baby in their mother's arms, being attended to and cared for in a way that is loving and attuned. *"As you lie cradled in your mother's arms, see how happy she is to gaze at you. She adores you. Feel the softness of her arms and the security she provides. She smells good, and her voice is soothing to you. Feel her stroke your soft head and rock you in her arms. You feel loved and at peace."*

As the client takes this in, add BLS. Again, some clients prefer continuous BLS as they imagine; others like shorter sets. Some clients really get into this and go into a deep reverie with the BLS going. They can *feel* themselves, as the baby, being loved.

When you stop for a break, ask your client how that was, or what's coming up. If it is positive, say, *"Go with that,"* and add BLS to take it in. If it doesn't feel good, or something comes up, ask them what they need to make it better. I tell the client that it's their imagination, and that they can create this experience in any way they want. This instruction can be quite freeing.

This whole process is fluid and creative. It is important to be flexible and go where your client wants to go. Some clients begin with birth and then reimagine their entire life with this new mother in one session. Others spend more time in stages that require more time to repair. For a client whose mother was an addict, for example, you might have a session in which you prompt your client to *"imagine what your life would be like if you had a sober, healthy, stable mother."* Encourage them to reimagine their life with that mother, with BLS. They might opt to spend more time at ages when they needed more support, allowing themselves to receive it with this new mother. If the client's mother was stable and sober during the client's first years of life, but became seriously depressed and drug addicted when the client was in first grade, the focus of the imaginary repair might begin at that age and move forward from there.

Take the example of a woman who is struggling with bingeing or overeating. She has never had a healthy relationship with food and eating. She was either starved or overfed as a baby, then put on diets as a child and adolescent. Her mother, who was anorexic, was obsessed with what she ate growing up and constantly criticized her. She remembers sneaking food and hiding it so that her mother wouldn't find out. As a result, the client never learned to listen to and respond to her own body's messages of hunger.

To work with this client, you ask her to create an Ideal Mother who has a healthy relationship with food and her own body. This mother is happy to be pregnant and eats nourishing food. When the client is born, she is breastfed whenever her body tells her she is hungry, and she is allowed to nurse until she is satiated. She imagines herself as an older baby ready for solid food, receiving nourishing food whenever she is hungry. (To integrate the Ideal Mother with the client's adult experience, you can ask her to imagine healthy eating as she gets older, using BLS throughout as she moves through all the stages of development to the present time.)

I believe part of the attachment repair comes from the therapist-client interaction—through the fluidity and creativity with which this work is done. By attuning to our client's needs in the present with them, we are *in vivo* creating new adaptive, healing, neural pathways for a healthy relationship.

Common Difficulties in Creating the Ideal Mother

Many clients will resist the whole idea of creating an Ideal Mother, claiming it is silly and unreal. "But this isn't what happened to me. What good will this do? This isn't my reality."

It is important to acknowledge the pain and truth of what they didn't get, and to let them know that it *is* possible to change their nervous systems. I tell them, *"You didn't have the loving, caring mother that you needed. We can't change what happened to you, but we can change how you feel inside. You can change your nervous system. You are no longer a child living with your parents, are you? But you still feel like you are? This is because you have developed memory networks that light up in a particular pattern like electrical circuits, making you feel as though you are still a child. This isn't reality, is it? Well, we can change the way in which you feel by using your imagination and bilateral stimulation. We can change the way you feel by changing your circuitry. We can rewire you. You won't forget what happened to you; you just won't feel as if it is important to you anymore."* Most clients can accept an explanation like this. I might also use the example of athletes using imagination for peak performance.

Another common difficulty in creating an Ideal Mother can be a feeling of disloyalty. "My mother did the best she could. She had a bad childhood, too. I don't feel right replacing her." Many clients feel loyal to their mothers, whom they may have taken care of, and feel disloyal imagining an ideal one. I might say, *"What you are creating is only in your imagination. You aren't really replacing your mother,"* or, *"This is a mother who fits your needs and can care for you in the way you need her to so that you can grow up to be a healthy adult. Can you allow yourself to have what you have always wanted and needed?"* Sometimes, asking clients if they would like to imagine giving *their* mother an Ideal Mother—someone who could take care of *them*—frees clients to give themselves what they need.

Some clients don't want to relinquish the good things they *did* get from their mothers. For example, if their mother was playful and fun, but was inconsistent and unreliable due to her substance abuse, the client may not want to lose those good things. Sometimes what works in these instances is to allow them to keep their mother and ask if they would like to bring in a co-mother—a mother who can fill in the qualities and skills that their mother lacked and that they needed to feel happy and secure. You can invite your client to imagine bringing in a co-mother who was consistent, reliable, sober, and loving. If they can do it, then say, *"Imagine that,"* and add BLS. Sometimes it is helpful to ask whether they want to imagine someone who can *help* their mother be a better mother. Maybe their mother needed treatment or more support. They can imagine these things with BLS, too.

A few more suggestions for clients who need this process of developmental repair to support them in recovery, but struggle with it.[32]

1. Think of a time when they were nurturing to someone or something—even one time. Can they evoke that feeling of caring for another? If they can, tap in that memory.

2. Can they now take that feeling and use it to construct a mother figure?

3. Then, if they can do it, ask them to imagine themselves in the position of receiving the nurturing they gave. For example, if the client evoked a memory of holding and rocking their own daughter in their arms, tap that in, then ask if they can imagine themselves as the baby, receiving that loving attention. If they can, ask them to imagine it with the feeling and tap it in. (This can be difficult for many clients with relational trauma. Go easy with it.)

4. You can give your clients homework assignments to search for pictures of loving mother-infant interactions and examples of healthy bonding. The pictures can help stimulate their imagination to create what they wish they'd had. They can compile these pictures from the internet or from magazines and use them to create a collage—a physical representation of what they want in a mother. Try having clients collect pictures of mother-child interactions that represent each stage of development: pictures of healthy, happy, pregnant women; then, mothers who have just given birth, with their babies on their chests, bonding; mothers suckling their newborns, gazing down at them lovingly; mothers with babies at different ages doing different activities; and so on.

5. They can look at videos of healthy mother-child interactions to get ideas, as well as read books.

DEVELOPING AND TAPPING IN AN IDEAL FATHER

Many clients with addictions grew up without a stable, emotionally healthy father or father figure to provide them with the guidance and support they needed to develop into healthy adults. Sometimes, some of the client's developmental trauma is associated with the absence of a father, as is the case with many men and women today whose parents divorced and whose fathers disengaged or even disappeared. Some fathers were themselves substance abusers or had addictions, which affected their parenting. Others were distant and uninvolved with their children's lives. Fathers who were abusive may be a source of the client's PTSD. Certainly, the lack of a loving, healthy father has created emotional wounds for many.

If you suspect that some of your client's problems are linked to the need for a father figure, you can tap in an ideal father. *"If you could imagine the Ideal Father for you, what would he be like? What qualities would you want in an ideal father?"* Together, you and your client can create a list of the qualities they want in this ideal father: strong, supportive, nurturing, intelligent, fun, sober, caring, tender, patient, playful, a good listener, wise.

Maybe after listing these qualities, someone the client knows will come to mind. It could be a coach, a friend's father, or their sponsor. They can use that person as an ideal father or use his qualities as a base template from which to build their own. They can create a father out of a combination of qualities from several different people they know. They can even create an ideal father out of qualities they recognize in themselves, in their relationships with their own children.

When they have created an Ideal Father—when they have an image or a sense of him, from the qualities they have listed—ask them to close their eyes, go inside, and connect to the sense of this Ideal Father. When they can do that, add BLS.

If they have been able to create an Ideal Father, you can ask them if they would like to imagine their life with this new father. They can imagine having had him from the time of conception with their Ideal Mother, or they might want to imagine having had him in their life from the first time they felt the lack of a father figure. *"When did you first feel the absence of a father in your life? Can you remember that? Good. Now, imagine the father you have created, your ideal father . . . imagine him there for you at that time."* When they can do that, add BLS.

The client might want to imagine their life from the beginning all the way to the present with this new father, or they might want to focus on times when they really needed the guidance of a father and bring in this new father's advice and support. If they needed someone who would set boundaries and act as a good role model—someone they could talk to about things that were difficult for them—they can imagine their ideal father doing those things. They can imagine conversations with this new father and ask him for his advice. If they then wish to imagine this father in their life, through all the life stages and major events, they can do this with the BLS going. Some clients will do short sets of BLS; others will prefer long, continuous sets.

Many different family constellations can be healthy for children. Clients can imagine any family constellation they would like that fits their needs or preferences. For LGBT clients whose parents rejected this part of their child's identity, it can be helpful to imagine parents who accept and love them as they are. They can talk to the client about their problems. This can be important in healing the wounds of rejection, alienation, and damaged self-esteem many LGBT clients experience. If they wish, they can create same-sex parents.

Many people with addictions come from families where there was domestic violence, a pattern they often repeat. For that reason, it can be helpful to take some time to focus on the relationship between their ideal parents in order to strengthen the new neural network of healthy relating.

REPAIRING DEVELOPMENTAL DEFICITS

Once they have tapped in an Ideal Mother or an Ideal Father, clients can use these resources to repair developmental deficits anywhere in their histories. They can imagine the development that they wanted and needed with BLS. Entire sessions can be devoted to creating and tapping in an alternate birth, infancy, childhood, adolescence, and adulthood.

Because many people begin their addictions in adolescence during times of stress and social pressure, imagining ideal parents providing them with what they needed at that age can help with this repair. The therapist can ask, *"What would have helped you at that time? What did you need? Can you imagine your Ideal Mother or Father providing that for you?"* If they can, ask them to imagine it, and add BLS.

VARIATIONS IN TIMING AND PACE FOR REPAIR OF DEVELOPMENTAL DEFICITS

The timing and pace of repairing developmental deficits through tapping in the Ideal Mother or Father can vary widely from client to client, or even within one client's experience over time:

- Some clients may spontaneously move from conception and birth through their life in a single session, filling in developmental gaps throughout. Many people prefer continuous BLS as they do this.

- Sometimes clients need to spend more time in one developmental stage, repeating reparative scenarios many times during a phase of life remembered as particularly difficult.

- Others will focus one full session on a phase of life; and then, in the next session, when the therapist checks in with them, they have gotten older and wish to focus on a later time.

As with everything we do using an attachment-focused approach, we listen to our clients and adapt what we do according to their needs. For more information on how you might integrate an attachment focus to your EMDR therapy, see *Attachment-Focused EMDR: Healing Relational Trauma*.[33]

CASE STUDY: A CLIENT WHO NEEDED AN IDEAL MOTHER

Donna was a woman in her 20s who was in recovery from a 6-year addiction to narcotics. She sought treatment post-rehab for support in her recovery, as well as for treatment for long-standing depression and trauma from early childhood. One of her goals in therapy was to fulfill her desire to have a healthy relationship.

She reported being worried that she would relapse, as she had relapsed multiple times in the past after leaving residential treatment. Though she was very intelligent, because of her addictions she had barely managed to graduate from high school and had never held a steady job.

Donna grew up in an affluent family with neglectful parents. Both had successful careers. Donna's emotionally volatile mother was addicted to narcotics, which she obtained through her place of work. Her frequent bouts of rage sometimes led her to beat Donna. Her father put his head in the sand, ignored the chaos of the family, and focused on his work. When Donna was 10 years old, he moved out, leaving Donna and her older sister alone to cope without a functioning parent.

Donna withdrew, coping with her mother's emotional swings by spending hours alone in her room. She reported no stability growing up and had felt anxious and depressed for as long as she could remember. When she was in her teens, her older sister introduced her to narcotics, which she began to abuse.

Donna's early 20s was a time of even greater turmoil. Her drug use worsened, and she became involved with older men who abused her. Though her father left when she was a child, he always gave her money and paid for her treatment. He showed her love in the way that he could, by supporting her financially. She reported that she felt her father loved her; she appreciated what he did for her. Her contact with her mother, who continued to be emotionally unstable and addicted, was limited.

Donna responded well to therapy, had an AA sponsor she liked, and managed to use some of the coping skills she learned in treatment. She lived in a sober living house with others who were new in recovery. She realized that her family was not capable of meeting her emotional needs. Even though she knew this, she still felt empty inside and struggled with the urge to use again.

Donna lacked the internal infrastructure necessary for healthy, secure attachment. She couldn't recall times of stability in her childhood with a mother who was loving and stable. Her anxiety and depression were more than likely caused, at least in part, by the lack of secure attachment. There was no one to take care of her, no one to hold her when she was scared or calm her when she was distressed. She was left to do these things for herself, and she was not equipped to do so at a young age. Her drug addiction was probably her attempt to self-medicate—to lower her anxiety, help manage her emotions, and fill in the emptiness she felt because of the attachment deficit. Based on her mother's history, the therapist considered the possibility that Donna also had a genetic predisposition toward addictions.

To address the underlying causes of Donna's addiction, her depression, anxiety, and developmental deficits had to be treated. This could be done with a combination of medication to address the biochemical link to the depression and anxiety; Resource Tapping, using the four foundational resources; and developing and tapping in an Ideal Mother to repair developmental deficits. Later, when she was more stable and could handle it, Attachment-Focused EMDR could be used to reprocess the traumas. When the time came to use Resource Tapping in her treatment, Donna chose the Tac/Audio Scan pulsers as her form of BLS. She placed the pulsers under her legs, which left her hands free. The therapist began by tapping in the four foundational resources of Peaceful Place, Nurturing Figures, Protector Figures, and Wise Figures. Because of the lack of a stable, sober mother in her childhood, Donna needed to create an Ideal Mother. She said she wanted her Ideal Mother to be a sober version of her biological mother. She imagined a mother who looked like her mother but was sober and stable. She could readily imagine her, and the therapist used BLS to tap her in.

Because she felt that her parents didn't want her from the beginning— they were on the verge of breaking up when she was conceived—she wanted to begin her developmental repair with her conception. She felt her father was good enough and didn't feel the need to create an ideal version. With her eyes closed and the BLS going, she imagined her father and Ideal Mother meeting and falling in love.

She imagined that she was conceived in love and that her mother wanted her and enjoyed the pregnancy. In Donna's imaginings, when her mother learned she was carrying a girl, she delighted in this, too. (Her mother had wanted a boy and made her feel inadequate because of this.) She spent an entire session imagining her mother sober, eating well, feeling healthy, and enjoying her pregnancy.

Donna liked long, continuous BLS with few interruptions. From time to time, the therapist would ask her to elaborate on something or ask her a question that helped fill out her imagined scenes more fully.

In the next session, Donna imagined being born to her healthy, sober mother, with her father there to bond with her, too. She imagined being placed on her mother's chest and looking into her clear, loving eyes, feeling wanted, safe, and secure. Donna saw herself going home with her loving parents, having her first bath, being breastfed when she was hungry, and having her diaper changed when she was soiled. She imagined crawling and learning to walk—a secure, contented child. She imagined her parents happy and unstressed, present and confident in their parenting.

When the therapist checked in with Donna for the next session, she reported that the baby was getting older. She reimagined her sober Ideal Mother and father and resumed repairing her development, continuing from ages 3 to 5 years: preschool, making friends, play dates; her mother able to manage her life well and allow healthy growth and individuation for her daughter; and kindergarten, imagining what she needed from her mother to separate in a secure way.

She imagined her parents having a healthy, loving relationship and extended family with which to connect. After three sessions spent on this early developmental repair, she reported feeling less numb and less anxious. She was beginning to feel the development of a kind of inner core, out of which she could identify what she felt and what she knew inside. From this inner core, she was better able to express her needs and feelings. She reported standing up for herself with her boyfriend in a new way.

In subsequent sessions, Donna continued to reimagine her elementary school years and then her adolescence. She enjoyed doing this work; it empowered her and gave her a new sense of stability. When she felt anxious at home, she began to use her resources there. She would imagine her Ideal Mother, feel her nurturing and comfort, and then tap her legs right and left. In this way, she could soothe herself, using resources that were now readily available to her.

CHAPTER 7

Resources to Lift the Spirit: Antidotes for Depression and Inertia

*Wear gratitude like a cloak and it will
feed every corner of your life.*
—RUMI

I t is essential to address symptoms of depression when working with people in recovery. Research suggests that individuals with overt, mild, or even subclinical depression may abuse drugs or other substances as a form of self-medication. Depression commonly affects people with addictions, and research suggests that treating mood disorders may reduce substance craving and use and enhance overall treatment success. Addictions often take hold after a person discovers that a drug, substance, or behavior helps them feel better when they are depressed.

Research points to a range of overlapping causal factors for drug use and mood disorders, including underlying brain deficits, genetic vulnerabilities, or early exposure to stress or trauma. In many cases, it can be difficult to assess what came first—the addiction or the depression. Because substance use often begins in adolescence, clients tend to be unreliable in their recall of when and why they first began to use. Whether or not a genetic vulnerability to depression is present, addicted clients may have been exposed to early childhood trauma that changed their brains in ways that predispose them to developing PTSD and depression. Withdrawal from their substance can also induce symptoms of depression. Is the client's depression a condition that existed before substance use, or is it a physiological consequence of withdrawal? This can be a difficult question to answer—but either way, treating the depression is key to helping clients sustain their recovery.

In some cases, clients have become dependent on their drug of choice as though it were a friend. They experience the loss of the drug as an emotional loss.

Along with the loss of the substance or behavior, recovery may also mean they must relinquish friends and a lifestyle that has been unhealthy, but familiar. They may feel grief that is experienced as depression. Because mood disorders increase vulnerability to drug abuse and addiction, the diagnosis and treatment of the mood disorder can reduce the risk of relapse. It is essential to thoroughly assess clients in treatment for addictions to distinguish symptoms of affective disorders from manifestations of substance intoxication and withdrawal. In order to support their recovery and chance of success in treatment, their depression or mood disorder must be treated. Treatment may include psychotherapy and trauma therapies such as EMDR and Resource Tapping. Clients may also need the support of medications that have proven effective in the context of co-occurring substance abuse. Nonpharmaceutical alternatives exist as well; supplements such as EM Power Plus or dietary changes supportive of the brain, body, and mood may also prove helpful. Meditation, yoga, exercise, good sleep, and a healthy diet are other effective measures that can be integrated into a treatment plan for coexisting addiction and depression.

Research Suggests:

- A high prevalence of drug abuse and dependence exists among individuals with mood and anxiety disorders.[34, 35]

- A higher prevalence of mental disorders exists among patients with drug use disorders[36]

- Treating a comorbid affective disorder can decrease substance abuse and craving[37]

RESOURCE TAPPING FOR DEPRESSION

Resource Tapping techniques can be used to support and lift the spirits of clients in recovery. Resources can be tapped when clients feel sad, low, depressed, and stuck and when they need broader perspective and inspiration.

We'll begin with ways to tap in gratitude; next, we'll move on to tapping favorite things; and then, experiences of awe and wonder, beauty, and joy. The use of humor and creativity as resources will also be covered. Finally, you'll learn how to use inspiration and experiences of freedom and expansion to provide a broader perspective.

Please keep in mind that some clients with depression need biochemical support before they can feel and benefit from resourcing. If you find that Resource Tapping is not working, it may be that they need biochemical support first.

RESOURCES TO LIFT THE SPIRIT

Gratitude

Experiences of Awe and Wonder

Beauty

Joy

Inspiration

Freedom and Expansion

GRATITUDE

Gratitude is a feeling of appreciation or thankfulness. It is a positive mental attitude that can be developed—one that is particularly important for people in addiction recovery, because it can help to ensure their success in the future. Rather than dwelling on what the addiction has taken away, it can be helpful to focus on the opportunities recovery has opened up. Simple things in life such as friendship, the warmth of the sun, a laugh with a friend, or a child's delight can be experienced as blessings that make sobriety worthwhile. They can boost motivation for recovery and help prevent relapse.

Psychologist Robert Emmons at the University of California, Davis, has studied gratitude in depth. He identifies two key components: "First, gratitude is the *acknowledgment* of goodness in one's life. We affirm that all things taken together life is good and has elements that make it worth living. Second, gratitude is recognizing that the source (s) of this goodness lie at least partially outside the self."[38]

WHAT ARE THE BENEFITS OF PRACTICING GRATITUDE?

Hundreds of studies have shown that practicing gratitude has social, physical, and psychological benefit, even to people going through hard times. People who regularly practice gratitude by taking time to notice and reflect upon things they're thankful for experience many benefits. Here are some of the top research-based reasons for practicing gratitude that apply to supporting clients in recovery from addictions.

- **Gratitude increases happiness.** Through research by Robert Emmons,[39] Sonja Lyubomirsky,[40] and other researchers, practicing gratitude has been proven to be one of the most reliable methods for increasing happiness and life satisfaction. Cultivating gratitude also increases feelings of optimism, joy, pleasure, enthusiasm, and other positive emotions.

- **Practicing gratitude has been shown to reduce anxiety and depression.**

- **When people feel grateful, they sleep better.** They fall asleep more easily, are more likely to sleep through the night, and wake up rested.

- **Gratitude increases resilience.** Practicing gratitude increases our capacity to handle challenging situations.

- **Gratitude improves relationships.** Grateful people are more helpful, altruistic, and compassionate. Gratitude also promotes forgiveness.

- **Gratitude for sobriety reduces the likelihood of relapse.** Addicts will have the motivation to do what they need to in order to protect their sobriety.

WAYS TO SUPPORT CLIENTS IN BUILDING GRATITUDE

Ask clients to reflect on what they feel grateful about in their life. They can focus on people they feel grateful for, things they have that they enjoy, their health, or capacities such as the ability to appreciate beauty, music, or art. They can focus on gratitude for their intellectual, creative, or physical abilities.

Another way to help clients in recovery develop gratitude is to encourage them to give to others. In active addiction, people are preoccupied with meeting their own needs. Self-absorption in recovery can mean continuing the pattern of thinking of their own needs. When people feel grateful, their focus extends beyond themselves and their self-centered orientation. Gratitude stimulates the desire to help others, which in turn helps people in recovery feel better about themselves.

Gratitude can also be fostered by actively finding ways to help others. Cultivating gratitude can help counter old patterns of self-pity, resentment, and negativity, especially when life in recovery becomes stressful. Increased irritability often sets in after the "pink cloud" of recovery. In that irritable state, it can be easy to have a very negative focus on other people. Developing gratitude and helping others can counter this tendency and can help decrease feelings of isolation that can be triggers for relapse.

THE GRATITUDE JOURNAL PRACTICE

Research by Robert Emmons suggests that keeping a gratitude journal can significantly increase well-being and life satisfaction.

Many studies indicate that brief journal entries—recording a sentence or two apiece about five experiences from the past week for which the person feels grateful—are adequate for positive impact. Emmons's research, however, found that elaborating in detail about a particular thing for which one is grateful carries more benefits than a superficial list of many things. He also says that focusing on *people* to whom one is grateful has greater impact than focusing on *things*.

Clients in recovery may find a gratitude journal helpful. They can start by listing in their journals five things that they have felt grateful for during the week or can write in more detail about particular sources of gratitude. Therapists can ask clients to bring their journals to sessions. Entries can be shared between client and therapist or in a group meeting. Resource Tapping can be used to more fully integrate the feeling state of gratitude while journaling; you might read an entry to your clients and ask them to reflect on it and then add BLS when they can access a feeling of gratitude.

Allow plenty of time for the client to imagine the source of gratitude in vivid detail before bringing in bilateral stimulation (BLS). This helps the feeling become more fully activated, which facilitates its integration and embodiment. Ask your clients to focus on the feeling about the object of gratitude as a gift. Ask them to take time to *savor* the feeling before adding BLS.

On some days, clients will struggle more to find anything to add to the list. Remind them that simply being alive can be a source for gratitude. Support them in looking through their lives for any person, thing, or experience for which they are grateful. What would they not want to be without? What or who has enriched their life? Quieting the mind, going inside, and playing a mental movie of one's life may be required to find gratitude on a day when nothing seems worth being thankful.

Give clients the option to tap in their own gratitude entries while journaling on their own. After they have listed something, they can close their eyes, go inside, and imagine what they have written. They can savor the feeling of gratitude and take it in as a gift. Remind them to *emphasize the feeling in their being that arises when they feel grateful*, and remind them that they will be able to call on these feelings at a later time when they need to lift their spirits.

For some clients, it can feel invalidating or shaming to be told to look for gratitude when they are feeling pain. You might suggest that they imagine a vast space large enough to hold both their pain and their gratitude. As they imagine this vast space that can hold all of these things, add BLS. In this way, you validate and allow their painful feelings in addition to providing space for hope and change.

TAPPING IN GRATITUDE

Ask the client to take a few moments to quiet their mind and come to the present moment. Have them take some deep, relaxing breaths, filling their belly, chest, and throat. *"Hold your breath a moment; then, slowly let it out, relaxing with the exhalation. Take another deep breath, and then slowly let it out."*

Once the client is fully present, tell them, *"Bring to mind one of the things you wrote in your gratitude journal. When you connect with what you feel grateful about, put your attention there. Amplify the sensory information. Really feel the feelings associated with it. If there are memories associated with it, bring them in also.*

"Be aware of your feelings and how you relish and savor this gift in your imagination. Take the time to be especially aware of the depth of your gratitude."

When the client affirms their feeling of gratitude, even a little bit, have them begin to tap, 6 to 12 times at first. Have them pause and check in with how they feel. If they wish to tap for a longer period to continue to strengthen the positive feeling, have them continue, and let them know that they can tap for as long as it feels positive. Tell the client to pause tapping if any unpleasant memories emerge and to settle back into the memory of the thing they are grateful for before resuming with tapping.

The cycle can be repeated with another source of gratitude, moving through all the same steps listed above for each thing on the list—starting with tapping 6 to 12 times, checking in, and then tapping again until completion is felt.

OTHER IDEAS
FOR CULTIVATING GRATITUDE

You might recommend to your clients that they begin or end their day with a prayer or meditation of gratitude and then tap it in. Or they can spend time doing a life review, beginning at birth, with a focus on gratitude. Each time they find something to appreciate, they can tap a few times to strengthen it. For example, "I appreciate being born. I appreciate my mother's sacrifice to give birth to me. I appreciate all those who helped in my care as a baby. I appreciate my education, my teachers, having books to read, and more."

PRECIOUS LIFE MEDITATION

In 1975, at a retreat with Lama Thubten Yeshe and Lama Thubten Zopa, I learned a Tibetan Buddhist meditation that can be used as an antidote to depression and hopelessness. It focuses on appreciating our precious life. In the West, we enjoy extraordinary privilege in comparison with much of the rest of the world. This meditation brings us to focus on all of the rare, precious factors we have been born with: having a functional body and mind, having enough to eat and drink to sustain us, living in a country where we have many freedoms.

I have modified the meditation I was taught, making it applicable to a wider audience and adding tapping to help strengthen and integrate the feeling and understanding this meditation elicits in the practitioner.

TAPPING IN GRATITUDE FOR YOUR PRECIOUS LIFE

Tell the client, *"Bring your attention to your breath. Take some deep, relaxing breaths. Feel yourself present. Spend as much time as you need to bring yourself to the here and now.*

"Bring to mind all the good qualities and advantages of your life. You have an intelligent mind, a loving heart, and a healthy body. You have friends and family about whom you care. You have the possibility to pursue your creative, intellectual, and social interests. You can travel if you want. Compared to many in the world, you enjoy a good standard of living. You have the freedom to explore spirituality in whatever form to which you are drawn.

"Think of how few people on earth have the possibility to travel, study, work, enjoy life, or freely practice their choice of spirituality or religion as you do.

"As you consider this, realize how rare and precious your life is, and feel gratitude, begin to tap. Tap right-left, right-left. Tap as long as it continues to feel positive and the good feeling strengthens.

You may choose to modify this meditation further, depending on your client's situation. If you are a treatment professional working with addiction, your clients may not have healthy bodies, good living standards, or a supportive family. Many marginalized groups do not feel they are living in a country free of social and political oppression. The point is that there is always something for which to be grateful; to find the right way into this recognition may require modification based on our clients' circumstances.

EXPERIENCES OF AWE AND WONDER

People in recovery from addictions can be caught in a narrow view of their lives. They may have lived in fear, contraction, and self-centeredness. Experiences that inspire awe are awakenings that take one out of one's self. Such experiences often happen in nature: a brilliant sunset, a meteor shower, dolphins leaping out of the sea, flocks of birds flying in a dance of perfect unison, the golden moon rising out of the horizon. It might also include the birth of a child, a beautiful piece of music, or a stunning performance.

Experiences of awe and wonder serve as reminders of something much larger than us. Recalling experiences of awe, then adding tapping to strengthen and integrate them, can help reconnect our clients with a sense of something larger than themselves and support them in viewing their troubles within a broader perspective.

You can ask your clients to describe experiences they have had that inspire awe, wonder, and astonishment. They might wish to list them in their journals. As they think of these times, ask them to notice how they feel. How do these memories act on their whole system? They can recall these times and add BLS to integrate them more fully.

TAPPING IN EXPERIENCES OF AWE AND WONDER

Tell your client, *"Close your eyes and go inside. Take some deep breaths and slowly release them. Relax and release with exhalation. Bring your-self to the present moment. If you like, you can imagine that you are in your Peaceful Place or Sacred Place. Take as long as you would like to relax and feel at ease.*

"Bring to mind a time when you felt an experience of awe or aston-ishment—a time when you were struck by something beautiful or amaz-ing or had an experience that took you out of your ordinary way of perceiving things.

"When the memory comes to you, spend some time enhancing your senses. What are you seeing? What sounds do you hear? What do you notice in your body? When you have evoked a strong sense of the mem-ory, begin to tap. Tap 6 to 12 times. If it is continuing to strengthen, you can tap longer. Tap until it feels complete.

"Now sit a while longer with the feeling of the experience. Savor it. Allow it to give you its gift."

BEAUTY AS A RESOURCE

Another way to help clients in recovery lift their spirits is to help them recall and connect to things that are beautiful. Beauty inspires us, lifts us up, and opens us. When we are touched by beauty, we naturally expand. Places in nature, art, architecture, and music can all provide resources for beauty.

Ask your clients if they would like to try an experiment to see how their environment affects them and how beauty can change how they feel inside. Have them close their eyes and go inside. *"Now bring up an image or memory of being in a city with a lot of dirt, noise, and traffic. Notice how you feel when you evoke this memory. How does your body react? What do you feel in your heart center?*

"Now think of something beautiful. It can be a place in nature, a work of art, or a piece of music. It can be something as simple as a flower or as spectacular as the Yosemite Valley. Notice how you feel. What do you notice in your body? How does your heart feel? Are you expanded or contracted? Notice how you feel now when you bring

up this imagery. Do you notice a difference between the way you feel now and the way you felt when imagining the noisy city scene?"

This experiment can help your clients learn how their environment affects their emotional state and recognize that beauty can lift their spirits. It also can show the importance of bringing beauty into one's life. Even a few flowers in a drab room can create a positive shift.

Explore with your clients what they find beautiful. What inspires them? If they live in a city, they might go to a park, museum, or gallery or listen to live music. Encourage them to venture out into nature as much as they can.

TAPPING IN BEAUTY

Have your client begin with some deep, relaxing breaths. *"Bring yourself to the present moment. When you are relaxed, bring to mind something beautiful. It can be a work of art, music, a scene from nature, anything that inspires you. When you have found it, open your senses. What are you seeing, hearing, smelling, tasting, or sensing? How does your body feel when you think of this beautiful thing?*

"When you are feeling good feelings, begin to tap. Tap 6 to 12 times, right-left, right-left. If the feeling is getting stronger, you can continue. Stop when it feels complete."

If the client wishes to tap in another source of beauty, go on to another round of tapping.

THE RESOURCE OF JOY

Joy opens the heart, often evoking tears or laughter. Memories of joy can help inspire and uplift during times when our clients are feeling down and struggling to stay motivated. This is another resource we can help our clients tap into to lift their spirits when they are feeling stuck or losing momentum. Exploring joy as a resource is especially important for people in recovery who have depended on their addiction to make them feel better. If their source of joy has been their drug, they need a natural substitute—one that does not depend on something that ultimately brings suffering.

Ask your client to remember times when they have felt joy. Some of my most joyful moments include holding my newborn sons in my arms for the first time;

watching whales and dolphins leap by our boat; watching my dog running full tilt on the beach, herding the waves; seeing a flock of pelicans gliding synchronously together and then hurtling headlong into the sea with a great splash; catching a fish as a child; and skiing down the mountain with my son.

If the client has difficulty thinking of a time when they felt joyful, you can suggest that they think of someone they know who is joyful. They can think of a person they know, or a character from a movie, book, or television show. They can even bring to mind animals that evoke the feeling, such as playful puppies or frolicking otters.

Please keep in mind that for many people with addictions, feeling good can be a trigger to use. They may not believe that they deserve to feel good. It may not feel safe to feel good, or they may be in the habit of using drugs or alcohol as a celebration. If they are triggered, it is not an obstacle to treatment, but a chance to work with a trigger (see Chapter 12).

TAPPING IN JOY

Have the client take some deep, full breaths with slow exhalations. *"Relax and let go with the exhalations. When you are feeling some relaxation, bring your awareness to a quiet place inside yourself.*

"Now bring up a memory of a time when you felt joy. It can be from childhood, or from your life as an adult. You can also think of someone you know, a character from a movie or book, or even an animal that makes you feel happy.

"When you have the image, open your senses. Allow yourself to drop into the memory more fully. What are you seeing? What are you hearing? What do you feel in your body? What do you notice in your heart?

"When you can feel joy, even just a little, begin to tap. Tap right-left., right-left, 6 to 12 times. Tap longer if it feels good and continues to strengthen. Savor the feeling of joy. Let it permeate your body. Allow your heart to open and receive it.

"If you want, you can think of something else that evokes joy and tap it in also. Continue bringing up joyful images or memories and tapping as long as it is positive and feels good to you."

INSPIRATION AS A RESOURCE

We can use inspiration as a resource to help our clients lift their spirits. Can they bring to mind times in their lives when they were inspired, or think of others they find inspiring? What inspires them? Who has inspired them? Whom do they admire—Mahatma Gandhi, Nelson Mandela, Jane Goodall, Albert Schweitzer, Maya Angelou, Warren Buffet, Bill Gates, Franklin Delano Roosevelt, Eleanor Roosevelt, Mother Theresa, John Muir? A client's resource for admiration can be an historical, political, spiritual, business, or sports figure; it can be someone they know personally, a public figure, or an ordinary person whose story has inspired them.

TAPPING IN INSPIRATION

Have your client close their eyes and go inside. *"Bring yourself to the present moment. Now think of a time when you felt inspired, or bring to mind someone who inspires you. It can be someone you know or someone you have heard or read about.*

"When you think about inspiration, what image comes to mind? Notice what you see. If it is a memory of being inspired, bring back the sensory details of the experience as much as you can. If you are thinking of a person who inspires you, bring that person to mind as strongly as you can. Represent the person in a way that evokes the feeling of inspiration.

"Once you have the image and can feel the feelings associated with inspiration, begin to tap. Tap 6 to 12 times, right-left, right-left. Then, stop for a moment and check in and see how you are feeling. If it feels good, continue to tap, and keep tapping as long as it feels positive and continues to strengthen." Then, if they wish, the client can bring up another resource that inspires them and tap that in.

Have them imagine taking these inspiring resources with them into a future situation. Any time they are facing an obstacle, they can tap these resources to give needed strength.

SUGGESTIONS FOR DEVELOPING
INSPIRATIONAL RESOURCES

Offer to clients these additional tips if needed:

- **Draw your inspirational figures or your experiences of being inspired.** Add in whatever visual details will enhance your experience. After you have drawn, feel the feelings of inspiration that are evoked, and then tap to strengthen and integrate it.

- **Find photographs or pictures of inspirational resources in magazines or online.** Tap them in, then place them where you will see them often.

- **Make a collage of your inspirational resources.** Tap it in and keep it in a place where you will see it often. You can also use computer technology or a website to make a digital collage.

FREEDOM AND EXPANSION

People who have been consumed by their addictions may have narrowed their lives in order to continue with their behaviors. They may have lost friends, family may have distanced from them, and they may have lost their sense of pleasure with healthier activities. Consumed by addiction, they may have lost perspective on life's possibilities outside the world they inhabited during their use. If they began to use at a young age, they may never have developed those wider perspectives. In their bodies, they may have developed a feeling state of tightness and contraction while living this narrow life. Their hearts have been closed off and their focus placed on the maintenance of their habit.

Once sober, they may find that the absence of the driver for their lives—the addiction—may make them feel lost. The habit of living a closed-off life becomes ingrained. Any memory of an expanded life, with a body feeling of expansion and freedom, has dimmed. The addiction may be under control for the moment, but the habit of living a contracted life may continue. They may have lost contact with the capacity of feeling free and expanded without the use of substances.

This experience or feeling of freedom and expansion can be used as a resource and strengthened through tapping in. You can ask your clients to recall times in their lives when they were not in their addiction—times when they felt expanded, open, and free. If they have difficulty finding such a memory, they can use someone or something that demonstrates this quality. It could be an animal or some other image from nature, or even themselves in the future, free from addiction—a healthy future self. This resource can help open things up and make room for new possibilities when clients are feeling stuck and have lost perspective in their lives; it can boost clients' moods when they are feeling down.

Here are a few images that evoke the feeling of freedom for me:

- Standing on the rim of the Grand Canyon and opening to the vista
- Watching California Condors soar over the ocean by the Big Sur coast
- Walking by the ocean
- Hiking high into the mountains to viewpoints from which I could see vast distances
- Driving on the highway through the desert where the sky is wide open and the landscape uncluttered

When I bring these things to mind I feel light and happy, even a little giddy; my heart opens and expands.

TAPPING IN FREEDOM AND EXPANSION

Have your client close their eyes and go inside. *"Bring your awareness to your breath. Take some deep breaths in; slowly let them out. Relax and let go of all tension with the exhalation.*

"When you feel yourself present, think of a time when you felt free and open—a time when your body felt expanded and unfettered. It can even include a dream you have had that evoked the feeling of freedom. You can also think of someone you know who has this quality, or an animal, an image, or an experience from nature.

"When the image comes to you, open your senses. What are you seeing? Notice any visual details that help bring the experience more fully awake for you. What are you hearing? What are you smelling? What do you feel on your skin? As you evoke this image, how does your body feel?

"When you feel open, free, and expanded, begin to tap. Tap 6 to 12 times, right-left, right-left." Then, have the client stop and check in with how they are feeling; tell them that if it feels good, and they want to tap some more, they can continue and that they can tap as long as it feels good. Have them stop when they feel complete.

When they are finished, have them sit for a few moments, savoring the feeling of freedom and expansion they have evoked.

CHAPTER 8

Spiritual Resources

If light is in your heart, you will find your way home.
—RUMI

Helping clients in recovery from addiction to discover, develop, and embody spiritual resources can provide powerful support from within. Spiritual resources, when evoked and tapped in to help support recovery, provide a larger context within which our clients can view and hold their lives and their problems. These resources can help them feel more deeply connected to their spirituality and can sustain, empower, and inspire. Evoking spiritual resources can remind our clients of their true natures and essential goodness. Connecting to something larger than one's self is fundamental for maintaining a sense of hope and inspiration in 12-step recovery programs.

Not every client will respond to these resources, as they may associate them with religion. It may be helpful to clarify with your clients that authentic spiritual resources are not religious. These resources are *felt* and *experienced* and are not dependent on faith or belief. In this chapter, you will find a large selection of spiritual resources to choose from to help your clients in their recovery process.

HIGHER POWER

Higher Power is a term coined in the 1930s in Alcoholics Anonymous (AA), and it is used across 12-step programs. This Higher Power might also be called God, the Ground of Being, Pure Consciousness, Divine Intelligence, or the Great Spirit. Clients can choose Mother Nature or the universe itself as their Higher Power. Contact with a Higher Power—a power greater than ourselves—provides comfort and a sense that there is something much greater than one's self directing the unfolding of one's life.

The Higher Power provides wisdom, guidance, and a broader perspective. Your client may have had an experience of a Higher Power during a time of great duress or during meditation or prayer. They may have touched into their Higher Power during a time of great wonder, such as the birth of a child. Many people experience a sense of something greater than themselves in nature. Learning to listen and attune to the wisdom expressed through the Higher Power provides a foundation for healing work.

To help clients connect with their Higher Power, ask them to find memories where they had a sense of something larger than themselves. Nature is a good starting point: the bright, beautiful, powerful sun; a glorious sunset, lighting up the sky with brilliant colors; lightning streaking through the dark night; the rising of the full moon. Clients might feel the power of nature in storms, in ocean waves, or in the miracle of the unfolding of a flower.

We can ask our clients to contact memories of connecting with a Higher Power, or a sense of a Higher Power they can feel in the moment, and to tap it in to strengthen the feeling. In so doing, they can call on it to provide wisdom and direction to their lives.

TAPPING IN THE HIGHER POWER

Tell your client, *"Close your eyes and go inside. Take a few moments to find that quiet place inside yourself. You might take some long, deep breaths to calm your mind. When you are quiet inside, imagine going to your Peaceful Place—your special place where you are at ease and can be fully who you are. Spend as much time as you need in your peaceful sanctuary.*

"Now open yourself to experiencing a Higher Power. You may have a direct experience of it in the moment or you may recall a time when you had a strong feeling of it. Allow yourself to experience it in whatever form it takes. When you have a sense or feeling of Higher Power, begin to tap. Tap 6 to 12 times. If you would like to tap longer, you may continue as long as it feels positive and the contact with your Higher Power strengthens."

Tell your client that if they have a particular problem for which they need guidance, or if they have a question or request, they can speak to a Higher Power. Have them listen for the response. *"Be open to receiving it in the way in which it comes. You may receive it in words, in pictures, or in positive feelings. Imagine what your life would be like if you followed the guidance of a Higher Power. Tap as you imagine it."*

Remind the client that they can contact their Higher Power at any time. "It is always with you. You are never separate from it."

SPIRITUAL FIGURES

Ask your client whether they have ever had a religious or spiritual experience that involved a Spiritual Figure. Perhaps they have had such an experience involving figures from religious traditions, such as Jesus, Mary, Moses, Abraham, Buddha, Quan Yin, Mohamed, Vishnu, Kali, the goddess, the Dalai Lama, Tara, or with a spiritual figure from Native American or other indigenous traditions. Beyond this, is there someone or something they associate with spiritual energy or their own spirituality? Such figures can be called upon to provide comfort and support during times of duress. In times of loneliness or difficulty, or any time a deeper connection to spirituality is wanted, the client can evoke and tap in Spiritual Figures to provide help and support.

I've had clients tap in Native American wise men or women, power animals, angelic beings, spirit guides, or spiritual teachers. Remind your clients that their Spiritual Figures are always close at hand; clients need only focus inward, recall them, and tap to increase their felt connection with them.

It is crucial to our resource work that our clients have a body-based feeling of the resource before we tap it in. If it is just an idea or image, it won't integrate into their systems. The feeling of the resource can come in many ways: from a spiritual experience, a dream, a vision, a visitation of some kind, or simply a felt connection with the resource.

TAPPING IN SPIRITUAL FIGURES

Have your client close their eyes and go inside, take some deep relaxing breaths, and let go and release with each exhalation. *"When you feel more present and relaxed, imagine going to your Peaceful Place—your Sacred Place or sanctuary. Tap as you feel yourself there.*

"Bring to mind someone or something you associate with spirituality. It can be someone you have met, someone you have read about, some-

one or something from a dream, or a figure such as Jesus or Quan Yin. If you had a spiritual experience that involved the Spiritual Figure, recall the experience as strongly as you can.

"After bringing the figure to mind, focus on visual details. What do they look like? What are they wearing? What expression do they have on their face? If it helps you to feel the spirituality of the figure more, fill in more sensory detail. Notice any sounds, smells, or bodily sensations. Feel the spiritual vibration of the spiritual figure. Sense their spiritual qualities.

"As you imagine the figure and feel their spiritual qualities, begin to tap. Tap right-left, right-left, 6 to 12 times. Tap longer if the resource gets stronger and remains positive. If you would like, you can imagine the qualities of your spiritual figure emanating from it and radiating out to you, where you absorb them into your nervous system. When you can see and feel this, tap. Tap as long as it continues to feel positive. You are taking in the positive qualities of your spiritual resource.

"Imagine your being filling with these qualities. Remember that these are your own inherent qualities. They have always resided within you. Whenever you want to connect to the spiritual resource that is associated with the spiritual figure, you can imagine the figure, feel the associated feelings, and tap."

THE ESSENTIAL SPIRITUAL SELF

Another spiritual resource is the Essential Spiritual Self. This is the deepest part of the person: their essence, a core of goodness that has been there since the moment of conception, or before. This part has never been touched by any of the bad things that have happened in a person's life. It is the part of them that got them into treatment, has a drive toward wholeness, and recognizes when they have veered off a healthy life path. It is a wise witness to their life and is pure and loving. It has always remained in the background of who they are. It is also the part that loves their children, that can be a loyal friend, and that can offer help to someone in need.

Because many people have done things they regret while addicted, facilitating the connection to the Essential Spiritual Self and tapping it in begins to heal shame and self-loathing that can contribute to addictive behaviors. When clients can begin to feel their essential goodness—their own good hearts—they can begin to live more from that part of themselves and behave in ways that are healthy instead of self-destructive.

To help your clients contact the Essential Spiritual Self, guide them in a relaxation to their Peaceful or Sacred Place. When they are there, ask them to find the part of them that has always been there through all the stages of their life, and that has been untouched by life events. This is the part of them that is whole, wise, and compassionate. When they have a sense of this part of themselves, begin bilateral stimulation (BLS).

If this proves difficult, ask them to think of a time when they loved someone or something or helped someone in need. See if they can contact the part of themselves that recognized that they needed help and brought them into treatment. When they can find that part, add BLS and direct the client to tap on themselves. Continue with BLS as long as it remains positive, helping to integrate this more fully. At the end, remind them that contacting and tapping in this part of themselves can provide a reliable resource for wisdom and support whenever they need it.

TAPPING IN THE ESSENTIAL SPIRITUAL SELF

Have the client close their eyes and go inside. *"Feel yourself sitting. Take some deep breaths in and slowly let them out. Relax and let go with the exhalation.*

"Take another deep breath, breathing up from the center of the earth, filling yourself with breath; and then release your breath back down into the earth. Let go of all the tension in your body and mind as you exhale. Take some more deep breaths, relaxing with the exhalations.

"When you feel relaxed, imagine going to your Peaceful Place. Take as much time as you need to go there. When you feel good and relaxed, tap a few times to increase the feeling.

"Now, in your special place, allow yourself to connect to your Essential Spiritual Self. This essential part of yourself was there before you were born and has been there all your life. This is the part of you that has been with you through all you have experienced in your life, yet has not been touched by any of it. This part of you is pure, good, innocent, wise, and resilient. This is the core of your being."

When the client has a sense of this Essential Spiritual Self, have them tap 6 to 12 times and then stop to check in. If they feel a strong connection, have them tap some more and continue to tap as long as it feels positive.

Have the client name this Essential Spiritual Self, if a name comes up: *"Take note of it and tap it in."* Tell the client, *"If it seems right, allow an image of your Essential Spiritual Self to arise. If you have an image and would like to tap it in, feel your connection to that image strengthening."* If no image comes up, that is fine.

Remind the client, "Your Essential Spiritual Self is always with you. You can contact it whenever you need to. All you have to do to contact it is to imagine it, say its name, and tap. Or simply think of it and tap."

SPIRITUAL EXPERIENCES

Many people have had spiritual experiences that have impacted their lives. These experiences inspire awe and a sense of something much larger than ourselves. If your clients have had a spiritual experience of some kind during their lives, these can be recalled and tapped in.

Spiritual experiences—perhaps those had during meditation or prayer, in a dream, in nature, or during an athletic feat or other kind of peak experience—inspire awe, openness, and stillness. Often, there is an opening of the heart. Many people can recall spiritual experiences from childhood.

Help clients strengthen and integrate spiritual experiences by asking them to recall them and adding BLS. Recalling and tapping in a spiritual experience may help your clients more fully integrate the experience into their life. Ask, *"How did it affect you? What did you learn from it? How would you like to take the essence of the experience into your life now?"* After their response to each of your questions, you can add BLS to help them integrate the information.

When tapping in the memories of spiritual experiences, clients may not reexperience their original power, but evoking the memory and tapping can awaken its feeling or flavor so that it is more available to them. Helping your client remember their deepest experiences can help them feel that their life is spiritually oriented, set within a larger context and meaning than they may have previously believed.

Clients can recall and tap in memories and meanings of these experiences in times when they wish to get in touch with a broader perspective in their lives or when they need motivation in their recovery. Their lives have purpose and meaning beyond the restricted one they led in their addiction. These experiences can later be recalled to bring a sense of something larger than themselves, providing inspiration and support in their recovery process.

TAPPING IN SPIRITUAL EXPERIENCES

Have the client close their eyes and go inside. *"Bring yourself to the present moment. Feel yourself sitting; make contact with the seat. Take some deep breaths and exhale slowly, letting go and releasing with each breath. Take the time you need to let go and come into the now. You might even tap for a few minutes, right-left, right-left, to calm your mind. If it helps, you can imagine going to your Sacred Place or sanctuary first.*

"Think of a time when you had a spiritual experience: an experience of something larger than yourself that inspired awe. This can be an experience of opening to a higher consciousness, a spiritual insight, an experience of God or a Higher Power, or anything you feel was spiritual. It can include a vision or dream or an experience in nature. You may have experienced it in your adulthood or it may be a memory from childhood. Invite in whatever comes to you.

"Now see if you can recall the experience as much as you can. Where are you? What are you doing? If it applies to this experience, bring in sensory information. What are you seeing, hearing, smelling, or feeling in your body? Notice how you feel inside. Now open to the experience. Allow it to unfold in you. Take in the information it offers you. Let it fill you with its flavor—the essence of its message. When you have a feeling for the experience, begin to tap. Tap right-left, right-left, 6 to 12 times. If it continues to strengthen and integrate, continue tapping until it feels complete to you."

Have the client sit for some moments with the feeling; remind them that they can recall this experience and tap to contact and strengthen it whenever they feel the need. You can also invite them to imagine ways to integrate or incorporate these experiences into their day-to-day life and recovery. As they imagine doing this, add BLS.

INSIGHTS AND LIFE LESSONS

Everyone has had insights into themselves where the meaning of life deepens and important life lessons are integrated. Maybe they had a grandparent, teacher, coach, sponsor, or therapist who taught them something important. Perhaps, during their own life, your client has learned some important lessons—some things that they know well enough to tell someone else, but that they sometimes need to be reminded of themselves.

So often, our clients know what is best, but have difficulty applying their knowledge to their own lives. When clients attend meetings to support their recovery, they may learn something important about themselves that they need to take in more fully. You can see how smart they are and how much difficulty they have accessing this part of themselves when it comes to making healthy life choices. If you try to tell your clients something that you think is important for them to know, they may reject it, saying, "I already know that." Well—they do, but it isn't integrated into their overall system. They don't have access to this information.

Unintegrated memory networks usually explain this gap between what a client knows and the behaviors and thought patterns they fall into by default. The information, wisdom, and life lessons they need are inside, but they lie in networks that are not linked up to the ones from which they are operating. Tapping in their insights and life lessons supports them in having better access to the information already within themselves.

Ask the client to make a list of their major insights about life, themselves, and whatever they believe drives their addictive behavior. What have they learned about themselves from their therapy, from groups, from their therapist or sponsor? What have they learned about their addiction from the education they have received in treatment?

They can make a list of these things, and they can even begin to keep track of them in a journal. You can ask them to think of each thing on their list, take in the message, and then add BLS. If it feels helpful, ask them to imagine what their life would be like if they took in this information; ask them to add BLS as they imagine this.

In either case, check in with your client after a few moments of BLS. See what they report. If they are getting more positive associations, do more BLS. When it feels complete, move on to another insight and tap it in. Continue in this way with as many of these lessons as feel useful at the time.

Another way to do this is to ask your clients to imagine using what they've learned in their own recovery to give advice to someone else. For example, a client might give advice to an imagined younger version of himself, adding BLS for as long as the conversation goes on.

What we are attempting to do is link the part of the client that is wise and knows what he needs with the part that drives addictive thoughts and actions. When the two begin a conversation with BLS, they begin to link up, and the addicted self will then have access to the information held by the healthier, wiser self.

If the client has difficulty imagining himself giving advice to another part of himself, he could imagine giving advice to someone else, such as another person in the recovery program or a friend. Add BLS as the client imagines conveying his insights and life lessons to this person.

TAPPING IN INSIGHTS AND LIFE LESSONS

Have your client spend a few moments reflecting on their life. *"What are your most important insights? The most crucial lessons you have learned about life? Have you had spiritual insights or understanding? What insights have you had that would help you in your recovery? Maybe you recall something someone told you that is important to you. Spend some time writing a list.*

"Now review what you have written. Take it in. As you take in your own understanding, your own insights about life, tap. Continue to tap as long as it feels positive.

Then have the client think of a situation in their current life where they might be able to apply some of their wisdom. *"Imagine bringing your wisdom and understanding to the current problem. If you have a good feeling, and you can feel how your wisdom might help you here, tap. Continue to tap as long as it feels positive. Then, imagine using your wisdom and understanding in your life. What would your life be like if you lived more with this wisdom? Tap as you imagine it."*

Remind the client that these insights are theirs to hold close at hand— to live by and be guided by.

SPIRITUAL TEACHINGS

Along with insights and life lessons, your clients can tap in spiritual teachings. Ask the client whether there are teachings from a spiritual tradition that resonate with them. Have they been touched by a spiritual teaching and wanted to integrate it into their way of life, but then have struggled to live what they have learned?

Your client may have been moved by something they have read in spiritual or poetry books or heard from wise teachers or elders. Ask your clients, *"What are the most important spiritual teachings you have read or received?"* or *"What spiritual teachings do you wish to live by more fully?"* Or, ask your client to think of a particular teaching, meditate on it a while, and then add BLS to more fully integrate it. Try asking a client to imagine what their life would be like if they lived with the wisdom of this teaching, and to then add BLS. In this way, clients can integrate this wisdom and make it their own; they can then use it to better orient themselves in their lives. They can do this for themselves between sessions if they wish: simply take time to contemplate teachings that are important to them, then tap them in.

TAPPING IN SPIRITUAL TEACHINGS

Have the client close their eyes, go inside, and spend a few moments calming their mind. Then, ask them to review in their mind the most important teachings they have read or received. They might want to focus on just one teaching or saying for the day. Ask, *"What specific teaching would you like to focus on today? As you contemplate the teaching and can feel the wisdom in it, tap. Tap as long as it feels positive."*

Have the client continue to bring up any additional teachings they would like to tap in, and take some time to tap in each one.

Finish by inviting the client to imagine taking the teaching into their life. *"What would your life look like if you lived with this teaching?"* When they have a strong sense of this, have them tap it in, continuing to tap for as long as it feels positive.

CHAPTER 9
Connecting to Inner Strength

You must do the things you think you cannot do.
—ELEANOR ROOSEVELT

When working with clients in recovery from addictions, we want to help them integrate and embody their own inner strength to support them on the path to healing. Many of our clients have had difficult lives, yet have been able to overcome many of those difficulties. Somehow, they find the inner strength to begin the work of recovery. In supporting their healing journey, we want to help them connect with their own inner strength, courage, and resilience so that they have more access to these aspects of themselves. This will increase their capacity to stay the course through the challenges they are bound to encounter as they change the patterns of their former lives.

As I discussed in Chapter 2, many of our clients grew up in families where there was substance abuse and violence. These clients felt unprotected and powerless as children, and these feelings stayed with them as they moved into adolescence and adulthood. The substances or behaviors that fueled the addiction may have helped them turn down the volume on intense fear, feel a sense of pleasure or connection, or have a feeling of power. Their addiction helped them cope. With the loss of the addiction, these clients may feel vulnerable and overwhelmed. Helping them to connect to inner strength and empowerment resources can enable them to better manage these feelings, providing them with the inner support they need.

What follows are several ideas for increasing and integrating inner strength and empowerment. Each idea will be fleshed out in more detail in this chapter:

- Memories of being resourceful
- Inner strength and courage
- Memories of saying no and setting boundaries
- Lessons learned

MEMORIES OF BEING RESOURCEFUL

As we work to strengthen our clients to help them move toward their personal recovery goals or maintain their sobriety, continue their treatment or recovery plan, and keep motivated, we can help them locate and reinforce their stored memories of times of resourcefulness. If we help them look inside, most people can recall times when they were able to contact inner or outer resources to handle a challenge in their lives—when they recognized that they needed help and then sought it out or drew on inner resources that proved powerful. It could be a time when they went for help when they were in a dangerous situation, or when they found the solution to a problem, or when they were stuck with some difficulty until they discovered the answer.

I've seen many examples in my work with clients: the man who was having difficulty learning in school as a child then found a kind, understanding teacher who was able to help him learn; the woman who was being abused by her step-father and told a neighbor, who contacted the authorities. One client's parents abused drugs and alcohol and did not provide a safe, stable home life for her; she chose to spend time at a friend's home, where the parents were kind and caring and warmly welcomed her. Over time, she became a part of that family and minimized time spent around her parents. This woman recognized that her home life and parents did not provide the safety she needed and that her friend's family did. She was wise enough to act on this recognition by spending as much time as she could with the healthy family.

You can help clients strengthen connection to their resourcefulness by asking them to recall times in their lives when they recognized a problem and addressed it in a healthy, constructive way. Explore different times in their lives. If they have shared experiences of being resourceful with you—experiences they may not have recognized as such—help them reframe those recollections as examples of their resourcefulness.

When they have recalled a time or times of resourcefulness, ask them to go inside and bring up the memory as strongly as they can, paying special attention to the actions they took that were effective and helpful. Can they contact that part of themselves that recognizes a problem and then works to solve it? When they have the positive feeling of this resource or memory, add bilateral stimulation (BLS). After a few seconds, check in. How was it? If it is getting stronger and more positive associations come up, go longer. If it should go negative at all, stop and return to positive memories or feelings. You might also ask them to put the distressing images or memories in a container. Be careful here that clients don't associate to past traumas. Pay close attention and keep sets of BLS short.

In the above example of the woman who spent time at the neighbor's home as a respite from her chaotic family, the therapist might say something like this: *"Close your eyes and go inside. Bring up the memory of recognizing that your home was not safe and of spending time at your neighbor's home. Can you find that part of you that knew what was safe and what wasn't and did something about it? Can you locate that strong, resourceful part of yourself that kept you going to your neighbor's home, even when your parents complained? When you have an image and a sense of this resourceful part of yourself, begin to tap. Tap as long as it feels good to you and the feeling of strength increases."*

If the client reports that it feels good, you can ask if she has any other memories of taking care of herself, of being resourceful. If she says yes, ask her again for the image and the feeling associated with being resourceful; then, add BLS. If she begins to associate to the fear of living in her home and the abuse that was occurring there, ask her to put that information in a container with a strong lid on it and then return to the positive image or memory. If she can do that, reinforce again with a short set of BLS. If the trauma memories are too strong, ask her to imagine her Peaceful Place and perhaps even bring her child self there; she can also bring in her Nurturing and Protector Figures. This can be done with or without BLS, depending on how the client responds. I might ask her if she would like to incorporate BLS.

If the client has a series of positive memories and associations to times when she was able to take care of herself—where she was able to be resourceful— continue with the BLS, reinforcing these memories. At the end of the session, debrief by talking with her about her experience. You might even name this part of her so that she can call on it when she needs to remember her own strength and resourcefulness.

INNER STRENGTH AND COURAGE

I learned that courage was not the absence of fear,
but the triumph over it. The brave man is not he who
does not feel afraid, but he who conquers that fear.

—NELSON MANDELA

Many of our clients have gotten through difficulties in their lives by drawing on their inner strength. Some part of them got them into treatment or recovery. Perhaps they were able to face a challenge without the use of their addiction, or they otherwise experienced times when they were courageous and strong. We can help our clients develop and integrate this inner strength so that it is more available to them.

Inner strength is the resource that makes it possible to face life's difficulties; it is a part of our clients that has been there since they were born. Although at times they may have lost contact with it or had difficulty feeling it, it has always been there. This is the part of the client that has enabled them to survive and to overcome some of the obstacles they've faced. It can be helpful to explore with clients times when they felt contact with this part of themselves. Such memories can be tapped in as resources to help connect them more fully to this internal capacity.

TAPPING IN INNER STRENGTH

Have the client close their eyes and go inside. *"Now take a deep breath. Breathe in from the earth, filling your belly, chest, and throat. Hold your breath a moment, and then slowly let it out, exhaling from your throat . . . chest . . . and belly. Now take another deep breath. Slowly exhale, letting go of all tension. That's it. Let yourself relax. Bring yourself to the present moment.*

"When you feel relaxed, contact your inner strength. This is a part of yourself that has been there since you were born—even though, at times, it may be difficult for you to feel—and it is with you now. It's that part of yourself that has allowed you to survive and to overcome obstacles wherever you have faced them.

"You may recall times when you were able to face and overcome a challenging situation with courage and strength. Take a few moments to get in touch with that part of yourself. Notice what images . . . or feelings . . . what thoughts . . . what bodily sensations are associated with

being in touch with your inner strength. You may have a memory of when you contacted that part of yourself.

"When those images, thoughts, feelings, bodily sensations, or memories are clear to you, however they are coming to you, begin to tap. Tap as long as the feeling of inner strength feels positive or deepens in you. If it doesn't feel good, or something negative comes up, stop tapping and return to memories of feeling inner strength.

"When you feel the sense of inner strength and courage well activated and integrated, remind yourself that in the future, when you wish to get in touch with your inner strength, you will find that you can do so by calling forth these images, thoughts, feelings, and bodily sensations. This will bring you in touch with your inner strength again.

"If you would like, if it is appropriate, imagine yourself in a future situation with your inner strength. When you can imagine and feel this, tap. Tap as long as it feels good and the positive feelings strengthen."

Remind the client that at any time they want, they can get in touch with their own inner strength by simply closing their eyes for a moment and evoking the images, thoughts, feelings, and bodily sensations associated with that quality.

THE RESOURCE OF HEALTHY, WISE, EMBODIED POWER

This type of power is connected to wisdom and is well-grounded in the body. From it, skillful action can arise. Our clients may be powerless over their addictions, but they are not without power to make healthy changes in their lives. "Courage to change the things I can" is part of the Serenity Prayer used in AA meetings, and this courage is an important resource to support in treatment. This is a "can-do" kind of energy that connects the legs and feet to the ground. When engaged, this power can move them forward in action toward positive goals.

This resource is an antidote to inertia and helplessness. It is useful for clients who feel weak and powerless over their lives whom you wish to help connect to the part of themselves that can act in healthy ways. This is a form of power that is constructive, not destructive—an important consideration when clients may have abused power while under the influence of their addiction or have been the victim of someone who has abused power in a way that caused harm.

Some clients may be afraid of their power because they associate it with abuse. If this is a concern, talk with them about the use of power and their associations to it. Help them understand that power can be expressed with healthy control and wisdom, rather than without control or concern for others.

What follows are some ideas you can use to help cultivate healthy, wise, embodied power. These can include body postures, power figures, overcoming obstacles, setting healthy boundaries, saying no, and integrating life lessons.

TAPPING IN BODY POSTURES

Clients in addictive processes may have lost touch with their bodies. Yoga postures such as the Warrior Pose or other simple standing poses in which the feet are planted firmly and the muscles of the legs engaged are great for generating a sense of embodied power. Employing imagery, such as the stance of a strong tree (see below), can help with embodiment and grounding. When that stance and the feeling of power, strength, or courage is evoked and felt in the body, add BLS.

For clients who tend to dissociate when strong feelings arise, I use the image and stance of a strong tree to help them ground and root themselves and to feel the power of their legs and feet. Ask them to imagine themselves as strong trees with deep roots. If they wish, they can reach their arms up like branches. Their branches are high, reaching to the sky; their strong roots pass deep into the ground, connecting them to the earth. Standing up straight and feeling their feet on the floor may be helpful; some clients may wish to remove their shoes to feel their feet more firmly on the floor.

When they have a sense of this and can feel it, add BLS. If it is comfortable for them, you might do this by tapping on their shoulders. Check in from time to time to see how they feel. If they wish, you can go longer, as long as it feels good to them and the feeling of strength and power increases.

A yoga posture that can also be used in treatment to increase the feeling of courage and power is the pose called Warrior I. This powerful stance can help develop inner strength and courage important for facing the challenges of recovery. On a physical level, it engages the feet, hamstrings, quadriceps, and gluteus muscles, helping to build core power.

HOW TO DO WARRIOR I (VIRABHADRASANA)

1. Stand with feet parallel and hip-width apart.

2. Step the right foot 3.5-4 feet back, raising both arms perpendicular to the floor and parallel from each other, reaching actively through the pinky finger sides of each hand toward the ceiling, palms facing in toward each other. At the same time, draw the shoulder blades down the back of the rib cage, lowering shoulders away from ears.

3. Keep the left toes pointing forward. Turn the right foot out 45-90 degrees, keeping the right leg straight and strong. Take care that your left knee does not jut out past your left toes; you should be able to see your left toes past your knee if you glance down toward them.

4. Firm both legs and reach high with the hands as you sink deeper into the lunge in the legs. If it's comfortable, bring the palms together, gaze upward, and take a gentle lift of your chest.

5. Stay for 30-60 seconds, breathing deeply and regularly. To switch sides, straighten your left leg, turn your left toes in, and face sideways, so that both sets of toes face to the left, legs spread wide. Pivot the rest of the way to execute Warrior I with the right leg in front.

6. Once the pose is completed, shift back through the way you went to change sides, then step forward, back to the posture in which you began—feet hip-width apart and parallel, facing front.

If you guide your client into this pose, once it is achieved, ask the client to notice how they feel. If they report positive feelings of empowerment, courage, and self-confidence, add BLS to help them more fully integrate the experience the posture evokes.

POWER FIGURES

Another way to develop the resource of wise, healthy power is imagining figures that represent it. You might ask your clients, *"When you think of a figure that represents healthy, wise power, what figure comes to mind?"* Power Figures can include someone they know personally, or historical, religious, political, or sports icons. They can be figures from movies, television shows, or books. Power Figures can include Spiritual Figures such as Kali, the Hindu goddess; Jesus; or Moses.

Figures my clients have chosen include Nelson Mandela, Oskar Schindler, Harriet Tubman, Abraham Lincoln, Joan of Arc, Frederick Douglass, Martin Luther King, Jr., and the Dalai Lama. I encourage clients to choose figures who integrate power with wisdom and compassion.

TAPPING IN POWER FIGURES

Have the client close their eyes and go inside. *"Take a few moments to bring yourself to the present. Find that still place inside yourself. When you are quiet inside, bring up an image of a figure you associate with power that is expressed with wisdom. It can be someone you know, a historical, religious, spiritual, mythological, political, or athletic figure, or a figure from a movie, television show, or book.*

"When the image comes to you, bring in more visual details if you can. What does the figure look like? What expression do they have on their face? What posture are they in? What is the figure doing? You want to evoke as strongly as you can the feeling of strength and power. When you have the image, notice how you feel. Can you feel the sense of power the figure is evoking in you? Where do you feel it in your body?

"With that image and the feelings of power activated, begin to tap. Tap 6 to 12 times. Check in with yourself. If it is getting stronger and it is positive, you can tap longer.

"Now imagine a situation in which you would need to feel powerful. See if you can bring to the situation the power resources you have tapped in. If you can, and if you feel more powerful in the situation, tap to increase the feeling and integrate the resource." Have the client tap as long as it feels positive and they feel strong.

OVERCOMING OBSTACLES: DEVELOPING RESILIENCE AND PERSEVERANCE

Clients who hit obstacles to their motivation can develop resilience and perseverance by activating and integrating memories of having overcome difficulties in the past. By helping clients to link in times in the past when they were able to accomplish something challenging for them or to move through a difficulty, we help them draw from the strength and power they already have within. For those clients who have difficulty recalling times when *they* were able to overcome an obstacle, you can use examples of *others* who have done so. It is important that the examples used are healthy and do not include their addiction.

When one perseveres despite challenges, it naturally feels good. Work with the client to identify times when they found the strength within to move through a difficulty and get through it to the other side. The associated feeling of mastery and empowerment can be strengthened and reinforced with BLS. By recalling and tapping in these resources, clients can remember that they have it within themselves to do what they need to do to stay the course on their healing journey and move through the rough patches.

TAPPING IN MEMORIES OF OVERCOMING OBSTACLES

Tell the client, *"Close your eyes and go inside. Take some deep breaths and slowly release them, relaxing and letting go with the exhalation. When you feel yourself settled, find that still place inside yourself.*

"Now bring to mind a time when you were able to overcome an obstacle. Think of a time when you were able to triumph over something difficult for you. It could be something from childhood or adulthood. Allow yourself to drop into that experience and notice what it feels like to move through difficulty in a way that is healthy and empowering. Notice what you feel in your body.

"When you have imagined the scene and have a strong bodily sense of overcoming the obstacle, begin to tap. Tap 6 to 12 times, then stop and see how you feel. If it is getting stronger, tap longer.

"You might ask yourself, what did I learn from this experience? When the answer comes to you, and if it is a positive one, tap it in to strengthen and integrate it. If you would like to, think of another time you were able to overcome something difficult for you. When that memory is well elicited, tap it in. What did you learn from that experience? Tap to integrate that information."

This may be all that you do in this session; however, if it has gone well, and you wish to help the client bring this resource into a future situation, continue. *"Now bring to mind a situation from your current life that is difficult for you—a situation that could be helped by this information you have tapped in about overcoming difficulties. When you think of it now, bring the information you have learned from the past to this experience.*

When you have a positive feeling of it, tap. Tap as long as it feels good."
To finish, have the client tap while imagining themselves in the future,
using the information they've received in this tapping in.

USING EXAMPLES OF OTHER PEOPLE OVERCOMING OBSTACLES

You can also help clients draw from stories of other people who have overcome difficulties in their lives. Whom do they know who has overcome their addiction and is living an exemplary life? Who has inspired them with their life story? These stories can be about overcoming addictions but can also include any stories that illustrate the resource of resilience, perseverance, and courage. Many inspiring books and stories describe people overcoming great difficulties and life challenges—famous people such as Mohammad Ali, Oprah Winfrey, Michael J. Fox, Bill W., Franklin Roosevelt, Helen Keller—or ordinary people who accomplished extraordinary things in the face of adversity. Characters from movies and works of fiction and mythology can be used if they elicit the strength and power you are wishing to develop.

TAPPING IN AN EXAMPLE OF A PERSON WHO HAS OVERCOME OBSTACLES

Have the client close their eyes, go inside, and take a few moments to calm themselves and arrive at the present moment. *"Now think of someone who has overcome obstacles. Who has persevered through difficult situations? It can be someone you know, someone you have heard or read about, or a character from a movie or book.*

When you have the image or memory of the person exhibiting this quality, notice how you feel inside when you think of them in this situation. What sensations do you experience in your body? Can you feel, inside yourself, the strength and determination the person displays?

"When you can feel the feeling of perseverance and determination to move through a difficulty, begin to tap. Tap 6 to 12 times. If it is getting stronger, tap longer. Feel that quality in yourself. As you recognize it in this other person, realize that it is within you.

"Is there someone else you would like to imagine who has overcome

obstacles? Bring them up, too, and when you have a strong sense of them, tap to strengthen the feeling."

This may be all that you do in this session. However, if it has gone well, and you wish to help your clients bring this resource into a future situation, continue. Have the client think of a current situation in which they are facing something difficult. "Bring in the resource person you would have tapped in. Feel the quality they would express. Feel the quality as it would manifest in you. Tap as you feel this applying to your current situation."

SAYING NO, SETTING BOUNDARIES

There are times when our clients must be able to say no—to set boundaries with people, themselves, or their addiction. Some of our clients may find it difficult to find the strength and self-assurance to say no to someone who is making demands of them, especially if it is someone with whom they have shared their addiction.

You can help clients strengthen their resolve and their ability to say no and set boundaries. Start by asking them to find memories of times when they *were* able to say no—to someone offering them their drug of choice, to their friends, or to their spouse or partner. Have them write a list of times they were able to say "no," then read it back to the client and have them tap in each example by tapping their own legs or knees as the list is read back to them. Clients may also choose to tap in these memories on their own. The key is to imagine the scenes and the body sense of limit-setting in order to activate this memory network.

TAPPING IN TIMES OF SAYING NO

Spend a few minutes reviewing past moments when the client has successfully set boundaries and limits. *"If you would like, write down times when you were able to say no to someone and set a limit or boundary. This list could include times when you were able to say no to yourself about engaging in a behavior that you knew wasn't good for you."*

Have the client begin with the most powerful "no" they can recall. *"As you think of it, fill it in with as many visual and sensory details as you can. What was happening? Who was there? What were you feeling as you say no? Help your body remember what it feels like to say no, to set a limit. What does it feel like in your body when you say 'no' and follow through with it? When the image and feelings are strong, tap. Tap as long as it strengthens and feels positive."*

The client can repeat this with another time they said no and were able to set a limit. Have them access and strengthen that memory by adding sensory information until they can feel the "no," and then tap for as long as it feels positive. *"If other memories of setting limits arise that are positive, you can continue tapping."*

If negative associations occur, have the client stop tapping, return to the positive memory of saying no, and tap it a few times; or they can go to their Peaceful Place. *"Put any unpleasant material in an imaginary container with a strong lid. You can bring in your Nurturing Figures, Protector Figures, or other allies if you would like them to help you."*

This may be all that you do in this session. However, if it has gone well, and you want to help your client bring this resource into a future situation, continue: *"If you wish, you might imagine a future situation in which you will need to put this resource of strong 'no' and boundary-setting to use. Can you imagine bringing this feeling of 'no' to the imagined future scene? If you can, tap to link them together."*

If they wish to bring up more than one future scenario where the boundary-setting resource could be brought to bear, have them imagine that, too. Each time, have them bring in the feeling state of the "no" and then tap as it is brought to the imagined scene. When this feels complete, lessons learned can be discussed and debriefed.

If your clients have difficulty coming up with times when they were able to say no, ask them whether they can think of an example of someone other than themselves who has that ability. It could be someone they know personally, someone from history, a character from a movie or book, or a religious or spiritual figure. The figure they choose can be real or imaginary. It is important that when they imagine this person setting limits and boundaries, they can also *feel* it. Brainstorm with clients; offer up possible candidates. They might choose one of your ideas, or they might be inspired by your ideas to come up with someone else. When they can call up in their imagination the figure that expresses this capacity, add BLS. Keep going as long as it seems positive and the feelings increase. If they think of other examples, add more BLS. If this spurs them to recall times when they were able to set limits, add BLS and follow that thread to reinforce and integrate it.

TAPPING IN OTHERS WHO CAN SAY NO

Have the client think of someone who is good at saying no. *"It can be someone you know, or someone from a movie, book, or television. It can be someone real or an imaginary figure. Bring the person to mind setting a limit, saying no, or creating a boundary. As you bring this person to mind, what do you notice? What do you feel in your body?*

"When you have a strong sense of the feeling of boundary setting, begin to tap. Tap 6 to 12 times. Right-left, right-left. Stop and see how you are feeling. If it is positive, you can tap some more. If you would like, you can bring to mind another person who is able to set limits and say no. Tap that figure in also."

Encourage the client to tap in as many figures as they like.

These resources can be used to help clients say no and set appropriate boundaries when their recovery is challenged. After clients have tapped in their inner strength and limit-setting resources, these resources can be applied imaginatively to current life situations that might challenge their recovery. This is a protocol for applying these boundary-setting resources to present-day challenges.

APPLYING LIMIT-SETTING RESOURCES TO PRESENT-DAY CHALLENGES

Have the client spend a few moments coming into the present moment. *"Take some deep breaths and slowly let them out. Relax with the exhalation; let go of tension; settle into the now in your body.*

"Think of a time recently when you had difficulty saying no—setting a limit or boundary with someone. It might be a time when you had difficulty saying no to your addiction. Bring the scene to mind as clearly as you can. What are you seeing? Who is there with you? What is happening? What are you feeling?

"Now bring to mind a time when you were able to say no to someone—a time when you were able to set a limit. It could also be a time when you said no to your addiction. Accept whatever image or memory comes to mind."

If the client cannot think of a time when they were able to set a limit, ask them, *"Can you think of someone else who can?"* It can be someone they know, or even someone from a movie or book. Let the image of the person come up for them. Encourage them to accept what comes. Once they have the memory or image, have them feel the feelings associated with saying no. Ask them: *"What do you feel in your body?"* When the image and feeling of no is strongly felt, have the client begin to tap, right-left, right-left, 6 to 12 times. If it is continuing to strengthen and feels positive, have them tap some more.

"Now return to the image you started with from the present where you had difficulty setting a boundary. How do you feel now? If you feel stronger, tap as you feel your capacity to set a limit in the present situation. If you need more strength, think of another time when you were able to say no, or think of another example of someone else. Tap that example in also.

"Return again to the scene from the present. How does it feel? If it feels good, and you feel better able to set a limit, imagine yourself setting a limit with a person, or with your addiction, in the future. Tap as you imagine it."

INTEGRATING LESSONS LEARNED: HARNESSING THE POWER OF INFORMATION

Many people struggling with addictions know all they need to know about overcoming them, yet have difficulty applying what they know to their own lives and addictions. One way of creating these link-ups is to have clients recall and imagine the information they learned about their problem and then add BLS. By engaging the left frontal lobe where rational, linear information is stored and linking it with imagination using BLS, we can help connect these disconnected brain regions. What follows are some suggestions for achieving this end through the harnessing of the power of education and lessons learned.

Tapping in Education about Addiction

Ask your client to write down everything they have learned about their particular addiction or problem. What do they know about its physiology? What do they know about how their substance of choice affects the brain and body? What do they know about the long-term effects of this particular substance? What drives it? What helps to control it?

After they have compiled this information, review what they have written. Then, ask them to close their eyes, go inside, and listen as you read back the list of things they have written. As you read the list back to them, add BLS. They can tap their own legs or knees, or you can use BLS devices. After you have done this, check in with them and see how they feel.

You might also ask the client to imagine that someone they know and care about has a similar problem. They can imagine that they are teaching this person about the addiction. As they imagine doing this, add BLS. To apply this idea to triggers, you might ask the client to imagine being triggered, and then have them imagine using the lessons they have learned with BLS. This is a means to link lessons with triggers in order to help integrate the information more fully in a practical way.

Tapping in Information from Various Sources About Maintaining Recovery

Ask your client to make a list of things they have learned about maintaining sobriety. This can be wisdom gleaned from a sponsor, family members, friends, reading, web research, or in treatment. What have other people done that worked? Which of these things do they think might also be helpful for them? As they think through the list, add BLS. They can also imagine taking the advice they've been given. What would that look like? What would it feel like in their lives? As they imagine taking this advice, add BLS.

Tapping in Coping Strategies for Recovery

Many people in recovery have learned coping tools from other therapies that they find difficult to apply in their own lives. Ask your client to make a list of the coping strategies they have learned; then ask them to imagine applying one of those strategies in their life. As they imagine doing that, add BLS. They can then imagine another coping strategy and imagine applying that strategy to their lives as well. Use BLS with each addition. Throughout, check in with your clients and see how they are doing. You can continue with the imagination and BLS as long as it remains positive and seems to strengthen their connection with the information they have linked in.

CHAPTER 10
Resources for Restoring a Sense of Inner Goodness

When we feel love and kindness toward others,
it not only makes others feel loved and cared for, but it
helps us also to develop inner happiness and peace.
—DALAI LAMA

Many people in recovery from addictions feel as though they lost a part of themselves during the time they were using. They descended into a dark place where they engaged in behaviors and activities that did not feel good to them on a deep, spiritual level. They may have hurt people they cared about or committed acts that went against their basic moral code. This dark place is where they resided for the time of their addiction—where they engaged in activities and behaviors that they regret and feel shame about. They may feel tainted by this darkness, as though it now defines who they are. They may feel disgust and loathing toward themselves.

Even though they may have left that life, they may still feel this darkness resides inside them and defines their sense of self. It is as though they have lost the connection to their inner goodness. For people in recovery, or for those who are struggling to get there, feelings of shame, unworthiness, and self-hatred may feel intolerable, thus triggering relapse behavior that temporarily relieves the pain. They simply can't bear feeling so bad about themselves. They feel they are bad people who don't deserve to be happy.

I once worked with a man in his early 40s who was in treatment for porn and meth addiction. He was big and burly, built like a lumberjack; he kept his head down when he spoke and avoided meeting my eyes. His shoulders were slumped, and he spoke in a low voice, claiming he was "fine." When we explored more deeply the time when he was using meth and compulsively watching porn, he described it as a time of darkness. He felt lost, doing things that he did not feel good about but had lost control over. He felt stuck in an intractable morass of negativity—so full of ugliness and shame that he couldn't find his way out of it.

To bring some light to this inner darkness, I asked him about people he loved and cared for in his life. He brightened as he told me about his children and family. I could see right away that he felt better. I asked him to focus on those people and feelings he had for them, and I added bilateral stimulation (BLS). When I checked in with him, he sat up straighter, gave me eye contact, and smiled. It looked like a weight had lifted off his broad shoulders as he began to feel his inner goodness again. We continued down this line of resourcing, bringing in memories of good times with his children and adding BLS. More light entered his darkness.

I began to understand more clearly that the time of his addiction was a lost, corrupt time about which he felt deeply ashamed. His inner goodness had not been entirely extinguished, however, and it was important to him that I recognized his good heart. We continued to use BLS to tap in those he loved. As we did so, he told me that he felt the darkness inside subside. He was also able to talk about what he had done in the past more openly. Before this, he had been able to abstain from the addictions, but was so overcome by shame around his past behavior that he couldn't admit what he had done or do any real recovery work.

To support clients in recovery, it is essential that we bring compassion for them to the work and help them connect with their higher self. When we align with their wholeness and see their inner goodness, we help to strengthen that part of them, providing positive motivation and hope for healing. Many people who are new to recovery or who are trying to get there need to feel they are good people, despite having done bad things. They may have left a trail of destruction that they feel too ashamed to face.

Facilitating clients' connection to their better selves—to their goodness, kindness, generosity, and capacity to love—is an important part of addiction treatment. This is not to deny any of the bad things they might have done or the wreckage they have created in their lives; it is to give them hope—something to build on.

Because feelings of shame can be so global and are experienced as the "truth" about whom one really is, providing resources to counter these negative feelings and internal constructs is essential for healing. What follows are some resources useful to restore a sense of inner goodness and facilitate the rebuilding of self-esteem on the path of recovery and healing from addictions. These resources help to create a distinction between harmful behaviors and the person engaging in them—so that the behaviors don't define who they are.

LOVE RESOURCES

When we help our clients recall and tap in love resources, we connect them to a wellspring from which they can draw inspiration and support through the tumultuous course of recovery. By tapping in memories of loving and being loved and experiences with cherished family and friends from the past and present, they can connect more fully to their good hearts—the best antidote to self-loathing and shame. Even though they may have lost contact with that part of themselves, the love they have received is never lost. It continues to abide in their hearts.

Tapping into love resources serves to increase self-worth and inspires motivation to withstand addiction urges. It decreases the experience of physical and emotional pain and increases oxytocin, the bonding hormone.

When we help our clients recall those who have given them love, even for a very short time, this recollection can provide a light in the darkness that sustains the client and provides hope. They are worth something. Someone has loved them. This reservoir of love can be tapped in to help clients become better able to make use of that gift. What follows are several love resources that you might integrate into treatment with clients with a history of addiction.

LOVE RESOURCES

- Those you love
- Those who love you
- The heart as a place of refuge
- Circle of Love
- Loving-kindness meditation
- Kindness and generosity

When working with these resources, as with any of the others, it is important to pay attention to individual clients' responses. Which resource seems easiest to contact? I always advise going in the door that is simplest to access and that provides the most benefit for the client. In particular, go slowly with clients who have attachment trauma. The pain of not being loved enough may cause them distress. I find it is best to begin with memories of giving love, help, or kindness to others before working with memories of receiving. Here, it seems in most cases, it is easier to give than to receive. When we bring up memories of giving, it facilitates receptivity to receiving—perhaps because when one gives to others, one feels like a person more worthy of receiving love or kindness in return.

Those you love. One of the easiest ways to tap into love is to ask your clients to think of the people *they* love. By accessing memories and images of those they love, they can contact their soft, open heart, which in turn can help them feel less self-critical, anxious, sad, lonely, or unsupported. If they were unloved as children, they may believe that they are unlovable. But when they are able to contact memories of feeling loving toward others, they can feel themselves to be a loving person. Their belief that they are bad becomes less compelling. How can they be bad and loving at the same time?

This resourcing exercise can be triggering for some people struggling with addiction, bringing up guilt and shame because their behavior toward these people has not always matched their love. Keep this in mind, and be prepared to shift to other resources that are less triggering for your client.

Ask your client to compile a list of all the people or animals they have loved in their lives. They might create a time line with these people and pets, grandparents, aunts and uncles, childhood friends, a beloved teacher, a neighbor, or their parents. They could do this as a homework assignment or create the list during a therapy session. Once the list is created, have the client recall each figure, feel the specific kind of affection that arises, and add BLS. Systematically going through the list and tapping in love figures can be done in one or more sessions.

You can also focus on whomever the client loves now. They can imagine each person (or pet) and, once they fully feel love, add BLS. Sometimes, as clients do this exercise, more memories come up of others they have loved. If the list grows, continue to tap in the new resources.

After tapping in these love resources, tell the client that they can call them up in their imaginations and tap them in when they are feeling the need for comfort or if they are feeling the urge to engage in their addictive behavior. In this section are many ideas and scripts you can use for tapping in or installing the resource of love. Most are adapted from my 2008 book, *Tapping In*.

Here is a script to help you guide your clients in tapping in those they love. You can direct the BLS using equipment, or by tapping on clients' knees, or by having clients tap themselves using the butterfly hug or tapping on the sides of their own legs.

TAPPING IN LOVED ONES

Tell your client, *"Take a few moments to go inside and quiet your mind. Find that still place within yourself and rest there a while. Now, think: Who are the people or animals from your past and present that you have loved?*

"Go all the way back to your childhood—to parents, grandparents, nannies, friends, or teachers. As a child, did you have a special pet with whom you felt a special bond? Or, you can focus on those who are alive and special to you now: your children, grandchildren, nieces and nephews, dog, cat, or horse. Do you have a close friend you love?

"If the people or animals are deceased and you feel sad when you think of them, see if you can put these feelings aside and focus only on your love for them. Remember that this love never dies. What they gave to you continues to be a resource for you throughout your life. You might want to imagine a container made of something strong into which you can put your grief or sadness or any other painful thoughts or feelings. The container can be a treasure box with a strong lid that you can open when you like. In the meantime, putting these less pleasant feelings in there will allow you to focus on the good feelings.

"Now bring up an image of one particular person or animal you love or have loved in the past. Bring the person or animal to mind as strongly as you can. The image should evoke only positive feelings. For example, you might imagine your daughter as a little girl, sitting on your lap as you read her a story. As you bring this image to mind, let yourself feel your love for her. Let that feeling of love fill your heart as much as possible.

"When you can hold the image and the loving feelings, begin to tap. Tap 6 to 12 times or longer, provided that the feelings strengthen or remain positive.

"If it should become negative in any way—if sad memories or regretful feelings come up, for example—stop tapping. Bring up the image you began with again and try to find the loving feelings. If you find them, tap again, but only for a short time. If you cannot find the positive feelings, look for another being for whom you have loving feelings, and evoke the image and feelings with tapping again. This time, only tap a short while." Have the client repeat this process with many beings for whom they have loving feelings. Guide them to bring each one to mind, feel the feelings of love and affection, and then tap to strengthen those feelings.

Here's how this might go. Let's say your client begins with his son, then brings in his wife and best friend, and then his dog. Your client recalls playing with his son when he was a little boy; ask the client to tap when he feels the feelings of love and to continue until it feels strong, integrated, and complete. You could then ask him to bring up an image or memory of loving his wife—maybe when they were first together and went on vacation to a beautiful place. When he can feel that strongly, you would direct him to tap and to continue until it feels fully embodied. Next, you might ask him to think of a time when he was close to his best friend, perhaps during a challenging time in his life where this friend came through for him. Direct him to tap in the image and affection for his friend, too. Then, finally, ask him to imagine his dog sitting next to him on the couch, his warm body nestled against him, his head on his lap. When he can imagine that, and he feels an upwelling of affection for the dog, direct him to tap and to continue tapping until he feels complete.

Receiving Love: Those Who Love You

Ask your client to think of a person or pet who loves them now or who has loved them in the past. They can make a list of all those who have loved them throughout their life and then bring each person to mind and add BLS. They can think of people or animals from their current life, or they can go all the way back to their childhood. It may be more difficult for clients to recall receiving love than giving it. Tell them that they can include experiences such as feeling affection from a beloved childhood pet. If this is too difficult for your client, keep working with different love resources that don't evoke feelings of inadequacy.

Here is a script, a variation on the one that appears in my book *Tapping In*, to help you guide your clients in tapping in those who love them. You can do the BLS, or clients can do it for themselves.

TAPPING IN THOSE WHO LOVE YOU

Have the client find a quiet place inside, closing their eyes and attending to their breath. *"Take some deep breaths and slowly let them out, relaxing and letting go with the exhalations. Do this for a few minutes, until you feel yourself present.*

"Now bring to mind someone who loves you. It can be someone from your life now or someone who has loved you in the past. They can be alive or they can be friends or family members who are deceased. They can include parents, children, grandparents, aunts, uncles, brothers, sisters, friends, teachers, caretakers, counselors, and others. You might bring up a memory of being with that person when he or she was expressing his

or her love for you. Or, imagine them expressing their love in some way, such as holding you or gazing at you with warm, tender eyes.

"As you imagine your loving resource person, increase the memory by activating the sense. What are you seeing, smelling, hearing, or feeling? Take in their loving presence. Feel it in your body. Remember what it feels like to be loved, to be seen. Focus only on positive imagery and feelings. Put aside any memories or feelings of disappointment or loss. "When you have a strong sense of your resource person's love for you, begin to tap on your knees or shoulders using the butterfly hug. Tap 6 to 12 times, right-left, right-left, strengthening the feeling of being loved. Really let yourself take in the feeling of being cared for. Let the feeling permeate your cells, bringing warmth and well-being to all of you. If the feeling keeps getting stronger, you can tap longer.

"If anything negative should come up while you tap, stop tapping and return again to the positive image. Try to stay with only positive feelings. If you cannot do this, bring up another memory of being loved by the same resource person, or think of another person and tap to strengthen that one.

"After tapping in the first image, bring another loving resource image to mind—a friend, child, partner, or other person or animal. When you have a strong image of being loved by that person or pet, tap that one in to strengthen it." Have the client continue bringing up images of loving resources and tap as long as they like.

CIRCLE OF LOVE

The Circle of Love uses loving resources that have been tapped in to give your client even more comfort and support. The client imagines resources surrounding them in a circle, then imagines each one sending them love that has a color and a warm feeling. Each of the figures surrounding them sends love light from their heart into the heart of the client. When the client can feel this, BLS is added.

After imagining receiving love, clients imagine sending this love light back to their loved ones. They might imagine a circuit of love light emanating from their loved ones, into them, and then back again. When they can imagine and feel this, they add BLS. Clients can imagine themselves surrounded by this love light, at the center of it, in order to feel loved and cared for. This can be deeply resourcing for the client, creating a feeling of connection that they have been missing—a sense of being part of a greater whole of love and support. They can use this resource when they feel low or alone and need support, before going to sleep at night, or if they are feeling the urge for their addictive substance.

As with any of these exercises, the Circle of Love can bring up strong emotions. If this happens, stop BLS and check in with your client. It may be time to refocus just on positive feelings or to stop BLS.

Clients can call up their Circle of Love to combat feelings of shame and worthlessness and to defuse addictive urges and triggers. If we can bolster the client's feelings of being loved and supported by tapping into this resource, they will have a tool for managing their lives without addictions. The activation of love also reduces the experience of pain and increases self-worth. For clients whose addictions serve as a way to manage pain, love resources may be the nonpharmaceutical means to the same end.

TAPPING IN THE CIRCLE OF LOVE

Once the client is centered and focused on their breath, have them imagine themselves surrounded by the loving resource people they have tapped in. *"Look around at these people who love you. Feel the sense of support that comes with being encircled by their love.*

"Now focus on each loving person, one at a time, and imagine a ray of warm light coming directly from each person and entering your heart center. Imagine these rays in the color you associate with love. Focus on one person at a time, seeing and feeling their love light radiating into your heart center. Open to each one until you are receiving love light emanating from each person in the circle surrounding you, radiating from each of them into your heart center.

"When you can feel their love, begin to tap, right-left, right-left. Continue tapping as long as the feelings are positive. Feel yourself at the center of a wheel of love, with your resource people and their love light as spokes. Take in this love light. Let it enter your heart and then permeate and radiate throughout your body, until you are filled with it." Have the client look at each resource and feel their love for them, one at a time. Have them see and feel their heart radiating love light back to each of them. *"The love light goes from them to you, and you to them, as a continuous circuit of blissful energy. Stay with this*

image and the feelings associated with it as long as you can. Bathe in it. Soak it in. Let it support and nurture you. Continue to tap as long as it feels positive.

"Realize that this love is in you, always available. Feel the connection to those you love and who love you, also. Let this connection support you and bring you comfort when you need it. Remember, it is always there. If you would like, you can imagine taking the love and support with you into a future situation. Tap as you imagine it."

Grief is a common experience when doing this exercise: grief related to loss of loved ones or to regret for closing one's heart. I have found that people often close their hearts to love as a defense against grief.

The use of BLS can help clients process through grief more quickly and come to a heart that is open and feels cleansed. Sometimes, after exploring the sadness, you can ask your clients to imagine being held by their other loving resource figures; then add BLS. This can help them process through these feelings quickly and in a way that feels supportive.

THE HEART AS A PLACE OF REFUGE

Your clients can use their heart center as a place of refuge—a kind of safe space that can serve as a gathering place for their loving resources. They can create this by focusing on their heart center and then evoking and tapping in each resource, one at a time. Suggest that they imagine their resources, or just the feeling of them, in their physical heart space. By focusing on their heart center and tapping in loving resources, they are creating a resource that they can return to during times of difficulty.

TAPPING IN THE HEART REFUGE

Direct your client to bring attention to their heart center. *"Let your heart become soft and warm. Breathe easily, in and out of this center, and let yourself become very relaxed. Imagine your heart as a place of refuge, a sanctuary, a place of safety and repose.*

"Now bring to mind someone you love. As you think of that person, feel the love in your heart. If it feels right to you, you might even imagine

holding the person in your heart center, or you might experience in your heart the feeling of love that person evokes for you.

"When you have the image and feeling, begin to tap. Tap right-left, right-left, 6 to 12 times. Tap longer only if it strengthens or remains positive.

"Now think of someone else you love. As you think of that person, tap. Feel your heart center radiating love and warmth. You might experience a string of positive memories or associations. That is fine. Tap to strengthen the positive feelings."

LOVING-KINDNESS MEDITATION

Martin grew up in a home where he was neglected and unloved by a harsh mother who had been neglected herself. This deprivation of affection in his childhood created feelings of low self-worth and of shame, which in part fueled his addictions. Along with Attachment-Focused EMDR on his early traumas and the tapping in of attachment-repair resources, we used this loving-kindness meditation with the butterfly hug to close our sessions. He found that the loving-kindness meditation was such a powerful healing tool for countering his negative self-talk and shame that he began to use it at home on a regular basis. Over time, he found that doing this meditation with the butterfly hug helped to soothe him, increase his self-worth, and support him in his recovery.

Loving-kindness meditation is a method for developing compassion. Though its origins derive from the Buddhist tradition, it can be practiced and adapted by anyone, regardless of religious or spiritual orientation. The practice is very simply about cultivating and developing love. In this meditation, the meditator generates thoughts and feelings of tenderness, love, care, peace, kindness, and wishes for well-being toward self and others. The practice begins with softening the heart; then, thoughts and feelings of loving-kindness are directed toward the self or others, slowly expanding farther and farther to include others as the person is capable. This practice helps develop self-acceptance and acceptance toward others.

I originally learned a version of this from Sharon Salzberg at a Vipassana meditation retreat she co-taught with Joseph Goldstein in 1976. I also learned meditations from the Tibetan Buddhist teacher Lama Thubten Yeshe that served to develop love toward self and others. I have combined elements from these meditations and have adapted them according to the needs of different practitioners, and I have been teaching therapists in my EMDR trainings to use loving-kindness meditations as I have in my clinical practice for over 30 years. I've written about them in several of my other books.[41] Adding BLS to these meditations further strengthens and integrates the feelings they generate.

Have the client begin their meditation by sitting quietly and bringing awareness to the sensation of sitting: the contact with the seat, their feet on the floor. It can help to direct them to take full, deep breaths and then to exhale slowly, relaxing and letting go with the exhalation. Filling the belly, chest, and throat with long, slow inhalations and exhalations serves to calm the mind and body before beginning the meditation. If it is helpful for the client, the breathing may be followed by guided imagery taking them to their Peaceful Place.

Some clients with trauma, especially severe childhood trauma, may feel *unsafe* relaxing. Letting go triggers feelings of anxiety as their guard is dropped, making them vulnerable to potential attack. These clients can imagine erecting a protective boundary around themselves and bringing in resource figures to protect them while they relax. If they choose, they can imagine doing the loving-kindness meditation in their Peaceful Place, protected by their barrier and supported by their resources.

What follows are several variations on this meditation. You can use BLS continuously throughout the meditation, beginning as soon as the client experiences positive feelings; or use BLS intermittently, using short sets. Clients can tap on their own knees or cross their arms across their chest and tap on either shoulder in the butterfly hug. You can read this script into a tape recorder for your client to listen to later. This meditation can also be done in groups, and you can close meetings or therapy sessions with it. It is most important that you discover what works best for your clients and adapt it according to their needs.

LOVING-KINDNESS MEDITATION BEGINNING WITH ONE'S SELF

Have the client close their eyes and ground into their seat. *"Be aware of the places of contact, your bottom on the cushion or chair and your feet on the floor. Be aware of your breathing, in and out. Feel the breath in your body. Let yourself relax into the present moment.*

"Now bring your attention to the area of your heart. Breathe in and out from your heart. Let the breath be gentle and natural. In and out . . . in and out. Feel your heart becoming soft and warm. Mindfully observe your breath until you are calm and your awareness is focused on the here and now.

"Begin to send loving-kindness to yourself, repeating phrases such as 'May I be peaceful . . . May I be happy . . . May I be free from suffering . . . May I be filled with loving-kindness.' Find the words that work best for you. Let the sound of your voice be gentle, with a rhythmic cadence. Think of a parent gently rocking and soothing a child. The idea is to generate a feeling of warmth and tenderness toward yourself.

"As you send loving-kindness toward yourself, feel your heart becoming soft, warm, and receptive. When you can feel some warmth in your heart, begin to tap. Tap right-left, right-left. Continue tapping through the meditation as long as the feelings remain positive. If for any reason negative thoughts or feelings should arise, stop tapping and return to generating loving-kindness toward yourself. Begin to tap again when positive feelings return.

"Now think of someone you love. As you think of this person, allow your natural good feelings for this person to arise. You might imagine your love as a warm, bright light glowing in your heart. Begin to extend loving-kindness to this person. Continue to repeat the phrases you chose earlier, now directed at them: 'May you be peaceful . . . May you be happy . . . May you be free from suffering . . . May you be liberated.' Use the words that work best for you to send loving thoughts to this person. As you do so, you might imagine light radiating from your heart to your loved one. Imagine this warm, luminous energy filling your loved one's heart with a feeling of well-being and loving-kindness. When you clearly feel the positive feelings, tap right-left, right-left. Continue tapping for as long as it feels positive.

"Now let your love flow out to others you care about. Let it extend to your family and close friends. You might even imagine them sitting near you. 'May you be peaceful . . . May you be happy . . . May you have ease of being. . . . ' Imagine warm, luminous energy radiating from your heart, touching them and filling their hearts. Tap as you feel and see love energy going out to others."

Have the client continue to send loving thoughts and energy out to all the other people around them. This feeling can be expanded to include their community, their town, their state, country, continent, the world, and infinity. As they send it out to others, they are continually replenished.

At the end of the meditation, have the client imagine sending loving-kindness to all sentient beings in the universe: "May all beings every-

where be happy, peaceful, and free from suffering." When the meditation is over, have the client sit for a few minutes longer and take in the feeling of love and expansion in their heart center. Have them continue to tap as this feeling expands. When the meditation is complete, remind the client they can always contact this feeling; it is their true nature—their warm, loving heart.

Many people in recovery from addictions have so much shame and self-loathing that it is difficult for them to send loving-kindness toward themselves. They don't believe they deserve love. In these cases, I've found it is best to begin the meditation by generating loving-kindness toward someone they love or care about first—even if it's a pet. Begin there; then, if they can, have them expand the feeling out to include others. If they are able to do that, see if they can begin to include themselves as one of the "beings" they send loving thoughts toward. You may need to build slowly here, with the focus of the meditation on kindness toward others. Over time, see if they can include themselves in this feeling.

LOVING-KINDNESS MEDITATION WITH TAPPING: BEGINNING WITH SOMEONE YOU LOVE

Once the client has relaxed and is breathing through their heart center, have them imagine someone about whom they care and for whom they have affection. *"Imagine them in front of you. As you imagine this person, begin to send him or her loving-kindness. You can say, inside your mind or out loud, 'May you be peaceful. May you be filled with loving-kindness.'*

"Imagine that warm light radiates from your heart center into the heart of your loved one. When you feel your heart expanding, begin to tap. Tap as long as it continues to be positive. You might tap a little and then stop, check in with how you are feeling, and then begin again, if it feels good. When you feel your heart expanding, begin to tap. Tap as long as it feels good.

"Now bring up another person toward whom you have loving feelings. As you imagine this person in front of you, begin to send him or her loving-kindness. Tenderly send your loved one loving wishes. When you feel the good feelings, begin to tap. Continue in this way, generating lov-

ing thoughts and feelings toward those you love and tapping when you fully feel those loving feelings.

"After you feel your kind heart expanding, begin to include yourself in your generation of loving-kindness. 'May I be peaceful . . . May I be happy . . . May I be free from suffering . . . May I be filled with loving-kindness . . . May I have ease of being . . . May I love and receive love . . . May I be free from fear.' When you feel loving-kindness toward yourself, begin to tap. Continue tapping as long as it feels good, the warmth emanating from your heart."

If your client responds well to this, and the feelings are increasing in a positive way, you can continue the meditation by inviting them to expand the feeling of loving-kindness further, as described above. You can ask to them to extend warm feelings to their community, state, country, world, universe—to all beings everywhere, in all directions.

This meditation can create a powerful feeling of openness, as if the heart expands beyond its human boundaries, filling the universe with love. It helps to cultivate compassion, self-love, and—in some cases—forgiveness. It can create a feeling of connection with all of creation, helping to alleviate the feelings of separation and isolation that so many of our clients feel.

The loving-kindness meditation can be adapted to send loving-kindness toward the child self. This can be especially helpful for clients who were abused or neglected as children and are frequently frightened, lonely, distressed, or triggered. If you and your client have done inner child work or are familiar with their child parts—those aspects that hold memories from a child's point of view—the loving-kindness meditation can be adapted to help bring comfort to those parts.

INNER CHILD LOVING-KINDNESS MEDITATION

Once the client is relaxing comfortably, with closed eyes, support them in going inside. *"Feel yourself sitting with your bottom on the seat, your feet on the floor. Take some deep, relaxing breaths. As you exhale, let go and relax; let go into the earth. Ease into the present moment.*

"Now bring your attention to your heart center. Let your breath be soft and relaxed. Begin to breathe in and out of your loving heart. Imagine your heart as a safe place—a sanctuary, a welcoming place of ease

and repose. Now imagine your inner child in your heart. Your loving heart is a safe place for your tender child. Begin to send loving-kindness to this child self.

Tell the client, *"Imagine sending these words to your child like a gentle caress,"* and then, in a soft, gentle voice, repeat with pauses between phrases: *"May you be peaceful . . . May you be happy . . . May you be filled with loving-kindness . . . May you be free from fear . . . May you be free from suffering . . . May you be joyful . . . May you feel free . . . May you love and be loved."* Tell the client to use the words that work for them and to repeat them silently while sending loving-kindness to their child self.

"When you can feel warm, tender feelings, begin to tap. If it feels right, do the butterfly hug. Tap right-left, right-left, and continue as long as it feels good. Stop tapping if it does not feel good, and return to thinking loving thoughts without tapping. "May you be peaceful . . . May you be happy . . . May you be free from suffering . . . May you be free from fear . . . May you be safe."

Continue this meditation for as long as it feels good and elicits positive feelings. It can be helpful to imagine the adult self holding the inner child in their lap as they repeat these loving phrases.

Other nurturer resources may also be in the space sending them loving-kindness. If they have created an Ideal Mother or Father, they can imagine the words coming from them. The meditation can focus completely on the child self, or it can expand to include others. If they have child parts of different ages, include all of them if they wish. The different children may have different needs and wish to hear different messages. For example, an older child may need to hear, *"You are good, you are kind, you deserve love and safety."* Again, check with your clients and discover what works best for them. Create a meditation designed for their individual preferences and needs.

Kindness and Generosity

We thrive on kindness. When someone is kind to us, it makes us feel worthy and cared for, and it feels good when we are kind to someone else. The warmth and kindness we show our clients helps them on their healing journey. They need to feel accepted and understood. It is important for close friends and family members of addicts to use kindness and compassion in their approach, too, although this may be difficult because of the damage clients with addictions have caused to those relationships.

Helping others is an important part of many recovery programs. When we help another person, we extend beyond ourselves. We leave the smallness of our self-centeredness behind, connect in a meaningful way, and feel better about ourselves. Being kind and tapping in these experiences is another way to help restore connection to inner goodness.

With this in mind we can help our clients connect to their good hearts in several different ways. A few suggestions:

- Ask your client to recall a time when they helped someone. It can be as simple as helping a child with homework or listening to a friend. Have them tap in each of those times.

- Ask your client to recall happy memories of receiving help from someone. How did that feel? It might be a time from childhood when his grandfather showed him how to bait a fishing hook and cast a line. It could be a time when a neighbor helped her balance on a two-wheeler and ride successfully. It could even be a time more recently in recovery, when a support group gave him helpful advice. When they can remember and feel positive feelings about these experiences, add BLS. Begin with one memory and tap it in, and then proceed to tap in others if it is going well and feels positive and helpful.

- To help heal some of the harm they have done in the past, encourage them to find ways in their lives *now* that they can be helpful to someone. How might they extend themselves to give back to others? Is there a way they can volunteer their time, help someone in need, or give to someone who is in pain? After they have done this, and they report back to you about their experience, ask them to focus on how it feels to be helpful to someone. If it was a positive experience, and it felt good to them, ask them to recall it and their feelings, and add BLS.

- Ask your client to recall and tap in times when they were kind to someone—a time when they were generous or compassionate. How did it feel? Begin with one memory, tap it in, and then move on to another. Continue to bring up more memories of their kindness to others, and tap them in using BLS.

- Have the client tap in memories of receiving kindness. Can they think of a time when someone was kind to them? Can they recall a memory of someone acting in a caring way? These can include simple memories of someone offering their place in line, paying for a meal, or giving them a hug.

Here are a few additional ideas for bringing love, kindness, and light to the places where clients struggle.

Bringing Light to the Darkness

The idea with this exercise is to bring in resources associated with love and kindness that feel light and good in order to heal the places of darkness in clients who have addictions. I described a version of this Resource Tapping technique useful for healing physical injury in *Tapping In;* here, we are applying the same principles to healing psychic injury. This healing technique was derived in part from teachings of Jean Klein and the yoga of Kashmiri Shaivism.[42]

Begin by tapping in love and kindness resources so clients have a strong sense of love and light and of their hearts being warm and expanded. What color, texture, vibration, or temperature is associated with that? If it seems helpful, ask them if there is an image that represents this for them. They can even draw or paint this image. Do whatever is necessary to elicit a felt sense of love resources.

After love resources are securely established, ask the client to bring up memories of being lost in their addiction. Evoke the feeling state associated with that dark time. They might imagine a time in their lives when they were behaving in a way about which they feel bad. Ask them if there is an image that represents that time for them. Offer the option of creating a visual representation of this feeling state.

Next, ask the client to recall again the feeling state associated with the love resources and their own inner goodness. Help them evoke this state again as fully as possible. If they have drawn it, you might refer back to the drawing. Then, ask the client to close their eyes and imagine or feel their loving, healthy part moving into the unhealthy dark part. They might imagine the love light infusing the darkness with light, diminishing it. As they imagine this, add BLS.

After 6 to 12 cycles of BLS, check in with them. What do they notice? Be open to whatever image arises for them. They may begin with just a sliver of the love light moving into the dark part and beginning to dissolve it. If it is positive and they want to continue allowing the light to heal the dark, keep going with the imagery and BLS. Follow your client carefully and see what works for them.

Some people will be able to very quickly imagine the light overlapping the dark, while others will move through the process more slowly.

If darkness still remains, ask them to return to the love resources again to reconnect fully with the felt sense of their inner goodness. When they can feel that, add BLS. Then, return to the dark again, and ask them what they notice. If it is changing in a positive way, bring the light part over to the dark again. They can go back and forth between the light and the dark, imagining infusing the dark with the light again and again.

TAPPING IN THE LOVE-LIGHT RESOURCE

Have the client begin by connecting to their love resources: those they love, those who love them, or their Circle of Love. *"When you have a strong sense of them and the feeling of love and connection, tap 6 to 12 times. If the good feeling is getting stronger, and feels positive, you may tap longer if you wish.*

"Is there an image that comes to mind associated with this feeling? Is there a color, texture, vibration, or temperature associated with it? Where do you feel this in your body? Bring your awareness to this part of your body that feels healthy. When you have an image and the feeling associated with the love-light resource, add BLS.

"Now bring up memories of when you were lost in your addiction. Is there an image that represents that for you? Notice what it feels like. Is there a color, shape, or temperature associated with it? Where is it located in your body?"

Once that is established, have the client invite the sense of inner goodness, the healthy part, to transfer over to the unhealthy part of the body. Use cues to help them integrate image, sensation, and temperature. *"You can imagine the healthy, loving part transposing onto the unhealthy part, mixing with it, or suffusing it with light and vibrancy. You can use an image such as white light to represent the feeling of goodness and allow it to fill the unhealthy part. As you imagine this, tap 6 to 12 times, or as long as it continues to feel positive.*

"You can go back and forth between the sense of the good, loving, healthy part and the dark, unhealthy part, repeating the steps as long as you like."

Then, have the client imagine themselves healthy and whole in the future. Have them tap as they imagine this.

This exercise can also be done using drawings. Ask your client to draw the love-resource imagery first and then tap it in. Then, they can imagine the addiction imagery and visually represent that on the page. Once both images are drawn, ask them to imagine the healing love energy image infusing the dark part with the love-light energy, and add BLS. Next, ask them to draw their experience. What has come up for them?

If darkness remains, ask them to bring their awareness to the love-light picture and to reconnect with that resource and add BLS. Then, again, ask them to bring that feeling and any image they have that represents that to heal the dark part. When they begin that, add BLS. After 6 to 12 sets, check in and see how they are doing. They can keep drawing what comes up for them.

If they are stuck, ask them, *"What is blocking the light? What is blocking the healing?"* You might then ask them to visually represent the solution for the blockage. They may choose to add in a color or shape or even to bring in one of their resource figures.

Healing the Darkness with Resource Figures

Another way to work with dark feelings is to bring in resource figures for healing. As the client connects with the image they associate with their addiction, what resource figure associated with love, mercy, and forgiveness could offer healing? What resource comes to mind for them? They might imagine Jesus, Quan Yin, Buddha, the Goddess, an angel, or some other figure with whom they feel a connection and that represents this pure, loving energy. If they can imagine such a figure, ask them to evoke the imagery and the feeling the figure generates, and then the therapist can add BLS. If they can feel a connection to this imagery and feeling state in a positive way, ask them to imagine the figure bringing healing energy to the dark state. If they can imagine this, add BLS, and continue for as long as it feels positive.

For example, if the client has a connection with Jesus as a forgiving, loving figure, she can imagine Jesus emanating love and compassion, and add BLS. Then she can imagine Jesus bringing this love and compassion to the darkness that she feels inside. When she has a sense of that, add BLS. Continue with the BLS as long as it feels positive.

BRINGING HEALING LOVE
TO THE ADDICT EGO STATE

Some clients have a distinct *addict* ego state associated with their addiction. When this ego state is active, it is as if the good part of them has disappeared, and this part has taken over.[43] The addict doesn't care about anyone else but themselves. It is the part that is consumed with the addiction, and it may be aggressive, hurtful, reckless, and cruel. Family members wonder, "What happened to the person I love—the devoted father, mother, friend, son, or daughter?" It's as though they've been overtaken by Gollum, the snarling, greedy figure from *Lord of the Rings*.

Clients in recovery may feel ashamed of this part of themselves and want to disavow it. They may want to shut it away behind a closed door. But this ego state needs love, too. It needs mercy, forgiveness, and compassion to help it heal the shame and badness it feels.

The suggestions offered in the previous section around bringing up the dark, addicted feeling state can also be applied to this addict persona. To begin the healing process, have the client evoke the addict part of themselves. To help them locate this part, ask them to recall a time when they did something they regret while under the influence. Can they locate that part of themselves that is selfish, harmful, and out of control when they are in their addiction? Can they connect with that part of themselves? If they can, ask them to come up with an image that represents that part. They might visually represent it by drawing or painting it. Then, ask them to connect with their resource figures that represent love and kindness, or memories of love from their love resources. When they have a sense of the love resources, add BLS.

Next, ask the client to bring the imagery and feeling of the love resources to the addict part. They may even begin a conversation between the different parts. See if they can begin to bring love and compassion to this part of themselves. If they can, add BLS.

If the addict part resists the healing love, inquire as to what blocks it. There may be blocking beliefs such as "I don't deserve love," or "I don't want to lose this part." Stay open to their responses. Ask them what they need to accept the healing; see what they say. It may be something that can be created in their imagination, or perhaps there is something in their life that they need to do to repair or make amends. If they come up with a solution, suggest they imagine doing whatever that thing is, and the therapist adds BLS.

Another approach to working with this ego state is to connect with it and then ask it what it needs. When we compassionately begin a conversation with this part with an open mind, we can begin to discover what drives it, and we can then begin to address its needs in healthy ways.

For example, the therapist might have a client close his eyes and go inside and connect with the part of himself that wants to use meth, the part that holds on to using and that way of life. *"When you locate that part, ask it what it needs. What does it long for?"* The client might respond, "He wants to feel good about himself. He wants to feel focused and in control. He also doesn't want to feel bored. He fears the empty, sad feelings." Then, the therapist can ask the client if he can imagine a resource other than the addiction that can fill those needs.

He might bring in one of his resource figures or memories of when he was able to focus and accomplish things without the use of drugs. In order to fill the emptiness, he might want to use love resources, or his Nurturing or Spiritual Figures. He could also use other healing imagery.

The important thing here is to develop an open, compassionate conversation with the addict ego state and to work to address the needs that the addiction is filling. If what is discovered is early childhood trauma or loss, processing these issues with EMDR will be helpful when the client is ready to do that work.

CHAPTER 11

Resource Tapping to Enhance Motivation

Our greatest glory is not in never failing,
but in rising up every time we fail.
—RALPH WALDO EMERSON

O ne of the hallmarks of addiction is the day-to-day challenge of staying motivated to remain sober while also doing the arduous work of rebuilding one's
life. Many clients struggling with addictions feel helpless and hopeless about their
ability to build a healthier way of being. There is so much wreckage from the past.
They may have lost touch with their strengths and capacities. Resource Tapping
techniques can be used to enhance this all-important motivation to keep moving
forward in recovery. This motivation is vital for relapse prevention.

Letting go of an addiction represents the loss of a false friend and an unhealthy
way of life, but is still experienced as a loss. There may be sadness or grief, clinging
to past patterns, and urges to hold on to an unhealthy identity. Sobriety entails
development of a whole new sense of self, free from the old patterns. Powerful
motivation is required to succeed in this journey into a new life, a new way of
living, and a new self. Several Resource Tapping techniques can be used as tools
to enhance motivation—integrating a new way of feeling and living into clients'
nervous systems, inspiring hope, and keeping them focused on a healthy future.

In this chapter, I'll provide many tools to help boost clients' motivation to
stick with their recovery. We'll start with a basic step-by-step guide for motivation
enhancement and will then describe a set of supportive tools and ideas.

LINKING IN RESOURCES TO ACCOMPLISH GOALS

Sometimes clients can imagine goals they want to accomplish but can't find the wherewithal to accomplish them. It is as if the power they need is located outside themselves, and they can't access it. By imagining goals and then using bilateral stimulation (BLS) to link in what is needed to accomplish them, the force to move forward to actualization is found and can be utilized.

If you are trying to help your clients feel more motivated in recovery, you may begin by asking them to imagine themselves doing whatever they are attempting to accomplish. If, for example, their goal is to get through the weekend without drinking, ask them to imagine that. Next, ask them what qualities or resources they would most need to be successful in accomplishing this. Do they have any memories of having these qualities or resources? Do they know someone else who does?

After they have found a memory or representation of the needed resource, ask them to activate the resource as strongly as they can, with all of the sensory information that accompanies it, and then add BLS to strengthen it. Then, return to the imagined goal to see how the client feels about their ability to accomplish it. If it feels better, and they would like more resources, add more. When you feel your client has all the resources needed, ask them to imagine bringing these resources to the current situation.

For example, if they have tapped in memories of being sober over a weekend and having enjoyed themselves without alcohol, along with memories of being confident, guide them to apply those tapped in feelings to imagining spending the weekend without alcohol in the future. In this way, you link the stored information networks of being sober and feeling happy and confident with the imagined future situation.

STEP-BY-STEP GUIDE TO ENHANCING MOTIVATION FOR MOTIVATION FOR RECOVERY

Ask your clients to bring up an image of themselves doing whatever they wish to accomplish. For example, if a client wishes to stay sober over the weekend, he might envision himself enjoying time with his family without drinking.

Ask him, *"What resource or quality do you need in this situation?"*

Listen to what he says. He might say, "I need to remember how good it feels to connect with my kids. I need to remember why I want to keep sober."

Ask him to think of a time when he experienced the resource or quality he needs. *"Can you think of a time when you were sober and had a good time with your kids?"* If he can, ask him to bring up an image or memory that represents that experience. With the resource, memory, or experience in mind, ask him to activate his senses. *"When you think of the fun times you have had with your kids, what do you notice in your body? What are you feeling?"* When the client has a strong sense of the resource, add BLS, then stop and check in to see how he is feeling. If it continues to strengthen, tap some more.

If the client can't think of a time when he had the needed resource, have him think of someone else who has it. It can be someone he knows, or someone he has read or heard about; for example, actor Robert Downey, Jr. famously was severely drug addicted and finally was able to build a new, clean life. If the client chooses him as an inspiration, ask the client to imagine him in a way that represents the desired resource.

Ask your clients to elicit the image and feelings associated with the resource as strongly as they can. In our example, you would bring up an image of Robert Downey, Jr. in his acting roles and perhaps engaging with his children. When the client imagines Downey, ask the client to notice how he feels. Can he connect with the inspiration that this person demonstrates? When the resource has been activated, add BLS to link it in.

Ask the client to return to the imagined goal. Check in to see how he feels about it now. Has there been a change? Is there another resource that would help accomplish this goal? If there is, ask again for a memory, an experience, or even someone else who has the desired resource. Perhaps the client remembers other times when he was healthy, strong, and sober. He can bring these memories to mind and add BLS to link them in.

In this process, you may also ask the client whether he can conceive of any encouraging or coaching words or inspiring music that go with the positive image or memory. The theme song to *Rocky* is a classic example. If he comes up with anything here, add BLS to the memory or image with the words or music.

After tapping in each set of resources, return to the image of the goal with which the client began. He wants to spend the day with his children having fun and being sober; what comes up for him now? If the client feels better and more confident, add BLS to strengthen these feelings. Add more BLS as the client imagines actualizing their goals.

To finish the session, the client can imagine himself in the future with his resources inside himself. "Imagine enjoying time with your family in the future." Add BLS as he imagines this.

MORE TOOLS FOR STRENGTHENING MOTIVATION

Many other resources can be tapped in to enhance motivation for health and recovery:

- Inner Sponsor
- Sober, healthy self
- Role models
- Recovery support dream team
- Memories of being successful
- Strengthening successes
- Reasons for recovery
- Imagining your goals actualized

As you read through this section, consider which resources will best serve your clients' particular situation. For many people, a combination is most helpful. For example, to decrease anxiety, you might tap in the Peaceful Place first. Then you might boost self-esteem and self-confidence by tapping in an Inner Sponsor and a recovery support dream team, adding in memories of being successful. After that, you could ask your clients to imagine themselves living a healthy life free of addictions, and tap that in. To help maintain motivation, you can suggest that your clients imagine achieving their goals for recovery and that they tap in this positive visualization on a regular basis. They might imagine running a mental movie of a sober day, using BLS to tap in all they need in order to accomplish this successfully.

Inner Sponsor

The Inner Sponsor is a resource that can be imagined and tapped in to provide clients with support in recovery from addictions or problematic behaviors. The Inner Sponsor can be someone clients know personally, such as a 12-step sponsor, life coach, therapist, clergyperson, friend, or someone they have read or heard about who inspired them; or the client can use a part of themselves as the Inner Sponsor. This figure, like the Inner Wisdom Figure, can be accessed when clients need advice and support.

TAPPING IN THE INNER SPONSOR

Ask your client to close their eyes and go inside. *"Take some deep breaths and slowly let them out. Relax and let go with the exhalation. Spend all the time you need to quiet your mind.*

"When you feel yourself present, imagine your Peaceful Place. Imagine yourself in this special place where you feel relaxed and at ease. Take the time that you need to really feel the serenity and peace of this place. When you can feel it, begin to tap. Tap right-left, right-left, 6 to 12 times. If you want to tap longer to strengthen the feeling, you can do that.

"Now bring to mind someone real or imagined whose support and encouragement would be of value to you whenever you needed it in your recovery process. Accept whatever image comes up for you. It can be someone you know or someone from a movie or a book, or someone you have heard about elsewhere. This is your Inner Sponsor.

"When you have an image of your Inner Sponsor, notice how you feel in your body. If the feelings are positive, tap right-left, right-left, 6 to 12 times, to strengthen it. If you want, you can tap longer.

"Does your Inner Sponsor have a name? If you like, you can give it a name. Tap as you imagine this figure with its name and feel whatever feelings come up as you imagine it.

"Now imagine your Inner Sponsor giving you the advice and support you need at this time. You may hear words, get a feeling, see an image, or receive the information in some other way. Just notice what comes to you. When you receive the message or advice, begin to tap. Tap as long as it feels positive.

"Imagine taking the advice your sponsor has given you. What would your life look like? When you have a strong image or feeling of this future,

tap. Tap as you imagine taking your coach's or mentor's advice. Tap as long as it strengthens in a positive way and feels good.

"Remember that you can contact your Inner Sponsor whenever you need their advice or support. Just bring them to mind, say their name, and tap. In this way, your sponsor will always be available to you."

Sober Self, Healthy Self

The sober, healthy self is the aspect of the client that is healthy. This self holds memories of being in a healthy state. In order to help clients get in touch with the sober, healthy self, ask your client to explore:

Who is the sober you?

What does the sober you like? What does this part look like?

Can you recall times of being healthy? If necessary, go back into your childhood to find them.

Can you recall times when you felt good in your body? What are the qualities of your sober, healthy self?

The key to discovering and strengthening the sober, healthy self is looking for any times the client has felt clear, healthy, and sober. These times can be enhanced with the senses and tapped in. If they can recognize health and sobriety in someone else, this is still the healthy self, recognizing health. You can tap this in, too. Go slowly, using BLS to integrate memories or imagined qualities of the sober self. Can they recall times in their lives when they were free from their addiction? Times when they felt healthy and strong?

What we are doing here is reinforcing neural networks associated with health. If, when you tap in these memories, they get stronger and create more positive associations, keep the BLS going for a longer period. If the associations should go negative at all, stop and return to positive memories of health.

Once these memories have been tapped in, tell your client, *"This is your healthy self—the part of you that is free from the addiction."* Ask, *"Can you now contact that part of yourself?"* If they say, yes, add BLS. The more the client can contact the part of the self that remembers health, the better. This provides them with an alternative identity to the addict and helps their bodies remember what it feels like to be healthy.

For example, if your client remembers how much he loved to ride his bike on the mountain as a child, you could ask him to bring up this memory and identify the feelings he has in his body and then add BLS. Once he has tapped in this memory, you could check in to see how this felt. If he says it feels good, ask him for another memory of being healthy and sober from any time in his life. He might then recall a time when he went backpacking: his body was strong, the heavy pack felt light, and it felt good to be alive in the clean country air. Once this is well activated, add BLS.

After that round of tapping in, you check in again. He says that he is having more memories of that time of feeling healthy. You continue with BLS, telling him to let you know when it feels done or if it should go negative at all. As long as it feels productive, you can continue bringing up memories of his healthy, sober self. At some point, you can ask him to connect with this part of himself that is healthy and nonaddicted, and then add BLS. Add that he can contact this part of himself whenever he wants to.

Is there an image that goes with his sober, healthy self? If so, he can bring that to mind and add BLS. If this client has a photo of himself slim and strong at the top of the mountain peak with his backpack, for example, have him keep it someplace where he can look at it and be reminded of this part of himself.

The more we activate the body's memory of health, the more the body is going to desire this state. The body wants to feel healthy and strong; this is why memories of health are inherently motivating.

Role Models

You can ask clients to think of people who inspire them—role models for overcoming difficulties and for healthy living in general. Who in their recovery community has inspired them? Who has been able to overcome difficulties? Who sets an example to which they themselves can aspire? These role models can be tapped in.

Clients can bring up images from movies, books, or history, or they can think of people they know, including family members and sober community members. As they bring up images of these role models, support them in noticing associated feelings. Guide them in identifying qualities of these role models that they can draw on for their own inspiration; add BLS for further integration. Where there are positive associations, or even memories of themselves having some of the qualities they see in their role models, continue with BLS.

Recovery Support Dream Team

Who would the client choose to be part of a dream team of support for their recovery? They may want to include all of their Nurturing, Protector, and Wise Figures, along with others who are especially helpful to them in their recovery process. They can add on to this team any time they wish, as more figures arise in dreams and in waking time. Someone may be helpful to them during their group therapy, or they may recall someone from their past they would like to add to their team. When the client has a good sense of their team, add BLS.

Some will imagine their recovery support dream team in a circle surrounding them, while others may imagine them assembled behind them. Clients often experience a feeling of internalized support—something new to them. They feel held and supported in a way they hadn't experienced before. Discovering this internal support can feel inspiring and motivating.

After the dream team has been tapped in, it can be called upon during times of need. For example, if the client is feeling shaky in her abstinence, she can imagine and tap in her team for support. If she is feeling low and down, she might call on the team to provide kind words to lift her spirits. If a client is afraid of relapsing, she can call on this team for advice and support. She is not alone; she is connected. If a client has a good connection to her 12-step therapy group or other support, she can tap them in, too. While tapping, she might recall words of wisdom heard in a meeting.

TAPPING IN THE RECOVERY SUPPORT DREAM TEAM

Ask your client to bring to mind all of their resources: *"Bring in your Nurturing Figures, Protector Figures, Wise Figures, Inner Sponsor, and healthy, sober self. You can include others if you wish, to make your team even stronger. When you can feel the support you get from your team, begin to tap. Tap 6 to 12 times, then stop and check in to see how you are feeling. If the positive feeling for your resource team is getting stronger, you can tap longer.*

"Imagine yourself surrounded by your support team. You are in the center of a circle of support. Spend a moment and look at each one of your support people. Feel their support for you. Take it in; feel it as strongly as you can in your body. Tap as you look at and take in support from each one of your team members.

"Now feel the combined support from your entire team. When you can feel the sense of support strongly in your body, begin to tap. Tap as long as it feels positive.

"Imagine taking this feeling of support with you into your life. When you have an image, picture, or sense of doing this, tap to strengthen it." Remind the client that their support team is always there; all they have to do is think of them and tap.

Strengthening Successes

It is a well-established fact that praise is a better motivator than punishment. Still, far more time and energy are spent—both in therapy and in life—focusing on what clients have done wrong than on acknowledging and celebrating successes. Many people feel perpetually inadequate, stuck, and spinning in the negative circuitry of their minds.

One way to counteract this negativity and feeling of helpless inadequacy is by activating and tapping in experiences of success. In doing this, we help our clients strengthen and integrate those experiences. Whether tapping in successes large or small, we can help clients raise their self-esteem and bring a more balanced perspective to their lives.

Try working with both present-day successes and memories of success from the past:

• **Present-day successes:** It can be helpful to do a review of the week or the day and to tap in any successes you can identify. Did the client get through the day without using? Tap that in. Did he call his sponsor when he felt triggered and worried about relapse? Tap that in. Did she exercise and eat a healthy diet this week? BLS. If it helps, clients can practice a positive life review on a regular basis. At the end of the day, they can review what went well. Where were they successful? As they review these successes and can feel them in a positive way in their bodies, they can tap them in. If your clients have set goals for themselves, it is helpful to review what they accomplished and then tap to strengthen and integrate the information. In sessions, you can take time to support them in specifically recognizing and absorbing into their systems what they got done. Ask them to hold the positive image, body sensations, and emotions, along with any positive self-statements such as "I did it," and add BLS. In my therapy work, I have devoted entire sessions to tapping in successes so that clients could more fully take them in.

• **Memories of being successful:** People with addictions can find themselves crippled by their addictive behaviors. Their ability to follow through on simple life tasks may be impacted. Helping them to find the part of themselves that can follow through helps them to strengthen these memory networks. Doing so begins to create a foundation for more hope and capacity to actualize. You can strengthen self-confidence by asking clients to look for any times in their lives when they have been able to accomplish something they have set out to do.

Maybe it was showing up for work on time or completing a year of school. Even small successes can be located and tapped in to strengthen. The beliefs, "I'm a loser; I can't do anything," can be countered with memories or experiences of completing something they set out to do. This begins to create new pathways to possibility and changes self-limiting beliefs and behaviors. You can apply memories of being successful to present-day situations that are challenging for the client. For example, if the client is worried about meeting her friends at a restaurant and abstaining from alcohol, she could imagine a time in the past when she was able to do this. As she recalls this, ask her what she is seeing and feeling; make space for her to add any other sensory information that comes up to fully activate the memory. When she has a good sense of this experience, add BLS. She may then think of another time she was able to remain sober with friends. She can recall this and add BLS to strengthen it. She can then return to imagining seeing her friends for dinner. How does she feel?

TAPPING IN MEMORIES OF SUCCESS

Ask your client to close their eyes and go inside. *"Take some deep breaths and slowly let them out. Let yourself relax and let go with the exhalation. Spend the time you need to quiet your mind. Then, think of a time when you were able to accomplish something you set out to do. It can be a time recently or a time from the past.*

"When you bring up that experience, notice what you see. Look around you. What are you hearing? What are you feeling in your body? Notice what it feels like to follow through with something you have set out to do. Feel the feeling of satisfaction. Take that in if you can."

Once the client has a strong sense of the experience, have them tap, right-left, right-left, 6 to 12 times. If it is getting stronger, have them tap for longer, and have them continue to tap for as long as it feels completely positive. Once that cycle is complete, the client can bring up another time they were successful at something and tap it in also.

Guide the client to strengthen and integrate this experience: *"Now imagine yourself in the future being successful in something you wish to accomplish. Take the body-memory sense you have tapped into the future situation. When you can feel it strongly, tap it in."*

Reasons for Recovery

Often, therapists working with clients who are new in recovery find themselves trying to convince their clients why they should let go of the addiction. We find ourselves providing reasons that the client knows and agrees with, but can't take in. It is as if we are speaking to one part of them, and another part is not absorbing it.

One way to help with this might be to ask clients to make a list of all the reasons they have for wanting to free themselves from their addiction. Then, when they have their list made, ask them to close their eyes, go inside, and connect to the first reason on their list. When they have connected to it, you might ask them to imagine what it would be like to have accomplished it. For example, if it is to not live in fear of being arrested and put in jail, the client might imagine what that might be like and add BLS. After doing that, bring up another reason for wishing recovery; imagine it, embody it, and add BLS. In this way, you are helping your clients to *embody* and *own* their own reasons for recovery. It changes the mental ideal of recovery into an integrated and embodied knowing. Clients can even be instructed to keep this list nearby, refer to it, and tap in the items as a way of reminding themselves why they are on this new path.

Imagining Goals Actualized

Many athletes make use of the imagination to help them achieve peak performance in their sport. By visualizing themselves performing at their best and evoking the feeling in their bodies of "being in the zone," golfers, baseball players, tennis players, ice skaters, runners, and others can improve their performance. These same principles can be applied to managing addictions and problematic behaviors.

Focusing on actualizing their goals and imagining a positive, healthy, addiction-free future can help boost clients' motivation. Ask, *"What would your life look like if you attained your goal?"* As they use their imagination to fill out what this might look like and begin to embody it, add BLS. *"Imagine living a life free from addiction. What would that look like? What might that feel like? Imagine living a healthy life with healthy relationships. What kind of a life would you like to have?"*

If you have a client who is trying to abstain from drinking, for example, you might ask your client to imagine what her life would be like in the future if she could enjoy her children and feel healthy without alcohol. In what positive ways would her life change? When she can imagine it, add BLS to strengthen and integrate this future projection.

You can reinforce your clients' goals by asking them to regularly imagine them and tap them in. Some clients will really get into this with their imaginations; others will have more difficulty. Some will like long sets of BLS and others will like short sets with more check-ins. It is important to follow your clients' lead and learn what works best for them.

TAPPING IN ACTUALIZED GOALS

Ask your client to close their eyes and go inside. *"Take some deep breaths and slowly let them out. Relax with the exhalation. Feel yourself coming to the present moment. Take as much time as you need to quiet your mind.*

"Think of a goal you have in your life right now. If you didn't have the problems you have right now, how would you like to live your life? What would a life free from addictions look like? What would you like to be doing if you could do what you most want to do?

"Now imagine yourself accomplishing your goal. Fill in details with your imagination as much as you can. See and feel yourself doing it. When it feels strong and well activated, tap to strengthen the feeling. Continue to tap as long as it feels positive."

Then, ask the client what other goals they have. Encourage them to write down their goals and to go through them to tap in a positive future with each.

EXAMPLE OF TAPPING IN AN ACTUALIZED GOAL

Imagine a client who is a young man in his 30s who is a maintenance meth user. He is new in recovery and having difficulty motivating himself. He has been using drugs since his teens and living an outlaw lifestyle that he wants to shed, but with which he is also quite identified. In order to help motivate him and provide an alternate view of a life he could aspire to, the therapist asks him to imagine the life he would like to live if he were not using.

The therapist starts out by asking, *"If you could live the life you really want—a healthy life free from drugs, doing work that is fulfilling to you— what would that look like?"* The therapist and client then spend time brainstorming about what would feel good to him. Where would he like to live? What kind of work would he like to do? What kinds of relationships would he like to have? The client recalls how good he felt when he was sober and fit.

Once they have created some potential goals together, the therapist asks the client to close his eyes and go inside—into a dream state, a kind of reverie. The client is guided to imagine living the life he created, taking as much time as needed to enter into this fantasy. When he has a good sense of this goal, he signals the therapist, and the therapist begins BLS or the client does the butterfly tap or taps on the sides of his own legs. The therapist tells him to take as much time as he needs to really get into this. *If it should go negative at any time,* the therapist adds, *signal me, and then stop tapping.*

At the end of this exercise the client has a stronger felt sense and picture of where he wants his life to go. He may not yet know how he will get there, but he can now imagine the goal.

CHAPTER 12

Defusing and Deactivating Urges and Triggers

Something we were withholding made us weak / Until we found it was ourselves.
—ROBERT FROST

Many people struggling with addictions find their recovery hijacked by triggers that drive them right back into old patterns of addictive behavior. Despite their best intentions and motivation for keeping to their commitments, they relapse when triggered. It is as if a switch has been turned on, lighting up a circuit that runs its course independent from the circuits that would switch it off and light up healthy behavior patterns. Urges and triggers for addictions can include uncomfortable emotions, anxiety, a memory, or simply the time of day associated with use.

In my experience, the key to defusing and deactivating urges and triggers is to disrupt the neural circuitry that perpetuates them. When a person with an addiction is triggered by something such as an uncomfortable emotion and experiences an urge to use in response, a patterned circuit of neuronal firing is created. The more frequently this circuit is lit up, the more it is reinforced and strengthened.

The circuit might look like this:

- It's evening, time to have a drink.
- This time of day is associated with drinking. (This activates the craving for alcohol.)
- I feel the urge to drink.
- I have a drink, and another, and another.

Or like this:

- I feel anxious. I want to feel better.
- I know a stimulant will improve my mood. I find the drug. I feel better.

Another example:

- I felt disrespected at work today. I feel bad about myself.

This causes memory networks associated with childhood abuse to be activated, along with feelings of powerlessness and shame.

- I can't tolerate these feelings.
- I go on the internet and look at porn.
- The engagement in the porn addiction helps me feel a sense of control and power as addictions provide a temporary remedy for distressing feelings, they become habit. The behavior is repeated during times of stress.

Resource Tapping is useful for disrupting this cycle, and in this chapter, I'll review several strategies for defusing urges and triggers for addictive behaviors. In Chapter 13, I will present the Connecting the Consequences Protocol, which is also helpful for urges and triggers.

Urge: a strong desire or impulse
Trigger: an event or thing that causes something to happen

In addition to Resource Tapping techniques for handling urges and triggers, A. J. Popky has developed an EMDR-related protocol for this purpose called the DeTUR Protocol.[44] Robert Miller's Feeling State Addiction Protocol[45] may also be useful for EMDR-trained therapists.

USING A RESOURCING PROTOCOL FOR HANDLING URGES AND TRIGGERS

The key to this protocol is to have clients find a time when they experienced the urge to use; or, in the case of a trigger, to identify what was happening *right before* the urge arose, which is most likely the triggering thing linked to the addictive behavior. Help the client find a specific time they can identify, as this helps connect them more fully to the feeling state they were in before they engaged in the behavior.

Avoid going into the behavior itself. By that point, the client is probably in a dissociated state. Instead, explore: What was happening right before they felt the urge to use? What were the internal or external events or experiences? Help the client focus inside, paying special attention to what they are feeling in their body.

For example, if your client who self-harms has relapsed during the week, you could ask about what happened. What was going on that triggered the urge to cut herself?

"My boyfriend didn't call me when he said he would," she answers.

Once that trigger is identified, ask her to close her eyes, go inside, and find the moment right before she felt like cutting herself. What image goes with that?

"I am home alone after work, and I keep looking at my cell phone, and he isn't calling. When I call him, it goes right to voice mail."

You would then ask, *"As you imagine this, what are you feeling? What are you noticing in your body?"* See if she can focus internally and find words for her experience. Once the client has located a time when she was triggered or had the urge to engage in her addictive behavior, activate resources to link the feeling state that could provide the remedy for the intolerable feelings.

Instead of going directly into the experience, or using EMDR techniques like bridging or float-back to find an early memory to target with EMDR, we activate beneficial neural networks for the client to strategically link in through adding bilateral stimulation (BLS). If she is feeling unlovable, memories of being loved can be tapped in. If she is feeling lonely, memories of feeling connected to others can be tapped in. She may even link in the foundational resources that were tapped in earlier.

The key to this protocol is to light up an example of the trigger and connect resourcing networks that provide relief from intolerable emotional pain. You are helping clients activate and integrate healthy alternatives to their addictions. By activating the trigger and linking in healthy resources, you alter the trigger-addiction circuitry.

RESOURCING PROTOCOL FOR URGES AND TRIGGERS

First, help the client identify when they have felt the urge to engage in the addictive behavior. When do they feel the urge to drink, use drugs, overeat, or engage in other addictive or undesirable behaviors? Can they think of a time recently when they felt this? For some clients, there is a trigger for the urge; for others, it is a craving or urge that doesn't feel associated with any identifiable internal or external stimulus.

Direct your client to go inside and connect with either the trigger for the urge toward the addiction or the urge itself. For triggers, I want to find what is happening right before they feel the urge. What is the internal or external stimulus that triggers it? When they have located it, ask them, *"What is the most distressing part of that? What are you seeing? What are you feeling? What do you notice in your body?"*

Example:

THERAPIST: *Bring yourself to the moment before you took the drink the other day. What was going on?*

CLIENT: I had a fight with my wife. I hate it when she yells at me.

THERAPIST: *Can you find the moment when you felt that you had to have a drink?*

CLIENT: Yes.

THERAPIST: *What is most triggering to you about that moment?*

CLIENT: It's the fire coming out of her eyes and her yelling.

THERAPIST: *When you imagine that, what are you feeling?*

CLIENT: Scared. Mad.

THERAPIST: *What do you notice in your body?*

CLIENT: I feel empty here [he points to his heart] and shaky. My face is hot.

Next, ask the client what resources or qualities they would need to feel better:

THERAPIST: *As you feel those feelings, what quality or qualities, or resources would you need to do something different? What would help with these feelings?*

CLIENT: I would need self-worth. When she looks like that, I feel worthless.

Once you have this information, ask the client if they can think of a time when they experienced that quality or resource. If they can't think of one, ask them if they know someone else who has experienced it. It can be a character from a movie, book, television, or a historical figure. It could even be one of their resource figures.

THERAPIST: *Can you remember a time when you felt worthy, when you felt valued?*

CLIENT: Yes, when I was a child and I went fishing with my granddad. He took time with me, showing me how to bait the hook and cast the line. I felt that I mattered to him.

THERAPIST: *Great. Bring up that memory as much as you can, and feel the feelings of worthiness. Let me know when you have it.*

When the client signals that he has it, the therapist adds 6 to 12 rounds of BLS, then checks in.

THERAPIST: *How was that?*
CLIENT: That felt good.
THERAPIST: *Do you want to go longer with that memory?*
CLIENT: Yes, that felt great. Keep going.
THERAPIST: *Let me know when it feels like it is enough. If it should go negative at all, let me know.*

The therapist then resumes BLS.

After tapping in one memory or resource, return to the triggering incident. Has the feeling of it changed? See what the client reports. If the client reports change, ask what other resource might help.

THERAPIST: *Let's go back to the image we started with—the fight with your wife. What do you notice now?*
CLIENT: I feel better. Not so shaky. My heart feels fuller, but tender.
THERAPIST: *What are you feeling now? Do you still have a desire to drink?*
CLIENT: Not as much. It feels better, but I feel sad.

Repeat the step where you ask the client for a resource or memory that can help with this new feeling state that has come up:

THERAPIST: *What resource or quality would help you with the sadness?*
CLIENT: I need to feel loved and cared for.
THERAPIST: *Can you think of a time when you felt that, or can you imagine a resource that can provide you with that?*
CLIENT: When I think of my love for my son, I feel like I'm a caring person. That helps me, too.
THERAPIST: *Can you bring up an image or memory of loving your son?*
CLIENT: Yes. I remember when he was little and I comforted him when he was sad.
THERAPIST: *Okay. Bring that up and connect with those feelings of loving your son.*

> *If this should bring up any other memories that are at all painful, signal*
> *me, and we will stop and only focus on the positive feelings.*

At this point, use BLS as the client focuses on the positive memory and the feelings associated with it. Take care that the client doesn't associate to regret about past behaviors toward his son and only focuses on the resource he is trying to strengthen.

After tapping in that resource, return to the triggering incident and check in again. You can continue adding more resources to the feelings and filling in the needs according what works best for the client.

CASE EXAMPLE: OVEREATING

The client is a 37-year-old woman who wants to get control over her binge eating. When she is triggered, she dissociates and begins bingeing until she "comes to" and is filled with shame and self-loathing. She has been educated about healthy eating, but can't stop the pattern. It is imperative to find the moment before the behavior—to find the trigger—as the client may dissociate as soon as the behavior starts. In this case, the therapist uses the idea of a video to find the trigger.

The therapist begins by tapping in the foundational resources of Peaceful Place, Nurturing Figures, Protector Figures, and Wise Figures, as well as a dream team of support. They decide to focus on the trigger for a recent binge.

THERAPIST: *Can you bring up what happened the other day when you binged? Close*
your eyes and go inside. Bring yourself to the moment right before you
began to eat. You might play a video in your mind of what led up to the
moment when you began to eat. Can you find that moment right before
you felt the urge?

If the client has a hard time finding that moment, the therapist could have her find the moment in the mental video where she was engaging in the addiction, and then have her "rewind" to before the behavior began.

CLIENT: This is what typically happens when I binge. I came home from work tired and cranky. No one was there. I am living alone now, and it is hard for me.

THERAPIST: *What emotions are you feeling as you imagine this?*

CLIENT: Sad and lonely.

THERAPIST: *What are you feeling in your body?*

CLIENT: I have this empty feeling in my solar plexus. I start to feel dizzy and spaced out, panicky. I open the refrigerator and have a feeding frenzy.

THERAPIST: *As you imagine this, what quality or resource do you need? What would help you?*

CLIENT: I need to feel connected to someone or something. I feel like I'm floating in space all by myself.

THERAPIST: *Can you think of a time when you felt connected to someone or something? It can be sometime in the past, or more recently.*

CLIENT: Yes, I remember a teacher who was kind to me. She let me stay after school and work on art projects.

THERAPIST: *Bring up a memory of this experience with the teacher and the feelings of being connected. When you have a good sense of that, let me know.*

The client nods her head and the therapist begins BLS. After 12 right-left taps on the client's knees, the therapist stops and checks in with the client.

THERAPIST: *How was that for you?*

CLIENT: It felt good. I began to remember other people in my life who saw and connected to me. I have a good friend now who has been great.

THERAPIST: *Do you want to go some more with those memories?*

CLIENT: Yes.

They begin more BLS.

THERAPIST: *How was that?*

CLIENT: It felt good. I feel less alone now.

THERAPIST: *When you return to the memory of yesterday when you came home to the empty house, what do you notice now?*

CLIENT: I feel better. I don't feel so alone.

THERAPIST: *Is there another resource or quality that might help you?*

CLIENT: Yes, I need self-control.

THERAPIST: *Can you remember a time when you had self-control?*

CLIENT: Yes, there was a time when I had to walk every day and do exercises to prepare for a trip to Europe, and I wanted to be able to enjoy it. I knew that there would be a lot of walking involved. I stayed with the walking plan and exercises and had a good time.

THERAPIST: *Bring up the memory of using this self-control and following through on your exercise plan. Notice how it feels to have self-control and how your body feels. Let me know when you have a good sense of that and I will begin the BLS.*

BLS goes until the client nods her head, indicating she wants to stop.

THERAPIST: *How was that? What did you notice?*

CLIENT: That felt good. Again, I had other memories of following through with things and having self-control. I feel stronger.

At this point, the therapist wants to check the work and see what has happened with the trigger.

THERAPIST: *Can you now return to yesterday when you came home to the empty house? What do you notice now?*

CLIENT: I feel good. I feel strong. I no longer imagine eating so much. I make myself a healthy meal on my meal plan, and I call a friend to connect. There are things I can do, and I am not alone.

THERAPIST: *Would you now like to imagine coming home and calling a friend and eating in a healthy way?*

CLIENT: Yes.

The client then imagines a positive future with BLS.

CLIENT: Now I am not coming home to an empty house. I have imagined calling a friend and we are going out to eat together at a place I know that serves food that is good for me. I have choices. I have options, I don't have to do the same thing every day. I could even have a healthy meal prepared at home that I could eat and then go for a walk.

The therapist adds more BLS as the client imagines more positive future scenes.

A version of this protocol described in my book *Tapping In* has been used for performance enhancement as well as the treatment of problematic behaviors.

TAPPING IN STRATEGIES FOR HANDLING URGES AND TRIGGERS

Another resource-based technique that can be used for handling urges and triggers is to link in with BLS strategies clients know but have yet to apply in their lives when urges or triggers arise. Very often, clients with addictions know what they should do when they are triggered but don't use what they know. They have all the information they need, but when they are triggered, they are off and running with the addictive behavior before they can utilize the tools they have learned in treatment.

I believe this happens because the information that they need to use is stored in a part of the brain that is not connected with the part where the urge and trigger are located. When they are triggered, they can't access their tools. It is as if they are stored somewhere off-site. This is not necessarily a case of denial; it is not purposeful. Rather, the integration of needed information has not occurred. It is a form of dissociation. With this in mind, we want to find ways to link in the important strategies clients have learned to handle urges and triggers.

Start by making a list of all the things your clients can do if they feel the urge to use or are triggered. What has she learned in her therapy or recovery group? What techniques might he imagine using in a stressful situation? As they imagine using their tools, add BLS to link them in. They might imagine and tap in advice from their recovery support dream team, 12-step group, or other supports. As they imagine doing this, ask them to take in the *feeling* of support and help, then add BLS.

Some of these strategies might include:

- Call their sponsor or a friend
- Go for a walk
- Remember why they want to maintain their sobriety
- Read a book
- Watch a movie that distracts them
- Take a warm bath
- Go to the gym
- Or any other plan they can come up with that is healthy and helpful

After the list has been compiled, ask them to think of each strategy—you might even read the list back to them—and add BLS.

Then ask the client to imagine something that has triggered him or her recently, or at some time in the past. Have them bring it up as strongly as they can. Find the internal or external trigger for the desire for the addiction. What is the scene they are recalling? When they have activated the scene and the feelings associated with it, ask them to imagine using one of the strategies they tapped in with the triggering situation. As they imagine using the strategy, add BLS.

For example, if the trigger for the client was anticipating visiting her family—which brings up feelings of anxiety and the urge to drink—you can ask her which tools or strategies might help her cope with this. If she says, "I need support, so I think calling my sponsor could help me," you can suggest that she imagine the entire scenario from the triggering moment, feeling the anxiety and then that she imagine calling her sponsor. The therapist then adds BLS. After 6 to 12 rounds, check in and see how she feels. If it feels good, ask her if she wishes to continue the BLS, or if there are other things she might imagine doing. If she says "yes" to the latter, ask her to imagine doing those things; then add BLS. Then ask her to return again to the urge or trigger and check it. *What do you notice now?*

Keep going: What other tools or supports might help her in a situation like this? Tap them in once she has imagined them fully.

You can help defuse future triggers by asking her to imagine things that might trigger her in the future and to imagine employing the strategies she has identified and tapped in. As she imagines these future situations, add BLS.

Another technique you might employ for urges and triggers is to facilitate communication between the part of the client that knows what to do and the part that is caught in the addiction. You can do this by asking clients if they can imagine someone they know and care about experiencing cravings or triggers like the ones they themselves experience. What advice would they give this person? As they imagine giving this person advice, add BLS. In this way, you help clients connect the disparate parts of their circuitry, giving them better access to the wise, informed part of themselves.

TAPPING IN MEMORIES
OF HEALTH AND STRENGTH

Another Resource Tapping technique useful for urges and triggers is to link memories of health and strength with the urge or trigger. When your client recalls the urge or trigger, ask them to remember times when they were able to behave in a healthy way. For example, can they remember a time when they were able to resist an urge or trigger? If they can, ask them to bring up a memory of doing that, then tap it in to strengthen it. They can also bring up generic memories of wellness and strength—times when they were healthy or were able to overcome a difficulty. These memories may have nothing to do with addictions but may serve to reinforce memory networks that are associated with health and strength.

FOCUSING DIRECTLY ON THE URGE
OR TRIGGER WITH BLS

If there is no clear stimulus for the urge to arise, you can use BLS directly on the urge feeling itself. For example, you can ask your client to recall a time recently when she felt the urge to drink. She might reply, "When I drove past the liquor store. I used to always stop and pick up a bottle when I drove past that store." She has done this many times, and the stimulus response pattern is well established. We want to disrupt this pattern by adding BLS to it.

Direct her to close her eyes, go inside, and bring up that memory as strongly as she can, paying special attention to the feelings in her body and the urge or craving. You might even ask her to rate the urge on a scale from 0 to 10—where 0 is no urge or craving and 10 is the highest. Then, ask her to focus on the image and the feeling and add BLS. Often, when this is done, BLS begins to process out the feelings associated with the urge or trigger, unlinking them. Have the client tap 6 to 12 times, right-left, right-left. Then check in with them. Ask what the urge to use is now, from 0 to 10; see whether it has diminished. If it has, ask the client to bring up the triggering image again and add more BLS until it is at 0 or 1.

USING THE BRIDGING TECHNIQUE TO FIND EARLY ROOTS OF TRIGGERS

For therapists trained in EMDR, I recommend using the Bridging Technique to discover the links to the trigger and then to reprocess those links with EMDR. I developed the Bridging Technique from a hypnotherapeutic technique called *affect bridging*.[46] Over the years, I have been successful in deactivating triggers in many clients using this technique.

The idea with the Bridging Technique is to activate as many memory components as possible (pictures, emotions, body sensations, and immediate thoughts or beliefs); then trace the whole complex back in time to get an early scene that can be reprocessed.

Frequently, clients think that what has arisen in this process is *not* associated with the trigger, but I trust that the unconscious mind has its own logic. I nearly always explore the scene or image that has arisen with the client. Then, I use this image as the target image, *even if it seems irrational.* In my experience, in nearly every case, the image that arose was a significant target that led to important new insights and information. Bridging back and finding the roots of the problem and reprocessing them with EMDR can help change the behaviors, sometimes quite quickly. The trick here is to activate the memory network of the moment *before* they did the behavior. What was their internal state? What were their emotions, body sensations, and cognitions right before they acted? For example, loneliness might be a trigger for eating. Light this up; then trace it back. If the early contributors to the behavior can be targeted and reprocessed, the behaviors can shift. For more information on how to use the Bridging Technique, see *A Therapist's Guide to EMDR*.[47]

BRIDGING INSTRUCTIONS FOR TRIGGERS

Ask clients for an example of when they did the behavior. *"Can you give me an example of when you found yourself bingeing recently?"*

Ask clients to hone in on the scene, to bring themselves to the moment right before they began to do the problem behavior.

THERAPIST: *Can you bring yourself to the moment right before you opened the refrigerator? What picture do you see?*

CLIENT: I am walking in the door to the house and my family is upstairs playing a game. I'm all alone.

THERAPIST: *What emotions do you feel?*

CLIENT: Sad, lonely.

THERAPIST: *What do you notice in your body?*

CLIENT: Empty in my gut. My heart is heavy.

THERAPIST: *What are your immediate thoughts or beliefs?* (For bridging, this does not have to be a negative, self-referencing belief.)

CLIENT: No one cares about me.

Bridge back.

THERAPIST: *Trace it back in time; go back as far as you can without censoring it. Let whatever comes up, come up.*

Whatever image or scene that comes up for the client is your target for EMDR processing. For example, "I'm in my childhood home. My parents have gone out and I'm all by myself. I'm sad, alone, and scared."

Target and reprocess the scene to completion. Let's say that, at the end, the client has a subjective unit of distress scale (SUDS) number of zero and a positive cognition of "I matter." Return to the recent picture or situation and check for any changes: *"When you go back to that scene, what do you get now?"* If cleared and close to positive resolution, add BLS.

For example, the client might say, "It feels different. I am not alone. I am loved. My heart is full and so are my insides. I go upstairs and give my family hugs. I no longer feel compelled to go to the refrigerator."

Do a future pace.

THERAPIST: *Can you imagine coming home in the future? How does that feel?*

CLIENT: It feels okay. I can connect with my family instead of eating. I am loved.

THERAPIST: *Go with that.*

Add BLS.

In Chapter 15, you'll see many of the techniques from this book— including the Bridging Technique—utilized in a case study of a client with a serious drinking problem.

CHAPTER 13

The Connecting the Consequences Protocol

Remember that sometimes not getting what you want is a wonderful stroke of luck.

—DALAI LAMA

Why do people continue with their addiction or addictive behavior even when they know that it is harming them and those for whom they care? Why don't they apply what they know about themselves and their addictions to changing their behavior? These are questions that many of us working with addicted clients have asked ourselves. The answers eluded me for years, until a stroke of insight I experienced one day in a session with a client who was struggling with an addiction. It was from this insight that I developed the Connecting the Consequences Protocol for addictions.

I had been working for many years with a man who was rapidly developing a dangerous addiction to cocaine. Although he had used substances throughout his life, his use was mild and did not affect his social or occupational functioning. As a highly regarded professional athlete and coach, he was dedicated to his work and his own emotional and spiritual development. He was high-functioning in most areas of his life. Still, he suffered from bouts of low self-esteem linked to an impoverished childhood, maternal deprivation, and abandonment by his father.

We had worked on early traumas, including reparative work on early childhood neglect. He worked very well with his resources; I witnessed him developing love for himself and gratitude for his life. Yet, despite these gains and obvious healing, he was descending further and further into an addiction that could destroy his life. He knew this, too—and could not seem to stop.

One day, we talked about the sequence of events that linked to his use of cocaine: his urge to acquire the drug, the waiting until it was time to take it, staying up all night with the high, and the horrible aftereffects of fear, terror, shame, self-hate, and extreme physical depletion that lasted for days. I had the judgmental thought, *"How could you do this to yourself?"* followed immediately by a flipping of that thought into an open question or query: *"How* could *he do this to himself?"*

Here was a man with great self-knowledge and exquisite connection to his physical body who was hurting himself. How could he do this? My next thought was, *"Because it isn't connected!"* The urge, high, and consequences were not connected in his brain and body. This wasn't denial; it was actually a kind of dissociation. These different states were disconnected, existing in separate compartments.

My next thought was: if we could connect these pieces together—the urge, high, and consequences—then he would naturally lose his desire for the drug. In other words, if the high were connected to the consequences, his body would remember the bad experience and the bad experience would be linked to the substance.

I believe that we are wired for health and wholeness. We want to feel good, not bad. If we link the substance or behavior with the negative outcome, there is a natural letting-go of the substance or behavior. This is the premise for the use of Antabuse (disulfiram) in the treatment of alcoholism: after taking Antabuse, the patient will become violently ill if they drink alcohol. As no one wants to be violently ill, the result is avoidance of alcohol. Eventually, alcohol and sickness get linked together in the brain, creating a natural aversion to the substance.

Remember Hebb's Law: neurons that fire together, wire together. With addiction, an unpleasant emotional state or an urge for something leads the addict to use the substance or do the behavior, which temporarily makes the addict feel better. These things all get wired together in the neural circuitry. For some reason, the negative consequences of the addictive behaviors tend not to become linked into the loop of *feel urge, use, feel good/high/better.* Instead, the consequences are filed away somewhere else. They aren't linked in or associated with the substance or behavior that provided the high.

I don't believe this is purposeful. It is not *denial.* Rather, it is a kind of *dissociation*: the behavior and the consequences are not linked up. This is just how things get wired in the brain. What we have is circuitry that perpetuates itself because it isn't linking in the consequences. In AA, they say, *"Think through the drink."* Thinking through the drink simply may not work, because the addiction is not in the *thinking* part of the brain (frontal lobes). We can make better use of that idea if we can link in the consequences of use through bilateral stimulation (BLS).

It is my belief that BLS serves in part to integrate memory networks. It processes and integrates information. So, in the case of my client, the information that was not linking in was the consequences. He was fully *aware* of the consequences—he felt them and experienced great shame that he couldn't control his behavior—but the linkups I've described were not there. His drug use was a secret; if it came out, it could destroy his reputation and his career. I hypothesized to him and myself that if we could link up the consequences with the urge and the high, perhaps he would experience a shift in his desire to use. So, after my flash of insight, we gave it a try.

This is what we did: I asked him what his urge to use was in that moment on a scale from 0 (no urge) to 10 (the strongest). He said he was at an 8. Then, I asked him to play a mental movie of his recent cocaine use, beginning with the moment when he first started to want to score some, into the use, the high, and then into what came next: the consequences—including all the bad feelings and how his body felt.

"I want you to pay close attention to your body and your feelings through all of this," I told him. *"I want you to stay with this time only. If it should start to link to other memories, signal me, and we will go back to this time. You can play the movie in your mind silently or you can narrate your experience if you want. Whatever feels best for you. You can go for a while, stop, take a break, and report your experience. But we need to go all the way from beginning to end. It is important to ride the waves of feeling and not stop."*

I handed him the pulsers for the Tac/Audio Scan, which he placed under his legs. He closed his eyes and began the movie in his mind, with the BLS going continuously. For 10 to 15 minutes, he kept his eyes closed and processed like this. Then he opened his eyes to report his experience. He said that he felt it linking in and that he felt some relief. I asked him to run the movie another time from beginning to end with BLS and then tell me what he experienced. This took about 5 minutes, after which he reported a kind of consolidation. Then, I asked him to rate his urge to use cocaine on as scale of 0 to 10; and he said it had hit 0. He couldn't find it. When he thought of cocaine, he couldn't feel the urge. It seemed to have vanished.

As they say, the proof is in the pudding. He had to test the work—to see if the urge to use would come up again and if he would relapse. Here is the amazing thing: He never used cocaine again! It's now 10 years later; he never used cocaine again. Once the urge became linked to the consequences, his body naturally rejected the aversive experience.

This was done without any other treatment other than what we were doing in our sessions with EMDR. It seemed to be the missing piece.

Since this breakthrough session, I have worked with others using this protocol and taught it in my classes and consultation groups. Many other therapists have gotten remarkable results with this. There have been reported successes with addictions to cocaine, methamphetamine, alcohol, smoking, sex, bingeing and purging (bulimia), unhealthy relationships, and diabulimia. Some of these cases are presented in more detail in Part V of this book. I have added more elements to this protocol that can be used if desired, but the primary protocol is simply running the whole movie of use from beginning to end with BLS, paying attention to the body and linking in the consequences.

Some clients will need to repeat this sequence more than once; for others, it seems to work in one session. Therapists using this protocol also report that this technique works for the specific addiction or behavior and does not generalize to others. For example, a man abusing meth may stop using meth, but continue to abuse alcohol. The protocol would need to be used with his alcohol abuse, too. Some people also need to do the early childhood work, using EMDR on the traumas that drive the addictions.

THE CONNECTING THE CONSEQUENCES PROTOCOL (CCP)

This protocol involves the following steps:

1. Get the narrative of the addictive pattern, using a recent time: what led up to it, the urge, the use, the high, and the consequences.

2. Before beginning the process, ask the client their urge to use on a scale of 0 to 10.

3. Ask the client to play the movie in their mind from the beginning of the urge to use, the scoring of the substance, the use, the high, and the consequences, paying special attention to emotions and body sensations. Use continuous BLS throughout. Take breaks where needed, but then pick it back up and keep going to the end.

4. Check in with the client; hear what they say.

5. Run the movie another time, from beginning to end.

6. Ask for the urge to use, 0 to 10. If any urge remains, run the movie again.

ADDITIONAL STEPS THAT CAN BE ADDED TO THE CCP

1. *Install the negative consequences:* If you want to more intensely reinforce the negative consequences, ask the client to bring up the urge to use, then bring up the memory of the consequences, and add BLS. This more firmly links them together.

2. *Tap in a negative future:* Ask your client, *"Imagine what your life will be like if you keep doing what you are doing."* Then add BLS. This bypasses the frontal lobes and activates the part of the brain that imagines and can see and feel the consequences. They know this, but don't yet feel it. It can be very helpful to imagine stepping into this awful scenario. Like the scene from Charles Dickens' *A Christmas Carol* where the ghost from Christmas Future shows Scrooge what his future will look like if he keeps up his behavior, this part of the protocol can help shift behaviors without the lecture from the therapist. Again, clients know this in *part* of their brain, but not in another. We are helping to link them up.

3. *Tap in a positive future:* Ask your client, *"Imagine what your life will be like if you maintain your sobriety and healthy lifestyle."* Add BLS. Have them imagine and embody a healthy future as fully as possible. Open up the possibility of health and wholeness and have them try it on. In doing so, you are helping rewire the client—creating new, healthy neural networks.

CASE EXAMPLES: THE CONNECTING THE CONSEQUENCES PROTOCOL

Using the Connecting the Consequences Protocol in the Treatment of a Woman with Severe Alcohol Abuse Impacting Her Family

Mary McKenna, LMFT

Amy was 40 when she first saw therapist Mary McKenna—initially, to work through some marital issues with her husband. Cognitive behavioral therapy resolved the surface issues, but Amy's alcohol abuse remained a serious impediment to the future of the marriage. Because her alcohol abuse was found to be significant, Mary began to see her for individual sessions focusing on this problem.

Amy was raised in an intact family until her senior year of high school, when her parents divorced. Her mother was an alcoholic, which greatly affected Amy—she reported often being embarrassed in front of her friends by her mother's behavior. She began to drink heavily in high school, and by 18 years of age her drinking had become so problematic she was admitted to the Betty Ford Center for treatment. She remained sober for 7 years, until after the birth of her first son. Postpartum depression may have been a factor in her relapsing. "I never wanted to be like my mother!" she told the therapist. "I vowed I would never do that to my children."

When she began treatment this time, Amy was drinking almost daily. She drank wine at home while cooking dinner, which often led to her consuming an entire bottle in an evening. She had a group of women friends—she called them her "closest friends"—who went to restaurants and bars together, and all of them drank to excess. In spite of promises to herself to have only two drinks, she most often drank until she blacked out; her husband often retrieved her from local restaurants, or her friends would bring her home. She did not generally remember what happened after her third or fourth drink.

Amy had been married for 9 years and had three children, ages 3, 9, and 13 years. Her husband was a successful restaurant owner, and they entertained often. He was devoted to her, but he had made it clear that if she did not attain sobriety, he could not remain in the marriage. They agreed that should they ever separate and divorce, he would keep the children in the family home and she would move out.

Amy tried, unsuccessfully, to "white-knuckle it" by willing herself to not drink over the Christmas holidays. She resisted the therapist's referral to a local alcohol treatment program for assessment. On the other hand, she was quite motivated to get sober, save her marriage, and remain with her children. After receiving an explanation of the Connecting the Consequences Protocol, she was eager to give it a try. Here is the therapist's account of the 1.5-hour session:

In the beginning of the session, I reviewed the process with her and answered her questions. I introduced her to the Tac/Audio Scan pulsers and we set the speed and the intensity of the vibrations. After this, we tapped in her resources. Her Peaceful Place was her family home in a beautiful valley, in her bedroom looking out over a river. Her Nurturing Figure was her father, her Protector Figure was her husband, and she chose an Inner Wise Woman as her Wise Figure. We established signals for stopping and a metaphor for distancing herself from the process if she should need it.

I began by asking Amy to choose a specific example of her drinking to excess. She identified a specific episode of drinking with her friends, which had occurred several months prior, as a typical episode. The image that represented the consequences for her was her children questioning her the morning after a binge. She rated the level of disturbance at a 9 on a 0 to 10 scale. She said she felt "shame, anger at myself, guilt, and a sense of helplessness" and "constriction in my throat . . . my stomach is queasy." She called herself a "failure."

I asked her to run the movie of the entire sequence of events from what happened before to the consequences. Amy wanted me to keep the BLS going for the entire time.

CLIENT: I'm getting dressed, I don't have a drink at home, and I make the decision, "I'm not going to drink too much tonight." I arrive at the restaurant and greet my friends. Champagne is served. I'm taking awhile to loosen up; I finish my champagne. I have a glass of wine. "I'm not going to blow it." I eat and drink water.

I have a second glass of wine. I drink more water. I have a third glass of wine. I stop drinking water. The party continues. The group moves to a second restaurant in a cab.

I have more wine there. I am completely unconscious of what I am drinking at this point. I have no thoughts of my husband or kids. We move to a third restaurant, The Sardine Factory. I have more drinks. I am not remembering too much at this point.

It is very late. We go to a local bar, The Blue Fin. I know I am out of control. I black out. I get home (in a cab?). My husband carries me inside. I wake up in the guest room in the middle of the night. My head is pounding. I go into the master bedroom and crawl into bed. I wake up hours later with a terrible headache. My husband is staring at me.

I feel horrible.

The next morning, I wake up and ask, "What happened?" I cannot remember much of the night before. I am so embarrassed. I am thankful that the kids didn't see me last night, but later, Bobby, my three-year-old, says to me, "Mommy, I tried to wake you up and you didn't wake up!" I feel terrible. The next few days, I am beating myself up. I am worried, "What did I do while I was drinking?" I text my friends asking, "What happened?" I keep trying to piece it all together.

I realize the consequences of my drinking: I let my husband down. The kids talk about me to their dad. I know what it does to them. I realize the consequences on myself. I beat myself up for days and days. I am doing exactly what my mother did, when I was so embarrassed by her.

For days after that, I am overcompensating: cleaning house, driving the kids to practices and lessons, cooking, doing laundry. I am making it look as if I am back in control, that I am okay.

After she finished with this narrative, I wanted her to link the urge to drink with the consequences. I asked her to *"hold the urge to have a drink, anticipating the pleasure, and the consequences you just described,"* and then added BLS. When I asked her how disturbing this felt to her, she rated it a 6: "I see my children's faces." This was good, because I wanted her to feel this and to link it with the drinking.

Next, I wanted her to imagine a negative future—one that she would have if she continued with her drinking.

THERAPIST: *Can you imagine what your future will be like if you do not stop drinking?*

When she said she could, I restarted the BLS pulsers.

CLIENT: I am divorced. The children live with their father. I am not a part of their lives. I am very separate from them. It's like I am looking in on their life. My husband has a lot of hurt. The children are hurt and very, very sad. I do not have custody of my kids.

After this, I asked her if she would like to imagine a positive future.

THERAPIST: *Can you imagine what your future will be like if you do stop drinking?*

I then started the BLS as she narrated her imagined future.

CLIENT: It's not an issue at all (drinking). It's a wonderful picture: we are happy; there is more love between my husband and me; we are all together; I'm a model to my children. I am taking care of them.

When I asked her if there was any distress associated with the positive future, she rated it a 2. After inquiring what kept it from being a 0, she said, "I'd miss the taste." I decided to go ahead. I added BLS as she went with that, and she reported that the distress level went to 0. "It's just a taste. It's just a thought. It took the power away."

THERAPIST: *What do you believe about yourself?*

CLIENT: I am strong. I can do this; I've done it before. I have the capacity to be sober.

We then linked those positive statements with her imagery of a positive future and added BLS. We finished the session by recalling her resources and adding BLS to link them in, and then talked about what she had experienced in the session.

On follow-up sessions two and three weeks later, Amy reported a significant decline in her interest in drinking and even in her thinking about having a drink. She was incredulous that this could occur. At a Super Bowl party, she had only one drink, but had no desire to have more. One month following the original session of linking of the desire/pleasure/consequences, Amy reported that the impulse to drink was "up and down"—often, with no desire to drink whatsoever—and that she often felt "repulsed" by the thought of alcohol. Friends would pour her a glass of wine, and it would just sit there.

Amy told me, "I definitely feel different than I did before [the EMDR]. I am more in tune with my actions and my behavior and the amount that I drink." She reported that on a night her friends called her to go out to party with them, she went home after an hour. "I was able to stop easily after two drinks," she said. At a luncheon where champagne was served and everyone was drinking, she did not have any. She felt that the best part of this was that she "wasn't aware that I hadn't had anything to drink until I told my husband about the party later." And then, another day: "I went to a huge party at our restaurant for a close friend's 50th birthday. I was the first one to leave the party; I wanted to go home. That is the very first time that happened. I'm usually the last one to leave. I'm [now] very aware of the effects of my drinking. A couple of times, I had a few drinks, and it really hit me hard. The second glass of wine hits me very hard now."

I asked her, *"Have you had any time during the past month when you felt that you drank to excess?"*

She said, "No. No episodes of getting drunk." Then, "I'm very nervous about it. I want to keep working on it. I have a fear that it could change, and that I will go back to being the way I was before. I am struggling with this fear." Perhaps her fear of relapsing was not a bad thing; this realistic fear may help her maintain control of her drinking.

Amy was very motivated to quit drinking, as it was a grave threat to her otherwise very happy marriage and to her good life with her children. Her selection of an actual, recent episode of drinking was important to the success of this process. We both agreed that a composite picture or generalized story about her drinking would not have produced the same result.

Connecting the Consequences with an HIV Positive Methamphetamine Addict
Randall Faulkner, MSW, LCSW

Mike is a 35-year-old, gay, male, graphic designer who, at the time of this report, has been in treatment close to a year. He has been using meth for five or six years with increasing intensity in frequency, amount, and method of use, moving from smoking or snorting to using intravenously. Resourcing had been done earlier, and Mike was able to easily identify resources—although the Nurturing Figure was somewhat challenging. However, I noted the client not having an observable response to his resources: no affect, no somatic reaction. I had already noticed that client tends to keep things "on the surface" and generally only presents as pleased and pleasing.

Since early adolescence Mike has been confined to a wheelchair. He is the oldest of five children in a traditional Christian household. His father is very much a "man's man" who raised his sons to be hardworking men, placing emphasis on his sons marrying and having children. He also instilled in his children a strong work ethic, along with the belief that problems are worked through, not talked about. Mike is HIV positive and has had other health complications throughout his life. Some of these have necessitated an extended hospital stay, which he experienced as traumatic and triggering. Triggering in that the event in early adolescence that led him to be confined to a wheelchair required a lengthy hospital stay. This has been identified as a potential target. Mike works from home, so he spends most of his time alone—especially when he is working on a project. He will take on multiple projects at a time and overwork himself. Mike's appetite and sleep is typically poor, especially when working. This is true when Mike is using meth as well.

Mike's triggers for meth use include feeling sexual, lonely, or bored/having time on his hands. After completing a project, he will often use in order to celebrate. He is a binge user—going several weeks or even a few months between using meth and then using for one to a few days.

The particular session described here followed a binge. He used intravenously, which intensified this period of meth use, extending it over a four- to five-day period. Mike also became very paranoid, a state of mind he does not normally experience. He had missed his previous session due to using and was quite activated – visibly scared, anxious, paranoid – rushing the therapist into his office, his speech slurred. Mike asked that the therapist take Mike's cell phone and hide it somewhere outside the office, believing that someone could hear them through the phone.

He went on to describe having used and believing that someone he had chatted with online with was angry at him and was internet-stalking him. This individual, Mike believed, had contacted Mike's family and disclosed his HIV status and that he was a meth user. I assessed Mike's substance use, which led the client to report the recent meth use mentioned above, as well as having consumed a bottle of vodka early that morning in addition to Valium. During an evaluation for suicidal thoughts, the client admitted to a suicide attempt.

I walked the client to an emergency room, where he was admitted. Upon being released, he came back to see me. I realized at this point that Mike would benefit from a higher level of care; however, he was somewhat resistant to this. To aid helping Mike in more fully understanding the impact of his substance use and to assist in a referral to a higher level of care, The Connecting the Consequences Protocol was explained to Mike, and resources were tapped-in. This most recent meth use was used as a target, and Mike's desire to use meth was identified as an 8.

Mike was feeling lonely and bored. He had just completed a project and had time on his hands. Joe, a friend whom Mike uses with, called and Mike asked him to come over. This time, Joe suggested they use intravenously and, not wanting to displease Joe, Mike agreed. This led to an extended period of use across several days, which was unusual for Mike. After Joe left, Mike sought out more meth. At some point, paranoia set in, and Mike disconnected his computer and bought a prepaid phone, thinking this would be safer (again, as he was convinced people could hear him through his phone). However, he was afraid to make calls on this phone, so it was not used. Friends, family, and this therapist tried calling him on his phone, but he would not answer. Mike did not sleep or eat for four to five days. I assessed the negative consequences of this: feeling out of control, fear of people finding out, negative impact on work and relationships, negative impact on his physical and mental health, and loss of privacy.

BLS was started. The movie played out: what Mike's life will look like if he continues to use in this way, with increasing health problems noted as well as losing his job and his family learning of his HIV status and meth use. Here, Mike imagined he would eventually need to move in with his parents so they could take care of him. This was a sobering thought, as early messages of being self-sufficient were strong for him, especially directly following his accident. Perhaps most importantly, Mike did not want to be a burden on them—a fear he has had since being confined to a wheelchair.

An alternate movie of Mike's life without meth was then talked through and imagined with BLS. Mike imagined he would be healthier, in a happy relationship, and with an improved relationship with family and friends. He imagined having a "saner" work life and hoped he would be able to be more present in therapy so he could process the accident from early adolescence.

To end the session using his Peaceful Place, I asked him to call up this resource: his family's homestead, told in rich detail. As soon as BLS began, the client began to cry. I stopped the BLS and I asked what had come up. Mike said, "I don't deserve to be there [family homestead] anymore." As the session was at an end, I used a container where he put the distressing thoughts and feelings with the plan to revisit this next session. A new Peaceful Place was created and tapped in to end the session. Shortly after that, Mike then admitted himself into rehab in Minneapolis for over a month and made excellent progress. He connected differently with his meth use, its triggers, and its consequences. Mike also began to explore his relationship with his body, a focus he wants to continue in EMDR. As of this writing, he has not used for six months and continues to make positive changes in his life.

Note: In transcripts of sessions, the ">>>>>>" sign indicates a set of BLS. Unless otherwise indicated, assume that the client was directed by the therapist to focus on whatever material had just come up, and that at the end of BLS, the therapist asked the client a question like, "What came up for you?" or "What do you get now?" to elicit information about the client's experience during the set of BLS. Wherever a section includes scripted verbiage for therapists or counselors, that verbiage is italicized.

CHAPTER 14

Using Attachment-Focused EMDR, Resource Tapping Techniques, and the Connecting the Consequences Protocol to Work with a Young Man Struggling with Shame and Alcohol Addiction

Elena Felder, LMFT

However long the night, the dawn will break.
—AFRICAN PROVERB

My client, Miguel,* is a visual artist, a deeply creative man who responds strongly to music, art, and the beauty of the natural world. He is a gay man in his late twenties who grew up in a culturally conservative Catholic community. He found me through Gaylesta, a therapist association for sexual and gender diversity. In his initial phone conversation, Miguel reported that he was having a stressful time with "my work, my partner, my life, and my parents" and that his problems had been going on for a long time. He let me know he would be visiting his family overseas and then traveling for an extended period in a few months and was hoping to get some help before he left.

When I went to the waiting room to meet Miguel for the first time, he had headphones on and was nodding his head to the beat, his body moving with a nervous energy. I could smell alcohol, although the session was in the morning.

I was initially trained to send clients home with a safety plan should they show up for a session high or drunk. Through training in harm reduction and

---

* Miguel is a composite of several clients, with elements of their identity and history changed to protect their confidentiality.

clinical experience, I came to realize that sending someone home because they have been using drugs or drinking makes about as much sense as a medical doctor sending patients home because they have hives or are sneezing.

When I brought Miguel in, he appeared physically agitated, his body in motion almost constantly, tapping his feet, moving his hands. I initially wondered if he might be using a stimulant in addition to alcohol, but he was coherent and easily able to ground and calm down as the session progressed.

I asked about his reasons for coming to therapy. He talked about fighting in his relationship and a recent separation from his boyfriend and about struggling with depression, anxiety, and panic attacks. Like most of the clients I work with, he did not initially identify his substance use as an issue he wanted to work on. When I asked about his alcohol use, he said he had been so nervous about coming to see me that he had had a drink before coming to session. I let him know how glad I was that he felt comfortable enough to tell me this, and that we would work together to find other ways to manage his anxiety.

When I assessed his alcohol and drug use, he reported that he was drinking about half a bottle of whiskey a day, sometimes more. Alcohol use had played a big part in the fighting in his relationship and his drinking had escalated after the separation. I am aware that shame and self-protection frequently lead clients to underreport their drinking and drug use, but Miguel said in his sonorous voice, looking up to meet my eyes, *"If I'm going to get help, I have to tell you what's actually happening here."*

We talked about his goals around depression, anxiety, and self-esteem, and I also asked him if he had goals around his drinking. He said he wanted to be able to drink socially and not in response to feeling overwhelmed. I said *"Okay, we'll try for that and see how it's working."* Because Miguel was drinking large amounts daily and withdrawal from alcohol can be dangerous, I asked him to check with his doctor before changing his drinking habits and he agreed. I suggested that he could also check in with the doctor about other possible options for managing his overwhelm, but he reported that he had previously been on psychiatric medications and was not open to using them again.

When I first worked as a substance abuse counselor, I urged all my clients to work towards complete abstinence from drugs and alcohol. Typically, when someone is struggling with addictive behavior, they have an internal conflict: a part of them wanting to drink and use, and another part wanting to stop. When I imposed my own goals on a client, it was easy for this conflict end up being between me and the client. With Miguel, I wanted to create an alliance to explore his internal conflicts and his goals.

CLIENT HISTORY

Miguel reported that his parents hated each other but stayed married because in their community and religion, divorce did not feel like an option. He said his father was not an alcoholic but he would drink daily, frequently to the point of passing out, and that he could not keep a job. I asked gently why he did not consider his father alcoholic. Miguel looked confused, shrugged, and said he guessed he didn't know.

According to Miguel, his father never took him to school and never showed up at a sporting event or parent-teacher conference. He shared a memory of his mother grabbing him and his older brother and huddling with them in a locked bathroom while his father banged on the door. As he described the story, he began to get anxious. I let him know we would wait to work on specific memories, and that, for now I just wanted a general overview.

As a boy, Miguel excelled at art and sports and had a number of friends. As an adolescent, he realized that he was attracted to other boys and that his home and school were not safe environments in which to come out. This realization was confirmed when he came out to his mother and she told him not to tell his father or he would be disowned. He struggled with anxiety and depression, which deepened after a close friend committed suicide. It was during this period that he started drinking. His mother was concerned about him and sent him to a psychiatrist who put him on an antidepressant. He stopped taking the drug soon after, saying that it made him feel dead inside.

When Miguel graduated from high school, he moved away from his family to San Francisco in the hope of creating a new life and being able to live openly as a gay man. Shortly after moving he was gay-bashed, physically attacked by a group of men who called him derogatory names for gay men.

After the assault, Miguel's drinking escalated. He said the alcohol helped him feel more alive, less inhibited, and more comfortable connecting with men. He was charming and attractive, easily drawing people to himself. He had a series of brief relationships and often found himself connecting to men who had histories of trauma and used alcohol and drugs.

In his early twenties, Miguel began dating Carlo and they quickly moved in together. There was genuine love and connection in their relationship, but there were also intense conflicts that occasionally escalated to physical violence. When Miguel first came to see me, he and Carlo had agreed to a physical separation with phone contact while they both worked to stabilize emotionally. One of his goals in therapy was to find a way to have a healthier relationship.

CASE FORMULATION

Miguel had been an affectionate, artistic, athletic child, and was connected to his brother and the natural world. He was cared for by his mother, so he felt nurtured but not safe. His parents' marriage was characterized by loud and sometimes physical fighting. Because of their beliefs, they would not divorce, and his mother was limited in her ability to protect her children and herself from his father's anger. He watched his father managing his unhappiness by screaming at his mother, withdrawing from the family, and drinking until he passed out. Miguel felt rage at his father but was scared to express his own anger. The fights and his father's drinking were never acknowledged in the family. In response to the hostility, and uncertainty in his environment and his own unexpressed anger, he lived in an almost constant state of anxiety

The culture Miguel grew up in had been impacted by colonialism and occupation. One of the legacies of the colonization was a community that was strongly associated with the military and, in Miguel's words, *"toxic masculinity."* Miguel was explicitly told that being gay was sinful and wrong. He realized as a teenager that he was gay but recognized that he felt different from other boys at a much younger age. He also realized that the differences could put him at risk for loss of love and acceptance and even endanger his physical safety. He was socially adept and athletic and did not experience bullying from his peers, but he lived with the fear that if they or anyone else realized who he actually was, he would be rejected. The secrecy around the substance use, violence in his family, and his sexual identity exacerbated his sense of shame. The acceptance he did receive felt false because it was contingent on his hiding his authentic self.

Miguel's shame, anxiety, repressed anger, and grief around a friend who had killed himself all led to depression in his adolescence. He was sent to a therapist, but because he did not feel that it was safe to open up, the therapy was not particularly helpful. While he still found refuge in his art and his swimming, he also began drinking. With the alcohol, he felt less inhibited, more able to allow himself to feel and even act on his desires. In his words, he felt *"more alive."*

I could see from what he had told me that Miguel was courageous and resilient, and that he was suffering from both childhood and adult traumas that caused anxiety and panic attacks. He was also impacted by shame as a result of feeling different and unacceptable as a gay man. The pain of this shame felt unbearable, and he discovered from an early age that alcohol could help with feelings of shame and overwhelm—at least temporarily. As with many of the ways we develop to cope with pain, the solution became the problem. For Miguel, the alcohol that once helped to manage his pain led to destructive behaviors and relationship patterns that reinforced his belief that there was something fundamentally wrong with him.

As a handsome, socially-skilled, and talented young man, Miguel had no difficulty attracting men and enjoyed a period of dating and sexual exploration when he moved to San Francisco. However, he wanted the stability of a committed relationship. He brought to his relationship with Carlo all the longing he carried for love and acceptance from a man, all his fear around rejection and abandonment, the relationship template he had absorbed from his parents, and all the anger he spent his childhood swallowing. When either Carlo or Miguel felt criticized, the fighting between them would escalate. If one of them tried to take a step back, it would trigger fears of rejection in the other. The alcohol that helped manage the pain also loosened inhibitions, exacerbating the conflicts. After the fights, Miguel would feel angry at Carlo for lashing out, afraid of abandonment, and deeply ashamed of his own behavior. These feelings further reinforced his negative core beliefs that there was something fundamentally wrong with him and that he was not safe. As his depression and anxiety worsened and he continued to use alcohol—which is a depressant—to cope with the pain.

OVERVIEW OF THE CASE

Because Miguel was planning to leave to travel, our work together was focused and time-limited, lasting a total of three months and thirteen sessions. I wanted to work to help stabilize him, provide him tools and skills he could use to manage his anxiety, help him reduce his craving for alcohol, and relieve some of his trauma symptoms. I realized that because of the deeper underlying childhood traumas, shame, and history of alcohol abuse, our work would most likely be incomplete when he left.

The work with Miguel involved movement between tapping in resources to help him regulate his nervous system, the Connecting the Consequences™ protocol to strengthen and support him in recovery, and EMDR using the modified protocol* to work with trauma, at times using all of these things within a single session. Initially, we used only Resource Tapping in the sessions, which provided

---

* The modified EMDR protocol changes the order of the procedural steps and omits some of the elements, such as the positive cognition and the VOC so that clients can quickly activate the memory network and seamlessly enter into the processing while maintaining safety and the therapeutic relationship. See *A Therapist's Guide to EMDR* and *Attachment-Focused EMDR* for full explanations.

Miguel with immediate relief. He was also able to tap in his resources outside of the sessions, which increased his tolerance for strong emotions and anxiety.

For clients with addiction and/or complex trauma, the stabilization phase of therapy is an important part of the work, a part we revisit many times. In Miguel's case stabilization was particularly important because we only had three months before he left for an indefinite period of time. Unlike other clients with whom I have worked when there was no time limitation, I chose *not* to work on his early traumas—even though I believed they were linked to his present-day triggers and difficulty with emotional regulation. I was concerned that if we began to work on the earlier traumas, we would not have sufficient time to clear them adequately before he left, thus leaving him in a more activated state and at risk for uncontrolled drinking. Instead, we focused on present events in his life that triggered his drinking, using EMDR.

SESSIONS

Normally, in a first session, I begin to take a history; but because Miguel was clearly agitated and had been drinking, I did not want to open anything up that might increase his anxiety. Many years ago, I had a client who told me she used to go to therapy with cocaine in her back pocket so she could manage any feelings that came up afterwards. That experience taught me to stay aware of how clients manage intense emotions outside of sessions.

If possible, I wanted Miguel to leave the first session with some immediate relief. I also wanted him to feel seen and heard enough and to feel enough hope to want to come for a second session. We talked about harm reduction, mindfulness, and grounding for help with drinking and anxiety. I talked about creating and strengthening new neural networks, using the phrase "*neurons that fire together, wire together*," and also used the metaphor of creating deeper and deeper grooves in the sand when he practiced new coping skills. We talked about people in his life who were supportive of him and his love of art, music, and swimming. Then we started Resource Tapping.

After trying different forms of bilateral stimulation (BLS), Miguel chose the tactile pulsers from the Tac/Audio Scan. When I handed them to him and turned them on, his body went still for the first time. He told me later that the pulsers reminded him of a heartbeat. We added bilateral stimulation to three of the foundational resources: Peaceful Place, Nurturing Figure, and Protective Figure. I had him close his eyes and go inside and imagine a place that felt peaceful and calm, and then imagine what he saw, heard, felt on his skin, and smelled, and what it was like to be inside his body. He leaned back with his eyes closed, a smile on his face, and his body still. When I turned off the pulsers, he let me know he wanted them to stay on. When he was ready to emerge, he described a field of flowers in the spring, with a cool breeze and the warmth of the sun, the sound of songbirds, and the scent of grass and flowers and the woods beyond the field. His voice was deep and soothing and his description so vivid I felt my own body relax.

How clients respond to Resource Tapping is one of my best diagnostic tools. Many people struggling with substance use have great difficulty with self-soothing. The fact that Miguel's imagery was so vivid and he responded with such visible affect was a hopeful sign. He chose Nina, a childhood best friend, as his Nurturing Figure and easily took in her loving, accepting presence. Coming up with a Protective Figure was harder for him. I asked him if he had not felt protected in the past, and his eyes welled up. We talked about possible fictional figures, historical figures or animals, and I let him know he did not have to imagine the figure protecting him. Eventually, he came up with an older man in a flannel shirt.

I talked to Miguel about practicing the resourcing outside of the session, both on a regular basis and when he noticed he was feeling anxious or wanting to drink. I showed him how to provide his own BLS, using his hands to tap right-left, right-left on his knees, and the butterfly hug, where he crossed his arms and tapped his shoulders with the same alternating rhythm. Miguel chose to tap on his knees and even added toe tapping. I reminded him that practicing would strengthen his resources, again using the phrase "*neurons that fire together, wire together.*"

We had a few moments left, and he began fidgeting and bouncing his foot up and down as he prepared to leave. I decided to use a more active resource to help him channel his nervous energy. We talked about a few possibilities and added BLS as he remembered the feeling of his arms and legs moving through the water as he swam fast.

A few hours after our session, I got an enthusiastic email from Miguel reporting that he felt much lighter and sending me his own phrase to remind him to practice his resourcing: "*The deeper the groove, the more it moves.*"

The following week Miguel showed up to session smiling and appeared calmer. He reported he had tapped in his resources and had decreased his drinking. I then asked him to tell me about his childhood and growing up years so that I could understand him better. We also talked about how we would work together during the time that we had.

A week later, Miguel came in shaky and sweaty. The day before, he had had a severe reaction to a medication and took himself to the emergency room. He described being on a bed in the emergency room and having the doctor tell him that his liver might be damaged. He was sick and scared, and he thought that the medical staff were condemning him as an alcoholic. He was given Librium to help with an alcohol detox, but when he got home from the hospital he started sipping whiskey.

I could see that the experience at the hospital was clearly traumatic and I considered using EMDR to help reduce the effects of this trauma, but because of the immediate urgency around his drinking, we decided to use the Connecting the Consequences™ Protocol: running the story of what led up to the urge to drink, the urge itself, the drinking, and consequence of the drinking with BLS. I kept the pulsers on while he spoke and imagined and turned them off when I asked questions.

I started by working with Miguel to identify the experience and emotion that preceded his urge to drink. I asked him what was happening when he first became aware of the urge. He said he was in the car on the way home from the hospital, feeling anger at the hospital and the doctors and also anger at Carlo for not being there for him. I asked if there was anything that came before the anger. "*I was scared, very scared,*" he told me.

THERAPIST: *Start with the fear and tell me what happened next.* >>>>>>>>>>>

CLIENT: *My friend is taking me home. I'm in the car, playing the scenes from the hospital over and over and I'm so angry. And I'm angry at the doctors and I'm angry at Carlo. When I get home, I find a flask and take a few sips.*

THERAPIST: *What was happening right before you took the first sip?* >>>>>>>>>>>>

CLIENT: *I was so angry and agitated and I couldn't sleep.*

THERAPIST: *What did you feel after?* >>>>>>>>>>>

CLIENT: *Comforted.*

THERAPIST: *Then what?* >>>>>>>>>>>>

CLIENT: *Then I lay in bed feeling angry and alone. So, I drank some more and I started hating myself and thinking I deserved to be sick and alone.*

THERAPIST: *Then what?* >>>>>>>>>>>>

CLIENT: *I drank more and I guess I fell asleep.*

THERAPIST: *Then what?* >>>>>>>>>>>>

CLIENT: *I woke up foggy and groggy.*

THERAPIST: *Keep moving forward and include your feelings of self-hatred and then waking up foggy and groggy.* >>>>>>>>>>>>

I wanted to further reinforce the negative consequences by linking the urge to drink with the consequences.

THERAPIST: *Can you put that first urge to drink in one hand and those feelings of self-hatred and then waking up foggy and groggy in the other?* </DIA>

Miguel nodded.

THERAPIST: *Now, put them together and feel them linking up. I'm going to put the pulsers back on so you can feel the connection.* >>>>>>>>>>>>

CLIENT: *This* (Miguel indicated the hand holding the urge) *led to this* (shaking the hand holding the consequences).

Miguel could now imagine the urge and drinking not ending with the initial feelings of comfort, but was beginning to connect them instead to feelings of self-hatred and physical discomfort. After Miguel had connected the consequences, I wanted to use Resource Tapping to help reduce his urge to drink. He had learned to use alcohol as a resource to help him manage his overwhelm, his anger and his fear. Alcohol had become the way he comforted himself. For him to not drink, he needed other resources for comfort. I decided to return to the triggering moment and see what he *really* needed, instead of a drink.

THERAPIST: *Can you go back to the moment we started with when you were very scared?*

CLIENT: *Yes.*

THERAPIST: *What did you need?*

CLIENT: *I don't know.* </DIA>

I was not surprised Miguel didn't know. When we had first used resources, Miguel had a rich imagination and a strong affective response: but when he was remembering feeling afraid and craving alcohol, it was hard to imagine something else that could soothe him.

THERAPIST: *Do you think you needed comfort?*

CLIENT: *I guess.*

THERAPIST: *Could we bring in Nina* (his childhood friend and Nurturing Figure) *or the older man with the flannel shirt* (his protective figure)?

CLIENT: *I don't think so.*

I wondered if Miguel did not believe that comfort and protection from other people would be enough when he was so scared, or if he did not want to let others in when he felt so vulnerable. In the past, I'd had clients who were able to imagine a loving, strong or compassionate part of themselves as a resource, even when they were not able to imagine any other resources.

THERAPIST: *How about your future self—a wise and compassionate part of yourself coming from the future to help you now?*

Miguel smiled and nodded, indicating this was a resource that did fit his needs, and I turned the pulsers back on. At one point, I turned pulsers off to check in, but he waved his hand to show that he wanted to keep going. When he was finished with his internal processing, he opened his eyes and began to narrate.

CLIENT: *He came to the hospital to pick me up. He was me but older, more grounded. He said 'I know it's dark right now, but you are going to make it through this, you're going to be okay.' We sat together for the longest time and I could feel his understanding.*

At this point, as we were nearing the end of our session, I wanted to help Miguel imagine taking these newfound resources and capabilities and bringing them into his life outside of my office.

THERAPIST: *Can you imagine yourself in the week ahead?*</DIA>

Miguel closed his eyes and smiled and nodded. I then turned on the pulsers and kept them on until he opened his eyes and indicated with a nod of his head for me to stop.

CLIENT: *I imagined going to the pantry and taking out food, not whiskey. I imagined going to a bar and ordering a soda.*

THERAPIST: *That's fantastic. You know, though, stopping drinking is hard. I wonder what it would be like this week to not have whiskey in your pantry and not to go to a bar. Would that feel possible?*

He nodded. We talked about playing the tape all the way through while tapping himself, right-left right-left, when he had an urge to drink. We also talked about continuing to tap in resources for comfort.

Because of the immediate danger to his physical health, I talked with Miguel about inpatient or intensive outpatient treatment but he was not open to those options. He said he would consider support groups so I gave him referrals to AA, a harm reduction group, and Refuge Recovery, a recovery group connected with Buddhism. Then, I then asked him if he could imagine going to one of the groups. He nodded, closed his eyes and we turned on the pulsers. Again, he wanted the BLS on for quite some time. When he was ready, he opened his eyes and began talking.

> CLIENT: *I imagined going to the group, and I was so scared, but then I saw my future self. He was patting a chair next to him. I sat, and he stood up and started talking. He was talking about what alcohol used to mean to him, and how alive he felt now.*

Miguel was smiling and relaxed as he reported this.

> CLIENT: *I feel my feet on the ground for the first time in days.*

We strengthened that feeling with BLS and he went out into the world.

At his next session, Miguel shared that he was following up with his doctors about ongoing health concerns. He had gotten rid of the alcohol in his house and had been sober, except for one shot of whiskey. We talked about all he had been able to accomplish and added BLS to integrate his good feelings and reinforce his positive gains.

I then asked about his trigger for drinking that one shot. He reported he had a fight with Carlo. "After that, I just said 'fuck it, I'm going to get a drink' and then I did. Then I went out to the woods and tapped in my Peaceful Place."

"*That's great that you were able to go into the woods and tap in your peaceful place,*" told him. "*I wonder if you can imagine doing that before you drink next time?*" He nodded, then imagined doing that while I added BLS. I gave him a relapse prevention hotline number and asked if he had gone to a group. He shook his head. We looked through a list of meetings together and he picked a gay men's meeting at a time he could attend.

I could have gone through the Connecting the Consequences Protocol again but Miguel had very few resources outside of the sessions to help him with his recovery, so I decided to focus bringing in internal resources to help him connect with external resources.

THERAPIST: *Can you imagine walking into a group?*

He nodded.

THERAPIST: *Do you want to imagine your future self there?*

CLIENT: *This time I want to start creating my future self. I have butterflies in my stomach. I'll imagine the older guy in a flannel shirt. He's kind and welcoming. >>>>>>>>>>>>*

Miguel was engaged in the imaginative process and was giving himself what he needed. He was bringing in kindness and compassion for himself—a wonderful antidote to shame and self-hatred. This was a sign that he was beginning his own internal attachment repair.

CLIENT: *I'm talking to him about my problem with drinking, how it has been going on a long time, what happened in the ER and how I feel like I hit rock bottom. >>>>>>>>>>>>*

THERAPIST: (after a time) *What's happening now?*

CLIENT: *I feel a little bit released, but my heart is still scared, and it still feels painful.*

THERAPIST: *Just go with the feeling in your heart. I am right here with you. >>>>>>>>>>>>*

I wanted my support and the support of his resource figure to help him move through the feelings with the BLS.

THERAPIST: *What are you feeling?*

CLIENT: *Dizzy.*

THERAPIST: *Would you like to look at the man next to you?*

I wondered if he was feeling dizzy because he was overwhelmed or ungrounded and was hoping strengthening the connection to his resource figure could help ground him.

CLIENT: *I've been looking at him ... maybe if he held my hand.*

I felt myself smiling as he continued resourcing himself - repairing shame and unworthiness without prompts from me.

THERAPIST: *Maybe you've found a guide. >>>>>>>>>>>*

Miguel's eyes welled up.

THERAPIST: *It's okay if the tears come too . . . Just holding his hand.* >>>>>>>>>>>>
CLIENT: *Warm.*
THERAPIST: *Let yourself feel that warmth and connection.* >>>>>>>>>>>>
CLIENT: *He says I don't have to say anything ... I want to say something but I need to watch first.*

He looked upset.

CLIENT: *There's this guy talking. He just keeps talking and I'm annoyed by him. He just keeps talking. He is so annoying with his talking.*

I was not sure what was going on here. It seemed like there was something important about this figure. I didn't want to interpret in case I was wrong, so I asked a question.

THERAPIST: *I'm curious about this man who won't stop talking. Would you be willing to invite the man to talk to you?*
CLIENT: *Ugghh . . . now he looks like me.*

We all have different parts of us—different ego states. For the clients I've worked with who are struggling with addiction, there are often a strong shadow parts that hold anger, desire, vulnerability, or anything else that is not safe to integrate. Therapists and counselors can sometimes inadvertently reinforce these splits by counseling the clients to defeat the addict inside of them. Ultimately, these parts need to be invited out of the shadows and brought into the light and connected in. It is helpful to ask these parts questions, to get to know them, and attempt to meet their needs.

THERAPIST: *What does he need?*
CLIENT: *I don't want to be there for him.*
THERAPIST: *So ... who can be there for him?*
CLIENT: *The older man in the flannel shirt.* (Long pause.) *He's holding him and rubbing his back and he* (the wounded part) *is angry and crying and crying.*
THERAPIST: *Stay there as long as you want and then, when you are ready, open your eyes and come back to the room with me.* >>>>>>>>>>>>

After a while, Miguel opened his eyes.

THERAPIST: *What's there now?*

CLIENT: *I can just feel him there with me. I'm going to be okay.* >>>>>>>>>>>

We checked in. Miguel said he would go to a meeting, but I felt as if he was saying this for my benefit. We ended the session with Miguel imagining using BLS to tap in the older man in the flannel shirt when he needed him in the future.

Miguel came into the next session telling me he had been diagnosed with diabetes. He felt wounded that Carlo had not been emotionally available to him when he was diagnosed. He said he had had a drink but felt no current urge to drink. I thought about using the Connecting the Consequences™ Protocol or EMDR on the moment of diagnosis, reprocessing it as a trauma, but Miguel was most upset about Carlo. I was most concerned that the feelings of rejection were likely to trigger future drinking. That convinced me to use EMDR to process his feelings about the interaction with Carlo.

When I asked Miguel what moment felt the worst in his recent interaction with Carlo, he told me it was when he was telling him he was diagnosed with diabetes and he felt that Carlo was impatient to get off the phone. He felt anger, fear, and cold, tight all over his body. His negative belief about himself was *"I'm all alone."*

Miguel's processing was intense and rich with symbolic imagery. He processed well with some support from resources, arriving at a place of feeling warm, comfortable, and at ease with being in the present moment. Yet when I asked him how his body felt, he said there was sadness in his heart. *"I feel a loss,"* he shared.

I asked him if he could imagine having someone there with him while he felt that loss. I wanted him to use the comfort and presence of one of his resources so he could experience grief in a way that did not feel unbearable. He imagined the man in the flannel shirt with him, and then began to cry with the BLS going. He was then able to experience the sadness with this resource supporting him and the BLS helping him to get through it. At the end of the session he reported his distress level at a zero along with a belief that *"I can move through this."* We then linked the feeling of calm in his body and the belief that he could move through his sadness with the scenes with Carlo, and added BLS. We finished the session by going over his plan for self-care around medical care and drinking.

In the next few sessions, Miguel reported feeling good about not drinking, and he became somewhat dismissive of the idea that alcohol might still be a problem. We talked about how he would know if alcohol became a problem, and he agreed we could go back to working on his alcohol use if he started drinking. We did EMDR around his fear and anger around his diabetes diagnosis. Afterwards, he reported an acceptance around the diabetes and a commitment to taking care of himself.

Then he had another difficult phone conversation with Carlo in which he learned that Carlo had cheated on him. He got upset, started drinking, and then went out and had unprotected sex with a stranger. I thought that since he had successfully processed a recent incident in the past, he could try it again. In the session that followed, we moved back and forth between EMDR processing—focusing on the fight that triggered his self-harming behavior—and using the Connecting the Consequences™ Protocol to help him link the urge to drink and have unprotected sex with the consequences of these behaviors.

I began EMDR by focusing on the conversation with Carlo that had triggered his urge to drink and have revenge sex. Miguel described Carlo telling him and everything seeming to speed up, his body feeling hot and flushed, and wanting to have sex with someone else. As we proceeded, Miguel's body got even hotter, and his feelings grew more intense. At one point he seemed to dissociate, so I checked that he felt grounded and present in the room and refocused him on the triggering moment. He processed anger for quite some time, and was able to accept my interventions to aid him in getting out of some stuck places. Although the distress level was coming down considerably from where he started, he became caught in the fact of the betrayal. He said that he wanted to *"fuck the pain away,"* and that he also wanted to drink. He couldn't seem to move through it. It seemed to me it wasn't just about his partner's betrayal, but was linked to something earlier, possibly from his childhood. Because we had limited sessions and time, I didn't want to open up those early painful places during this session. Taking that into consideration, I decided to try the Connecting the Consequences™ Protocol and see if that might help reduce the impulse for self-harm.

THERAPIST: *What did you feel right before you knew you were going to drink and try to fuck the pain away?*

CLIENT: *Anger.*

THERAPIST: *Okay just play out what happened, from the moment you felt the pain and anger. >>>>>>>>>>>>*

CLIENT: *I was so angry. When I drank, I still felt angry. Then I got with the guy. After sex, I still felt angry, but then I felt some relief, some calm, more able to have a conversation.*

He felt relief after having sex but I didn't want the story to stop there.

THERAPIST: *Then what?*

CLIENT: *I put myself at risk (for STDs). Now I have a secret and I don't know if I should tell him. Shit, I don't know what I'm going to do.*

He had connected the consequences and was more fully realizing what he had done. I now wanted him to pair the desire to drink and have sex with the consequence. Given the homophobia Miguel had internalized, it was important that we were clear that sex and the desire to be sexual were not the problem. The problem using sex for revenge and trying to manage his pain by being sexual in a physically risky way.

THERAPIST: *Okay, can you put that desire you had to drink and have sex to get rid of the pain with putting yourself at risk and carrying this secret?*

He nodded and I turned on the BLS for a time. >>>>>>>>>>>>>

THERAPIST: *Now can you go back to the scene we started with, with Carlo, and tell me what's there?*

CLIENT: *I'm not angry, more peace. I'm commending him for telling.*

THERAPIST: *What do you feel in your body?*

CLIENT: *I feel love for him, an openness in my heart.*

THERAPIST: *How charged does it feel on a scale of zero to ten?*

CLIENT: *About a three.*

THERAPIST: *What keeps it at a three?*

I wanted to know what was still troubling him, and if it was something we could clear out before he left. I was concerned that if he left still feeling upset, he would be tempted to soothe himself with alcohol.

CLIENT: *Everything that happened, it's just still not resolved.*

THERAPIST: *Go with that.* >>>>>>>>>>>>

He processed for a long time, and as he did, I saw his body relaxing.

THERAPIST: *What's there now?*

CLIENT: *I can see a picture of Carlo and I am chipping away flakes of paint obscuring his face. He is getting brighter and more real.*

He reported that the charge was gone from the triggering incident, but that now he had a secret, and he might have exposed himself to STDs. He was relaxed and felt love in his heart for Carlo. At the end of the session he *"I have a lot of work to do and I'm going to be okay."* We used BLS to integrate these positive beliefs and feelings with the scene he began with. Then we talked about a plan for self-care after the session.

I checked my voicemail a few minutes before the next session and found two messages from Miguel. In the first message, which he left twenty minutes before the session, he said that he was feeling ill and he wouldn't be able to come in. The second he left five minutes later, and he said he would be coming in after all.

When I went to get him from my waiting room, he smelled like alcohol. The first thing he said to me was, *"Carlo broke up with me this morning."* I inquired about the messages he had left me and the alcohol I detected on his breath. He told me he went out and bought a bottle of wine and had a few drinks. He felt so upset and anxious he didn't think he could leave the house and left me the first message. After he left the first message, he started tapping in his resources. *"You know it actually works,"* he told me. *"I knew I needed to come here and I could do it then."*

Because Miguel was clearly upset, I opted to start with EMDR processing around the breakup to see if I could help him move through some of that pain. I knew it was a risk to use EMDR when he had been drinking, because the EMDR results might not integrate and he might not have the affect tolerance to move through it. However, I had seen from past sessions that he benefitted from the processing and I wanted to give him some relief from his distress in the fastest way I knew. I also knew that Miguel had strong resources that he had been able to utilize in the past, and I believed I could bring them in to support and stabilize him if needed.

In the EMDR session, we began with the moment when Carlo told him *"I can't do this."* He described feeling sad, shocked, and numb. He was very distressed, crying, and his nose running when I began the BLS. His grief was intense, nearly intolerable, and I kept reassuring him that he could move through it. At one point, he became overwhelmed by the intensity of the emptiness he felt without his partner. I believe that underlying the emptiness and his emotional fragility was an early injury in his relationship to his parents, but the needed attachment repair work would have to wait until we could work together more consistently over a period of time. Until then, I used my supportive presence and had him call in the resources he had developed to help fill the emptiness.

Although the resources Miguel brought in helped for the moment, he got stuck again in despair and feelings of emptiness, which were a large part of what drove his drinking. I wanted to make the connection explicit and not risk triggering more drinking through the processing, so I switched to specifically bringing in resources to address his urge to drink.

THERAPIST: *What were you hoping to find in that bottle of wine?*
CLIENT: *Something to relieve me.*
THERAPIST: *What did you need?*
CLIENT: *I needed something to fill that void. I'm bringing my brother in.* >>>>>>>>>>>>

He was able to name the need and bring in a resource without my prompting him. In the session before, we had not gone back and resourced his urge to use, and here it felt as if he were filling in the work we had not finished.

THERAPIST: *What's there?*
CLIENT: *It felt good to feel him.*
THERAPIST: *When we go back to the breakup scene what's there now?*
CLIENT: *I see a swathe of purple and behind that, green.*

At this point his face looked peaceful and relaxed. I now applied the Connecting the Consequences™ Protocol to see if we could get a reduction in his urge to drink.

THERAPIST: *Now go back to the moment before you felt the urge to get the bottle of wine.*
CLIENT: *My vision is blurred. I am walking, having conversations in my head. I need a drink because I am so anxious.*
THERAPIST: *Just play out what happened from there.* >>>>>>>>>>>>
CLIENT: *I went and bought a bottle of wine and started drinking.*
THERAPIST: *Then what?* >>>>>>>>>>>>
CLIENT: *I thought I was going to have a panic attack. I took my shirt off, lay on the floor, and stared at the ceiling. I needed something reliable, something I could count on. The alcohol made me calm down. Alcohol is my friend, steady and reliable.*

Miguel was using alcohol to meet attachment needs. The relationship with alcohol was an abusive relationship; parts of it felt great, and it was important for me never to deny that reality. Instead I tried to help him integrate the whole picture.

THERAPIST: *What happens if you keep turning to this friend? Play it out.* >>>>>>>>>>>

CLIENT: *It ends up in situations that feel so meaningless and then I get really out of control and can't stop drinking.* >>>>>>>>>>>>

THERAPIST: *Can you really feel that?*

He nodded. Now I wanted to link the negative consequence with the urge to drink.

THERAPIST: *Can you go back to that anxiety and urge to drink and put that together with feeling meaningless and out of control?*

He nodded and was quiet for a while. >>>>>>>>>>>>

THERAPIST: *Got it?*

CLIENT: *It's like the end of the book goes with the beginning.*

At this point, we were running out of time, and I wanted to be sure that he had sufficient resources to deactivate his trigger to drink so that he would be able to manage better when he returned home. With that in mind, I decided to bring resources to the trigger.

THERAPIST: *Go back to yourself when you were so anxious and felt like you needed a drink. What did you need?*

CLIENT: *I don't know.*

Again, the fact that he did not know what he needed when he was triggered made sense. I thought about suggesting a resource for comfort like his brother, because he was struggling with self-soothing. I also knew he had been saying repeatedly that he had a hard time having a sense of who he was without Carlo and was feeling scared of being alone, and I thought those fears about the future were fueling his anxiety.

THERAPIST: *Can you bring in your future self?*

CLIENT: *I forgot about him. He's telling me to get it together.*

Miguel was saying the words to himself without any harshness, in a way that sounded grounded and reassuring.

THERAPIST: *Imagine that.* >>>>>>>>>>>>

CLIENT: *He says to hold my head up high and stop forgetting who I am. Allow myself to enjoy being by myself.* >>>>>>>>>>>

I now wanted to see if he could imagine using this helpful resource outside of our session when he might feel triggered.

THERAPIST: *Can you imagine bringing him in next time you feel that anxiety and want to drink?*

He nodded. >>>>>>>>>>>

THERAPIST: *Got it?*

He nodded again.

THERAPIST: *Do you want to ask him if you will make it through this?*
CLIENT: *I know I will.* >>>>>>>>>>>

At this point, I wanted to check our work by returning to the breakup that had triggered him to drink.

THERAPIST: *Okay, now go back to the scene we started with, with the breakup. What's there?*
CLIENT: *I want to get back together with him. I'm really sad.*
THERAPIST: *Can someone hold you while you feel that sadness?*
CLIENT: *The man with the flannel shirt ... I still feel sad but I'm going to make it.* >>>>>>>>>>>

This was hopeful and appropriate for a recent break up. He was no longer feeling the overwhelming emptiness. I wanted to check, though, to see if there is anything left undone.

THERAPIST: *Scan the scene. Is there anything that feels charged or unfinished?*
CLIENT: *No.*
THERAPIST: *What do you feel in your body?*
CLIENT: *There's an underlying feeling of relief that there's going to be closure.*
THERAPIST: *What do you believe about yourself?*
CLIENT: *I'm going to be okay.*

I had him put that feeling of relief and belief that he would be okay with the scene and added BLS. We ended the session by developing a plan for self-care and I invited him to contact me if he needed to. I also asked him to check in with his doctor concerning the blurry vision, which I thought might be a symptom of the diabetes with which he had been recently diagnosed.

Over the next few weeks, Miguel followed through on many of his self-care plans. He consulted a physician about the blurry vision, obtained a blood glucose monitor, and reported eating well and working out. He did not go to any meetings, but he was not drinking. He was also relieved when his STD panel came back clear and he reported feeling physically strong. After hearing these encouraging reports, I asked him to focus on the good things he had told me and how good his body felt, and we used BLS to strengthen and integrate how healthy and vibrant he felt.

In the last session before Miguel left, we talked more about self-care: planning food ahead of time, physical exercise, recognizing if he was triggered and tapping in his resources and his connection to the natural world. I asked him to close his eyes, go inside and imagine himself in his Peaceful Place.

THERAPIST: *Now, can you bring in your resources - all the figures that have guided you through your journey here - and see them making a circle around you, a circle that is big enough for all the different parts of you? Invite all the different parts of you, all the ages and stages into the circle. Look around and notice who is surrounding you and who is inside the circle. Nod to me when you have it.*

Miguel nodded.

THERAPIST: *Now I want you to look at your resources and feel the love and complete acceptance in their eyes going into all the different parts of you.*
>>>>>>>>>>>>

I turned on the pulsers and when I turned them off, Miguel signaled for me to keep going. He went for a long time. When he was ready, he opened his eyes and began talking. He told me he went to his field of flowers, felt the breeze, heard the birds, and saw different parts himself inside the circle. He saw the man with the flannel shirt, his brother, his friend Nina, me and his future self in a circle around him. He also saw a golden tree, filled with light and wisdom. I asked what he felt in his body and he described a warm red glow filling his core. I asked him if he could imagine times during his travels when he might become triggered. He talked about feeling triggered around his family, loneliness or missing Carlo. I turned on the BLS as he imagined bringing his resources and the golden tree into those moments.

When Miguel left, his relationship to alcohol and self-care was a work in progress. He felt tremendous sadness about his breakup, but also joy and excitement about traveling and hopeful about his future. He was not having panic attacks. When he got anxious, he was able to use tapping and exercise to move through the anxiety. He had not gone to a recovery meeting and was not committed to staying sober. He may commit someday but I also know that there are many definitions of recovery and the journey is not linear. In the meantime, he was not drinking. When he got an urge to drink he was able to imagine and tap in what he would feel like physically and emotionally if he drank - or, in his words, *"put the end of the book with the beginning of the book."* He could also soothe himself by tapping in his resource figures, his profoundly felt sense of the natural world, his compassion for himself and his connection with a spiritual part of himself that is wise, loving, and always available to him.

FOLLOW-UP

It has been a couple of years since our last session and Miguel and I recently spoke on the phone. He reported he had a serious diabetic health crisis triggered by family stress. This crisis reinforced his desire to take care of himself physically and emotionally. He set boundaries with his parents and has taken a break from sexual relationships. He is currently sober and he recognizes the need to strengthen his recovery support system. He is about to go traveling, but when he returns he is ready for the deeper work in therapy to heal early attachment wounds, to continue to develop his future self and to allow him to feel more fully alive in the present.

Elena Felder, LMFT, is an EMDRIA-certified EMDR therapist, consultant, and Parnell Institute for EMDR faculty member who specializes in recovery from childhood abuse and trauma as well as substance abuse. Trained in psychodynamic and relational psychotherapy, she has a private practice with locations in Oakland and San Francisco, California.

CHAPTER 15

Using the Bridging Technique to Find the Early Roots and Triggers of a Male Client Who Binges on Alcohol and Has Early Attachment Deficits

Constance Kaplan, LMFT

Seek the wisdom that will untie your knot. Seek the path that demands your whole being.

—RUMI

CLIENT DESCRIPTION AND PRESENTING ISSUE

Dmitri is a likable, successful 41-year-old, first-generation son of Russian immigrants.* He is a responsible, entrepreneurial man who works hard as the owner of a restaurant. He sought treatment for a long-standing problem with binge drinking in social situations with "a certain group of buddies," some of whom he grew up with. His binge drinking often leads to blackouts, causing significant stress in his marriage. He was referred to me for EMDR by a concerned friend. When I asked if he had any insight into the origins of his behavior, he shrugged and added with a hint of bravado, "I don't have an off switch. Besides, it's a cultural thing. If you don't keep up, you're not a real man." While this seeming rationalization does have some validity, given his upbringing in an ethnically insular, tough, macho, Russian pocket of New York City, I was also struck by a certain casualness to his explanation that felt disconnected from the urgent consequences of the behavior that initially led him to seek help. It was as if these different aspects of him weren't communicating.

*Dmitri is a composite of several clients who have presented with similar issues over the years. Any identifying information has been carefully disguised.

When I asked Dmitri if he had any other insights into the early links of his drinking, which began around age 11 years, he said he wasn't sure; then, he paused and added, "I think I chase the feeling of euphoria. I guess I just want to let go." I asked, "Let go of what?" I was listening for the earliest and most charged target(s) that might be at the root of his presenting issue; this would be the target I'd desensitize. But Dmitri responded to my question with confusion: "I don't know." That was my cue that I would use the Bridging Technique to find the root target.

When I asked him for his specific *goals for treatment*, I got my answer in a compelling way. Dmitri's eyes watered, his bravado dropped, and he said quietly, "I have to stop. I have to. My wife is pregnant with our first child, a girl, and I don't ever want my little girl to see me this way." When I asked what "stopping" would look like, he said he wanted to be able to "enjoy a shot or two and that's it. I want to stay present and be respectable for my family."

DEVELOPMENTAL HISTORY

Dmitri is the oldest of four and the first-born son. His parents fled Russian oppression and settled in New York. Over the years, they have grown into a large and social extended family. He described his mother as a resilient woman who was loving to her children. His father, however, was portrayed as a collapsed, depressed man who felt bad about himself, struggled to provide for his family, and expressed his low self-esteem by minimizing the strengths and accomplishments of others. Neither my client, nor his siblings, nor his mother was spared from his father's denigration or indifference.

Dmitri's narrative was organized, though I noted some gaps as I conceptualized the case and considered my treatment plan. From our first meetings, I determined that Dmitri had enough ego strength and support in his current life to be able to handle the intensity of EMDR trauma-processing sessions. He was highly functional at work and was in a loving but increasingly stressed marriage to a younger, equally bright and decent woman who worked in middle management for a major corporation. Dmitri reported that he was often painfully triggered when he felt criticized by his wife, which conjured memories of his childhood denigration by his father.

CASE FORMULATION

I hypothesized that the likely roots of Dmitri's binge drinking were linked to the denigrating and conflictual relationship that my client witnessed between his mother and father and the one he experienced personally with his father. I believed that processing these roots would reveal whatever intolerable feelings he wanted to let go of. I thought that when we began EMDR processing of these early experiences, we would discover whether my hypothesis stood up.

SESSIONS

After the initial history-taking sessions, we began to prepare Dmitri to do EMDR trauma processing by developing and tapping in the four foundational resources of Peaceful Place, Nurturing Figures, Protector Figures, and Wise Figures, as well as others to support him in our work. Dmitri quickly developed robust resources, most of which were strong, real, and imaginary mentoring men. The qualities of each resource were individually tapped in, and he also chose to tap in all the resources as one team. During this time, I explained to him what EMDR was and what to expect from EMDR sessions, including ways to establish a dual focus of awareness such as choosing a metaphor to help with this. After I introduced Dmitri to the different forms of bilateral stimulation (BLS) available to him, he chose the Tac/Audio Scan pulsers, which he held in his hands and adjusted to the tempo he preferred.

In our first EMDR session, I had determined to use the Bridging Technique to discover the link to Dmitri's trigger for binge drinking. After first tapping in his resources, I asked him for the most recent time that he binged. He said it was last weekend, when he and his family attended the baptism of a close friend's son.

THERAPIST: *Focus on the scene and notice the moment just before you started throwing back shots of vodka without any mindfulness. What is the most disturbing image?*

CLIENT: Sitting at a banquet table with my parents, brothers, their wives, my sister, and her husband.

THERAPIST: *What emotions do you feel?*

CLIENT: Anxious. Sad.

THERAPIST: *Where do you feel this in your body?*

CLIENT: Kind of numb . . . Sick in my stomach.

THERAPIST: *What thoughts or beliefs go with this?*
CLIENT: Powerless.
THERAPIST: *Trace all this back in time, as far as you can, and let whatever comes up come up, without censoring it.*

I quietly waited for several seconds for a memory or a scene of some kind to emerge. Then, Dmitri landed on a very charged memory, which became the target for our EMDR processing session.

CLIENT: I am around 11 years old at a large family celebration, a cousin's wedding. Dad drank at parties like this and would become belligerent, a sloppy drunk. My family is sitting at the table, and suddenly, out of nowhere, my dad cursed at my mother and threw an empty vodka bottle across the table at her. I'm not kidding. Just missed her. It shattered behind her. Thank God no one got hurt. Everyone couldn't believe it.
THERAPIST: *What picture represents the worst part of that memory?*
CLIENT: The rage on Dad's face.
THERAPIST: *What emotions do you feel?*
CLIENT: Shock and embarrassment.
THERAPIST: *What do you notice in your body?*
CLIENT: My chest is tight and cold.
THERAPIST: *What do you believe about yourself?*
CLIENT: I'm helpless.

At this point, we were ready to begin EMDR processing of this childhood memory. I then turned on the Tac/Audio Scan pulsers, and we began processing. After just a few seconds, Dmitri opened his eyes, signaling me to stop the BLS.

THERAPIST: *What's happening now?*
CLIENT: I no longer feel helpless or hopeless. Just anger.
THERAPIST: *Go with that.* >>>>>>

Dmitri quickly began to process memories that held images, emotions, body sensations, and negative beliefs associated with the original trauma, but were not safe to experience at the time. Feelings of anger, hurt, disgust, humiliation, shame, and eventually sadness about his father's drunken outbursts started to link together into a context and a coherent narrative. He also processed body memories of thwarted defensive postures when he wanted to run over to the table, stop his imposing father, and protect his mother, but couldn't because of his young age. Instead, he felt frozen, helpless, and numb. We processed the tension in his arms, the tight feelings in his jaw and throat, and the things he wanted to say as a child but couldn't.

At one point, he was looping in helpless anger, which he was afraid to express. I decided to help him out of the looping by using a couple of interweaves. The first, a Socratic Interweave, was designed to link up his adult perspective with the child's.

THERAPIST: *It wasn't safe to shout at your father and tell him to stop back then, but is it now?*

CLIENT: Yes!

THERAPIST: *Go with that. >>>>>>*

When the client again became blocked with unexpressed physical sensations, I introduced an Imagination Interweave.

THERAPIST: *Would you like to express now the actions you couldn't take back then to protect your mother?*

He again responded in the affirmative, and we added BLS, this time with the pulsers in his pockets so he could freely use his arms and body as needed.

As his processing continued and then neared completion, he wept, "I will never be a drunk making a fool of myself. I will never do it again. I will never be like him." He was shocked and a bit embarrassed—he said he never cried—but he also reported feeling much relief. At the end of the session, he reported his level of distress to be between 0 and 1. When I asked him what belief now went with the memory, he replied, "I'm my own man. I will be a better father. I have the power to do that." This positive cognition was linked with the scene and then installed with BLS. When he scanned his body, he reported that his body felt good and clear. When Dmitri returned for his next session, he reported great progress.

During the week after our session, he had gone to a birthday party. Despite peer pressure from his friends, he had no real desire to drink. Dmitri reported with some amazement, "Some crazy progress this week. I was the odd man out, but I felt good, so there was no point." He added that when he began to sip just one shot, he felt the buzz more quickly. "There was no reason to finish the entire shot. I had an off switch and felt more present." He appeared to be regaining further connection with his body. He also said he had imagined his support team of resources around him at the party. In particular, he'd called from within an imaginary resource, a man with a strong, firm, and loving presence. "I asked myself, what's the right thing to do? What would he think? What would he say to me? It was all about accountability."

For the next three weeks, Dmitri had to travel for work and family obligations. We developed a plan to maintain his stability during his absence. We kept in touch by phone, and he agreed to continue to tap in his resources on a daily basis to access whatever quality he needed most to maintain his progress. Dmitri liked to work out, so I explained to him that tapping in resources is like building muscle; the more you do it, the stronger it gets. He did well while away and was able to pace himself, with very little urge to drink. However, he called in distress on the Monday after he returned and asked for an earlier session that week.

When he arrived Tuesday morning, he reported that he had binged again at a colleague's bachelor party over the weekend and didn't know why. He was genuinely puzzled. In order to answer his question and discover what might have triggered his bingeing, I decided to use the Bridging Technique again, to see if we could locate the roots of this trigger.

I asked him to recall the day that he binged and to see if he could roll the tape of that day back, and then play it forward and see if he could notice what was happening just before he started drinking too much. Dmitri closed his eyes and went inside himself for a few moments as he attempted to recreate what was in his mind that day. As he did this, he discovered that he felt the urge to drink to excess when, at the bachelor party, he was approached by an older male friend he respected who told Dmitri that he was a good and successful man who would be a good father. Dmitri added that it was usually hard for him to take in positive information, but there was something about this man that made it safe to do so. Even though neither of us understood the significance of this trigger, I believed it was important to follow this back in time to discover what it meant to him.

THERAPIST: *What picture represents that moment for you, right before you had the urge to binge?*

CLIENT: My friend's demeanor and look of respect on his face toward me.

THERAPIST: *What emotions do you feel?*

CLIENT: Powerful. Happy. Euphoric.

THERAPIST: *What do you feel in your body?*

CLIENT: Adrenaline rush, energized in my chest, wound up.

THERAPIST: *What thoughts or beliefs go with this?*
    CLIENT: I'm unstoppable.
THE2RAPIST: *Trace all this back as far as you can without censoring it. Let whatever comes up, come up.*

I quietly waited several seconds for him to land on an image or memory. Then, Dmitri opened his eyes and reported on what had come up.

    CLIENT: I am around age 8. Innocent. Wearing shorts and a T-shirt. Both parents are at work, but I know they will be home soon and start arguing.

This is the memory for EMDR that we then developed as our target. I still didn't know or understand how it related to his urge to binge drink.

THERAPIST: *As you imagine this scene, what emotions do you feel?*
    CLIENT: Anticipating the escalating look and sound of arguing parents. I feel sad.

He reported feeling pressure in his chest and the beliefs, "I'm on my own. There's no one to turn to. No guidance or male role model to help." He was beginning to cry; I could see that he was emotionally distressed. I began the BLS. >>>>> After a couple of minutes, Dmitri opened his eyes, which signaled me to turn off the BLS and that he was ready to report his experience.

    CLIENT: Pressure in my chest is released. There's a white, hollow place in front of my eyes. A breath of fresh air.
THERAPIST: *Go with that.* >>>>>>

After just a few seconds, Dmitri opened his eyes. I asked him what was happening.

    CLIENT: Nothing.

I wondered if the memory had been completely reprocessed or if he was blocking. I asked him to return to the childhood scene to check the work and see where we were.

    CLIENT: The boy feels kind of lost.

I could tell by his response that there was more work to do, so I instructed him to "go with that" and turned on the BLS.

THERAPIST: *What's happening now?*
  CLIENT: A void. >>>>>> Just lost. >>>>>>

Because this feeling of void and being lost wasn't changing, I determined that the processing was blocked, and I needed to do an interweave to get it unblocked and moving again. I decided to try a Resource Interweave.

THERAPIST: *What does that little boy need?*
  CLIENT: A dad to empower me.
THERAPIST: *Who could do that?*

Dmitri immediately came up with a classic male movie figure as a kind of co-dad, one he had not thought of before. As he imagined bringing this figure into the childhood scene with BLS, this figure provided inspiration, knowledge, pride, support, nurturing, and protection to his young self. Because this male figure was so helpful and seemed so healing for him, I asked if Dmitri would like to go through his developmental trajectory, positively empowered by this male resource—to feel, in an embodied way, the qualities that he never got to experience as a boy. This process of using resources for developmental repair is outlined in *Attachment-Focused EMDR*.[48] The client was eager to try this.

My sense was that if Dmitri could access his adult empowerment, then he might have the internal structure to grieve the very painful truth that what he wanted most from his father, he didn't get and never would—not the way he once needed it.

As he imagined the developmental repair with BLS, he chose to process out loud, narrating his experience. But instead of short sets of BLS, he asked me to keep the pulsers going continuously. >>>>>>

CLIENT: I wanted my dad to be around for my birth, not at a bar. I wanted him to come home at night, cradle all the kids and be interested in how we were, come to my hockey games, cheer me on, be proud, listen to my music, come to my high school graduation. I wanted him to celebrate my being the first in the family to get into college, even though he didn't even pay for it. My dad—so much negativity, undermining me, my school work, and my job. I needed a dad who told his kids they could be anything. I want to look proudly at my dad, instead of waiting for a stupid and embarrassing comment. I don't want to feel humiliated. I wanted to picture my dad busting his ass to provide for a happy family. But it was always about him. Not the family. No guidance. I was never held. Never told I was loved. He was too busy talking crap. I never got the adrenaline rush of his empowerment. (Pause.) I guess he wasn't a bad guy, but afraid to show his vulnerability. And he had a lot of his own trauma.

His eyes opened.

CLIENT: Wow. Empowerment and anger got all tangled up.

He paused.

CLIENT: I put Dad in his place. Feels good, more empowered, like when my friend was genuinely warm to me. I feel safer. Someone to lean on. I had it from Mom, but it wasn't enough. I needed it from my father, someone I respected walking in the door. I wanted the excitement of that.

THERAPIST: *What are you feeling now?*

CLIENT: Wow. Peace. No anger.

Dmitri reported his level of disturbance to be zero, and his positive belief was, "I am a good man, and I'm powerful," which we paired and installed with the childhood scene. He said his body felt relief. When I asked him to return to the original trigger to binge drink at the party, he said it no longer held any charge for him. In order to further check our work, I asked him to imagine partying with his friends and family in the future. I wanted to see if he still could locate triggers for bingeing. He closed his eyes, went inside, and then said that he could feel some worry. He was specifically thinking about what might happen at his daughter's future baptism. In order to help him with this potential trigger for binge drinking, I decided to use the Connecting the Consequences Protocol.

I asked him to recall a time recently when he had lost control and binged and then to play the entire sequence through in his mind like a movie—including the urge to use, the bingeing, the euphoria, the blackout, and the subsequent shame he felt. I then added BLS as he played through the sequence. After doing this, I also installed the negative consequences by linking the moment of the urge to use and with a negative future with BLS.

THERAPIST: *Imagine what your life will look like if you continue this behavior and its effect on your daughter.*

Dmitri had never been a father before, so I gently described his daughter's developmental stages and what she would witness if he continued to binge as he aged. He shuddered and opened his eyes.

CLIENT: I just went cold inside. She will never see what I saw.

I then tapped in the opposite: *"Imagine what your life can be like if you stop bingeing and where you become the man you long to be."*

He opened his eyes, nodded affirmatively, and said, "I get it. I really get it. I really do!"

After this session, Dmitri did not report more bingeing, but we believed there was more work to do. He was still afraid that the behavior would return. There was one more EMDR target to process that was feeding into his fears of bingeing again. When we explored what that link might be, he seemed startled to realize, "It's about the group of guys I drink with."

I asked him to close his eyes, stay close to the feelings, and notice what came up for him as he imagined drinking with these particular guys. As he did, his shoulders slumped, and he uttered, "It's about grief and loss." It was clear that a lot of feelings were coming up for Dmitri, and he asked if I could just hand him the pulsers while he expressed and processed his grief. I responded to his needs and turned the pulsers on to the tempo and intensity he favored. He spoke with anger, hurt, and sadness about the loss of his childhood.

CLIENT: I grew up with a lot of these guys. When I drink with them, I feel like the teenager I never got to be—a kid with no responsibilities, no burdens, just partying and making dumb decisions, not knowing my limits or even caring. Just having fun. But I never got to be that. I didn't even have a choice. When my friends were just screwing around, I worked in every kind of crappy job in restaurant kitchens to help support my family. I even left college. My dad couldn't cut it, and my mom didn't make enough.

He then paused and mused thoughtfully.

CLIENT: I guess in some ways, it was a good thing, because now I own my own place.

Then he became more emotional.

CLIENT: But the decision was made for me. I'm so pissed.

Dmitri went on to lament the excessive burden placed on him as the "parentified" oldest child, even as a little boy, and how adult responsibilities should have been shouldered by his parents. As he anticipated the birth of his first child, he asked me in a pleading way, "How can I be a father when I was never a kid?"

I decided to respond to his pained question with an Imagination Interweave, which I sometimes use as a stand-alone technique when a client is stuck in a negative belief. Dmitri was bereft about the childhood experiences he missed out on. He felt robbed. The Imagination Interweave I crafted was designed to repair additional developmental deficits and provide a new internal experience for him as he anticipated fathering his own child.

THERAPIST: *Would you like to imagine what it would feel like to be your child being raised by you, a loving and responsible man?*

I was asking him to attune to the experience of a child raised in safety, security, stability, and joy and to feel it in every cell in his own body. He was eager to give it a try. I turned the pulsers back on, and he narrated how it felt inside to experience healthy parenting from his daughter's point of view: the delight she saw on his face and the delight he felt for her; and his gaze, attention, and attunement from right brain to right brain. He imagined his child witnessing him and his wife in a loving, respectful, and affectionate relationship and her excitement as he returned home from a satisfying day at work, exuding pride that he could provide for all her needs. He continued to narrate her experience of being a teenager dealing with peers and forging an identity while having a supportive and mentoring dad who had her back. He imagined what it would feel like to be encouraged, to be helped with homework and activities about which she was passionate. He imagined the feeling of being taken to different colleges and then given the security and space to focus on growing up in an age-appropriate way. He also added with a wry smile that he would definitely give any of her boyfriends "the once-over." He signaled me to turn off the pulsers.

CLIENT: I feel relief. But also, sad, because it's true; it happened. I didn't get what I needed, and there's nothing I can do about that. But I don't feel as angry right now. I'm just determined to make up for the loss by giving my daughter a real childhood. And maybe, during some of those moments, I can relive my own.

I asked him to imagine drinking with his group of childhood friends in the future. When he did, he put a mild look of distaste on his face, shook his head, and said, "Yeah, that's over. I mean I'll still hang out with them, have a couple of shots and catch up, but I'm not 17 . . . And it's actually kind of gross to act like it."

As of this writing, it's been 10 months, and Dmitri hasn't binged. Since the session above, we've worked on additional self-esteem issues and processing his cigar- and cigarette-smoking habit that became linked into the drinking. His marriage is stronger, and he is now a proud, tired, and doting dad.

Constance Kaplan, LMFT, is an EMDRIA Approved consultant and faculty of the Parnell Institute for EMDR, where she is a facilitator and senior trainer.She is also Director of Training Trainers at the Parnell Institute and runs EMDR consultation, certification, and consultation-of-consultation groups. With over 21 years of experience specializing in treating PTSD, complex trauma, and early attachment trauma with EMDR, she has a private practice in Los Angeles, California.

CHAPTER 16

Using Attachment-Focused EMDR, Resource Tapping, and the Connecting the Consequences Protocol to Treat a Woman with Life-Threatening Diabulimia

Julie Probus-Schad, LCSW

The cave you fear to enter holds the treasure you seek.
—JOSEPH CAMPBELL

CLIENT DESCRIPTION AND PRESENTING PROBLEM

Brooke* came to me as a 23-year-old college student. She presented in my office suffering from many physical symptoms associated with poorly managed juvenile-onset diabetes. She was extremely thin and frail, and walking with a cane; her large, beautiful eyes looked tired, lacking the gleam often associated with youth. Neuropathy in her feet caused pain with every step. Her vision was deteriorating secondary to macular degeneration, and she had frequent hospitalizations related to unmanaged diabetes. One of the many life-threatening symptoms was diabetic ketoacidosis (DK) exacerbated by diabulimia.

The Mayo Clinic defines diabetic ketoacidosis as "a serious complication of diabetes that occurs when your body produces high levels of blood acids called ketones."[49] Insulin normally plays a key role in helping sugar (glucose)—a major source of energy for your muscles and other tissues—enter the cells. Without enough insulin, the body begins to break down fat as fuel, which produces a

---

*Brooke is based upon a conglomeration of clients who present with similar concerns. In order to protect confidentiality, aspects of history and identity have been changed.

buildup of acids in the bloodstream called ketones. Left untreated, this eventually leads to diabetic ketoacidosis, which in turn can lead to heart attack, kidney failure, and damage to other organs.

Upon assessment, I learned that Brooke was slowly destroying her body by practicing the dangerous exercise of diabulimia. The National Eating Disorders Association describes diabulimia as an eating disorder that may affect those with Type 1 diabetes.[50] In diabulimia, the diabetic purposefully reduces insulin use to raise ketone levels, leading to weight loss. This behavior may also be combined with bingeing, and this was the case with Brooke as well.

Before our initial meeting, Brooke had several hospitalizations related to DK. She was referred to me by her endocrinologist and chose to seek help after a 2-week hospitalization for cerebral swelling related to excess ketones. Her physician told her if she did not stop the diabulimia, she would likely suffer severe brain damage or die.

Brooke presented with severe anxiety and panic attacks. She also reported feeling sad and depressed almost every day. At our initial session, she shared that she was terrified that she would lose her feet and legs due to diabetes. She was haunted by photos of amputations a nutritionist had shared with her in her adolescence while trying to jolt her into healthier eating and compliance with her insulin. Her father, who also had diabetes, had had a leg amputated, and Brooke was also haunted by images of him in the hospital.

Though she had no active suicidal ideation, Brooke realized she was likely slowly killing herself. She was very confused about the fact that her desire to be thin seemed to supersede the known consequences of poorly managed diabetes and active diabulimia. I explained to Brooke that she needed an evaluation by a psychiatrist who specialized in diabetes and depression. Brooke agreed, and was placed on an SSRI antidepressant to help manage her anxiety and depressive symptoms.

CLIENT HISTORY

Brooke described a loving and happy early childhood, during which her father was her primary caregiver as her mother finished her education. Brooke and her sister, three years her junior, spent their days with her father and his extended family. She recalled time with her mother as infrequent but loving and connected. Brooke shared that her world changed when, at the age of 8 years, she was diagnosed with juvenile-onset type 1 diabetes.

Initially, the illness was challenging to manage. Brooke had several hospital-izations to stabilize blood sugars. She told me that her parents fought about her healthcare and were frantic about her wellness. From the onset of her illness, her parents stressed the need for Brooke to be able to take care of herself medically and understand her illness. She reported that she was required to learn how to self-administer her insulin; she felt that, at 8 years old, she had stopped being an innocent child and had begun to be her own medical caregiver. Brooke hated giving herself insulin shots, but felt she had to comply with her parents' wishes without argument.

A thorough education on the practical aspects of managing her own diabetes did not include anyone talking to her about the emotional impact of her illness. Brooke remembered an early doctor's appointment during which she was told she was a "brittle diabetic," which she had interpreted to mean that she could break or easily die. As a result, she spent many nights lying awake, praying she would live until morning.

Shortly after her diagnosis, Brooke began to feel deprived around food. Her diet had completely changed. Weekend trips with her sister and father to the sweet shop were immediately halted. When she was 10 years old, her parents divorced; and then, the following year, her father moved out of state for his work. Brooke longed for the days with her father, who had increasingly infrequent vis-its with her and her sister. She described her mother as a hardworking woman who was loving, yet a perfectionist. Brooke and her sister were expected to have excellent grades, play an instrument, and keep up with chores at the house as her mother worked long hours in a less-than-desirable job.

After the divorce, Brooke became increasingly responsible for her younger sister. Brooke's tween years were fraught with anxiety and frustration. She felt she was flawed because of her diabetes and that she was not enough for her father. Feeling hurt and abandoned, she coped by becoming increasingly rigid with her food intake, getting perfect grades, and participating in many school activities.

In her mid-teens, Brooke's father reestablished a relationship with her and her sister; unfortunately, by this time, he had developed a serious drinking problem. Brooke learned that her father had diabetes as well. She worried about his medical well-being. Because of his drinking, visits with her father were always chaotic. He would even drive while intoxicated with the girls in the car.

During this time, Brooke's food intake became even more rigid. She also increased her school activities so that she had an excuse to be unavailable for the monthly visits with her father. Her younger sister followed suit, and soon the visits ceased. Brooke was eager to get away from home as soon as she could. She finished high school a year early and went away to college.

As hard as she had worked in high school, Brooke was unprepared for the competitiveness of college, both academically and socially. One of her sorority sisters who also had diabetes shared with Brooke how she could control her weight by withholding insulin. As she followed her friend's advice, Brooke quickly lost fifteen pounds and began getting compliments from her peers about her appearance. By the time she arrived home at semester break, she had lost 30 pounds. Her tall frame became more and more slight. With each decrease in weight, secondary to diabulimia, her medical symptoms worsened.

By the time Brooke presented in my office, she had been hospitalized nine times and had suffered irreparable heart damage and vision problems. As indicated earlier, she could not walk without a cane. Her mother and endocrinologist told her she could not return to college unless she got therapy for her condition. Her endocrinologist had heard about EMDR and hoped it would benefit Brooke. I agreed to see her, with close medical follow-up from the endocrinologist.

CASE FORMULATION

Brooke's diabulimia began as a way to manage the stress and fear associated with performing well at college while maintaining the image of the perceived perfect body. She had a long-standing belief that if she looked good on the outside, others would believe she was okay on the inside. In addition to the bingeing-and-withholding cycle of diabulimia, she spent a significant amount of time and energy calculating carbohydrates, insulin doses, and weight loss.

At her diagnosis at 8 years of age, Brooke had experienced a change in her primary relationships related to a change in her body and medical condition. This link had carried through as an underlying belief that if she could control her diabetes and her body, she could be successful in other areas of her life as well. Anxiety and self-loathing about her medical condition were channeled into controlling her weight.

Brooke was so hyperfocused on the desired result of being thin that she did not connect the consequences of her diabulimia. This disconnect was made even more obvious when the death of her father from diabetes-related illness did not scare her away from diabulimic practices, but instead intensified them.

SESSIONS

Brooke identified her goal for treatment as staying alive while staying thin. She voiced concerns about taking her insulin as prescribed, fearing a complete loss of control if she were to gain weight. We developed a therapeutic contract to work with a team of medical professionals who would help her reach her goals. Brooke continued to collaborate with her endocrinologist, a personal trainer who specialized in working with clients with severe muscle loss, and a nutritionist who specialized in working with clients who have diabetes. This team became an integral part of the therapeutic container. A group of people with her best interests in mind, who would help her to manage this illness, empowered Brooke to feel safe and capable of doing the work she needed to do in order to get well.

An integral part of attachment-focused work is creating sufficient safety before beginning the EMDR processing. Following the completion of a thorough developmental history, our initial sessions were spent tapping in the four foundational resources to help keep Brooke in her window of tolerance and to create a foundation on which to build our work. In my experience, the ease with which a client can identify and connect to their resources is a good indicator of how well they can process difficult material. I wanted these resources to provide healthy alternatives to the many maladaptive means of coping Brooke had developed.

I hypothesized that Brooke used her diabulimia as a means of managing her emotions and anxiety. Because I believed that this anxiety was associated with the lack of support she had received as a small child, I suggested that we tap in ideal parents to begin repairing developmental deficits. Brooke rejected this idea. Even though she described her parents as largely absent in her childhood, she firmly believed they would have done much better with proper assistance. When I offered the option of bringing in resources for her parents, Brooke readily agreed.

I invited Brooke to bring in as many resources as she wanted or needed for her parents. She began by creating a nanny for her sister and herself as well as household staff and a skilled assistant for her mother, so that her time would be freed up to be with her daughters. For her father, she brought in an addictions coach who took him to meetings and helped him understand alcoholism. She created a private duty nurse for herself, who showed her how to care for her diabetes but did not make her self-administer insulin.

After further developing and tapping in resources, we spent an entire session imagining her development with the resources in place. Brooke closed her eyes and went inside, and with the pulsers going, she imagined being *in utero*; she imagined being born to calm, relaxed parents who lovingly awaited her arrival. Brooke then imagined her development up until the age of onset of diabetes. She noticed that her parents having proper support created more time for interaction and play. When we reached the age of onset of diabetes, Brooke began to cry, stating in a childlike voice, "I can't do it . . . I can't do it."

I turned off the pulsers and asked Brooke what she needed to continue.

CLIENT: I am afraid, because this was when everything changed in my life. I can't do it by myself again.

Brooke was required to take on many adult responsibilities as a very young child. This was an excellent opportunity for developmental repair, creating a new awareness that she did not have to go through her juvenile-onset diabetes or challenges in her adult life alone.

THERAPIST: *Who can help you?*

CLIENT: My nurse.

THERAPIST: *Imagine your nurse helping you. Take your time and let her give you everything you need.*

Brooke again closed her eyes and went inside, this time narrating her experience. As she imagined receiving education and more generous support for her diabetic care, we used continuous bilateral stimulation (BLS).

CLIENT: >>>>>> The nurse is sitting down with me and my parents, helping them understand that I need help, that I am too young to be responsible for my injections. My mom and dad let go of their expectations and listen like concerned parents. My dad whispers to me, using my childhood nickname, Benji, telling me that it is all going to be okay, and he holds my hand. My mom challenges the nurse, who gently but firmly tells Mom what I need. Mom smiles at me and agrees to give my morning insulin and have the private duty nurse come daily for help with nutrition and diabetes management. The nurse goes on telling us about diabetes in words that I can understand. I ask her if I am going to die or break because I am a "brittle diabetic," and she tells me that I am not going to break and that with proper management I can live a long and healthy life. I can go to sleep without fear and anxiety about not waking up. I go to school and play with my friends because I know I am strong and not brittle. My parents are not mad at me if my blood sugars are off; we figure it out together with the nurse. I can have fun and play; it is not my job to manage my illness. I can do it with the right help.

Brooke opens her eyes.

CLIENT: I can do this with the right help. I am not alone now; I truly do have my medical team to help me through this now.

I invited Brooke to take this information into her entire nervous system with BLS. Brooke smiled and breathed calmly as she further integrated this information.

At the end of the session, Brooke reported feeling calm and relaxed. In subsequent sessions, we continued with the developmental repair by connecting with and imagining her resources throughout her development. Brooke reported less anxiety and improved sleep after completing the resourcing. I explained to her that so much of her childhood was spent trying to regulate the family system that she had not learned to self-regulate.

In our next session, Brooke told me she was angry with herself for her diabulimia. She believed that she should have known better than to engage in behavior that would threaten her health and life. I spent time educating Brooke about eating disorders in general and diabulimia in particular and explained to her that we could tap in education about diabulimia as a resource. After she seemed to take in the information provided, I asked her to connect with what she had just learned about diabetes and diabulimia; then we tapped in the new knowledge by turning on the BLS to help her more fully integrate the information.

Brooke's therapeutic container was strengthening. She was beginning to develop the ego strength needed to start EMDR processing. Due to Brooke's fragile physical and mental state, I continued to use the resourcing as a means to facilitate developmental repair, increase affect tolerance, and develop adaptive self-regulation skills.

When the time came to tap in the four foundational resources, Brooke imagined a Peaceful Place very easily: her aunt's cabin. Brooke nodded when she felt connected to her Peaceful Place, and I turned on the pulsers. Brooke took in a deep breath and relaxed. We then moved on to making a list of Nurturing Figures. She named her mother as a nurturing figure, and because I knew that her mother was loving, I allowed her to be used as a Nurturing Figure. I knew she needed more than her mother, however, since her mother did not meet her emotional needs when she was a young child. When prompted to choose more Nurturing Figures, Brooke added her grandmother and her older cousin. After identifying these figures, she tapped each one in with BLS. She did well with this, smiling, her body continuing to soften and relax.

For her Protective Figures, Brooke listed her maternal uncle and a lion. She successfully tapped in each of these figures, too. When invited to choose a Wise Figure, Brooke wanted to use herself. Knowing that Brooke had needed to rely on herself too much growing up, I agreed to tap in her adult wise self, but with support from additional Wise Figures.

Since Brooke had to be so independent and self-reliant as a child, I wanted to strengthen her with additional resources. Brooke identified her current medical team as Wise Figures. We tapped in her endocrinologist, nutritionist, personal trainer, and therapist.

Brooke seemed to flourish with the resourcing, reporting in the period following a marked decrease in anxiety, improved sleep, and a general sense of well-being. Brooke regularly used Resource Tapping between sessions by tapping on her own knees, right-left, right-left, or by using the butterfly tap.

EMDR SESSIONS

Brooke's health began to stabilize. She had a clear commitment to therapy, and with the extensive resourcing we were doing, her affect tolerance and ego strength grew. I believed she was strong enough to begin EMDR processing. Medical clearance was given by her endocrinologist.

As explained in Chapter 2 of this book, when developing EMDR targets for addictions work, it can be helpful to identify the age when the client first engaged in the addictive behavior as well as the age when the client first experienced trauma. Typically, I would process the traumas chronologically, beginning in childhood and working my way up; but when I asked Brooke what, of all that we had discussed, she had found to be the most distressing, she immediately said it was the death of her father. Tearfully, she shared that her diabulimia had intensified and she had begun withholding insulin more regularly after his death.

Because it was the most traumatic event and was likely driving her present-day addiction, I decided to begin EMDR by targeting the death of her father first. I believed that if we did so, it would provide her the most immediate relief from her emotional distress.

Brooke reported that her father had died somewhat unexpectedly from a diabetes-related illness during her sophomore year of college. At the time of his death, Brooke had been studying abroad, and had been scheduled to return home the following week. Her family had chosen not to inform her of his death until her arrival at home. Brooke had been shocked to learn of her father's death and equally shocked to learn that he had been hospitalized for the three weeks before his death. She was sad and angry about not being given a chance to say good-bye to him.

Before beginning the EMDR processing, we tapped in the four foundational resources. To create distance, we established the metaphor of watching the scene like a movie, where Brooke had the remote control and could stop, pause, or fast forward at any time.

THERAPIST: *What picture represents the worst part of your father's death?*

CLIENT: It is just before the funeral. I'm standing alone by my father's casket, and I touch him. He is cold and dead, and I realize that I will never see him again.

THERAPIST: *What emotions do you feel?*

CLIENT: I feel deep despair, sadness, and blackness. I am blank and emotionally numb.

THERAPIST: *What do you notice in your body?*

CLIENT: I feel cold and numb. Wait, I have a very distinct body sensation of a sinking feeling in my chest and stomach.

Without being prompted regarding a negative cognition, Brooke indicated that she felt that nothing mattered. "I do not matter . . . It is all ending." At this point, I turned on the pulsers to begin the processing. I observed closely as the waves of affect began to rise and fall. After a long set of BLS, Brooke opened her eyes to report.

CLIENT: I am kneeling on the floor by the casket, crying hysterically. I feel so guilty that I did not get to say goodbye.

THERAPIST: *Go with that.* >>>>>>

CLIENT: All I can see is him dead. I feel numb. It is all ending. Nothing matters. All I can see is him dead. He is cold and dead.

Often, with grief and loss, it is reparative for the client to complete an incomplete act—to do or say something in imagination that they did not do in reality. I wanted to give Brooke the opportunity to say anything she would like to her father. I used an Imagination Interweave.

THERAPIST: *Would you like to imagine saying goodbye to your father?*

CLIENT: Yes.

THERAPIST: *Imagine saying whatever you need to say.* >>>>>>

CLIENT: I tell him I am so sorry he is gone, that I miss him and that I would have come home if I had known. He is hugging me and kissing me on the forehead. He is rocking me back and forth.

THERAPIST: *Go with that.* >>>>>>

Brooke then had a marked change in her affect, suddenly appearing flat and distant. She reported feeling numb and not present in the room or on the earth, repeating over and over that nothing mattered. She said she was outside of her body, looking down at the scene. I realized she had dissociated.

To help her return to her body, I used grounding techniques. I instructed her to feel her body connected to the chair, to look into my eyes, and to notice that we were present in the room together. Brooke reported being afraid of the numbness and feeling "floaty." I explained to her that what she had just experienced was dissociation and that this is something people do when their feelings are too much for them. I normalized her dissociation, and we agreed that she would let me know if she left the room or her body again.

Once Brooke came back to the room and acknowledged being fully present with me, I asked her what she needed to continue processing. I offered the idea of bringing in anyone on her resource team to be present with her in the scene. Brooke reported she wanted to do it by herself. I reminded her that she had the remote control and could stop, pause, or fast forward at any time, and I let her know she could process with her eyes open if she would like. Brooke chose to continue with her eyes closed, viewing the scene like a movie. She took out the sensory feeling of her father being cold.

THERAPIST: *Brooke, close your eyes and go inside. When you think of the scene with your father, what do you notice?*

CLIENT: I am so sad.

THERAPIST: *Go with the sadness.* >>>>>>

After just a few sets of BLS, Brooke began shaking and sobbing. She asked me if I could move closer to her and place my hand on her leg. I did as she asked and watched her breathing, affect, and movement, using my voice to let her know I was in the room with her, keeping a dual focus of awareness in the present as she processed a past trauma. The first time we had attempted to process this scene, she was numb; this time, her affect indicated that we were in the trauma network.

After a long set of BLS, Brooke took a deep breath and opened her eyes.

CLIENT: I see myself squatting on the floor by my father's casket, crying hysterically. I am saying that I cannot believe he is gone. I need my father; I need to know he is somehow still with me.

THERAPIST: *Would you like to imagine that?*

Brooke nodded her head, and I turned on the pulsers. >>>>>> She immediately calmed and began smiling and sharing the experience verbally as she processed with her eyes closed.

CLIENT: I can feel him here with me. My dad is hugging me, kissing me on the forehead, and rocking me back and forth. It starts out as comforting, but it is not comforting now because I cannot remember the smell of my father or the sound of his voice. I fade in and out of feeling his presence.

I suspected the fading in and out was related to Brooke's tendency to dissociate. Brooke appeared to be looping and stuck; I offered an interweave to get the processing back on track.

THERAPIST: *I am confused. Do you need to smell your father or hear his voice to remember him?*

CLIENT: No. It's weird. No, I do not.

THERAPIST: *Go with that.* >>>>>>

Initially, her eyes were moving frantically back and forth, and her brow was furrowed. Then, she began smiling, bouncing lightly in her chair like a child.

CLIENT: I know what his hair feels like when he hugs me. I can feel his soft, fine hair as if it is under my hands right now.

THERAPIST: *Go with that.* >>>>>>
CLIENT: My dad let me play with his hair when I was little.

Sensory experiences spontaneously emerged.

CLIENT: I can see us on the floor playing. I see his belly, it was a little larger, and I remember what it feels like to cuddle up to him. My dad is warm.

THERAPIST: *Go with that.* >>>>>>
CLIENT: I see myself and my sister in my father's car on the way to dance lessons. I remember he always had cherry Life Savers. Oh, my God, this is a smell I remember!

THERAPIST: *Yes, yes. Go with that.* >>>>>>
CLIENT: Now I am playing in my father's walk-in closet. He let me and my sister play in his closet and rummage through his clothing.

Brooke began smiling ear to ear.

CLIENT: I am digging through his clothes, and I can smell him. His clothes smell like him. I know he is here with me. I can feel him here with me.

She narrated as she continued to process.

CLIENT: I am back at the scene at the casket, but now my father is comforting me. I feel the numbness completely leaving my body like a rush of warm air. I feel here, fully present. My father hugs me; he is kissing me on the forehead and gently rocking me back and forth. He is telling me that he is all right. I am telling him that I am so sorry for not coming home to see him in the hospital. He cuts me off, saying he is proud of me for studying abroad, and that *he* told the family not to tell me he was in the hospital. He tells me it is not my fault and that he loves me. Oh, my God, I can hear his voice exactly as it sounded. My father looks me right in the eye and says, "Brooke, it is time to focus on *you.*"

Brooke opened her eyes and smiled, stating that she saw the words "focus on you" in the air like they were floating in the room.

THERAPIST: *Go with that.*

CLIENT: I can hear my dad lecturing me. I like hearing him lecture me. He is calling me by my childhood nickname. My father is telling me, "Benji, you are going down the same road that I did," and he says, "Let's not do that." My father hugs me and tells me that I need to let him go. I tell him that I am afraid, and I don't want to let him go. He gives me a big hug, tells me he loves me and starts to fade in the distance. I yell to him, "I love you, too, Dad," then it all goes blank, but not scary blank like before.

THERAPIST: *When you go back to the scene we started with, what do you notice?*

CLIENT: I cannot believe it. It feels so distant. I finally got to say goodbye. I feel calm and relaxed.

THERAPIST: *What do believe about yourself now?*

CLIENT: I believe that I *do* matter, and my health and life matter.

We paired the belief "I *do* matter" with the scene, then added BLS to integrate the new information that Brooke had learned about herself in this session. I asked Brooke if she would like to go back to her Peaceful Place, and she reported that she did not need to. I instructed her to write down any new insights or "aha" moments and bring them to the next session and reminded her that the processing might continue after the session. We briefly discussed Brooke's plans for after the session as a means of bringing her back to the now and my office.

Brooke returned in one week for her next session. She reported feeling less anxious and more present in her body. I checked in, asking Brooke whether anything came up when she thought about the scene we had worked on the previous week. She reported that she felt she had her dad back. Then, smiling broadly, she reported, "I even tapped him in as a protector, and it felt amazing knowing that he was with me and that I had lost him in the flesh, but not in spirit."

I asked Brooke if she wanted to add him to our team by tapping him in at the office, and Brooke indicated that there was no need to do so because he was already on the team. Brooke kept a journal during the week, noting that she was familiar with the feeling we identified as dissociation in the initial EMDR session. "It is the same sense I get when I am standing at the refrigerator right before I binge, which then leads to withholding my insulin." Brooke identified this dissociated state on her own; this was evidence that she was developing new insights.

Though there had been some improvement in her diabulimia, Brooke continued to binge and withhold her insulin regularly. I decided to utilize the Bridging Technique to explore further possible links to the triggers to binge. First, we tapped in her team of resources, which now included her father as a Protective Figure. I then asked her about her most recent episode of bingeing. Brooke reported that it had happened the night before, right before she was supposed to go meet friends for dinner.

THERAPIST: *Brooke, close your eyes and go inside. Go to moments before the moment you binged and tell me what you notice. What picture represents the worst part?*

CLIENT: I am standing alone at the refrigerator with the door open, looking for what I can binge on, paralyzed by the fear that my friends will judge me if I overeat at dinner.

THERAPIST: *What emotions do you feel?*

CLIENT: Sadness, fear, and frustration.

THERAPIST: *What do you feel in your body?*

CLIENT: Chest is tight, my arms feel tight, and then I go numb.

THERAPIST: *What do you believe about yourself?*

CLIENT: I can't handle this. I am out of control.

Brooke is breathing heavily and has an urgent look on her face.

THERAPIST: *Trace it back in time, as far back as you can. Let whatever comes up, come up without censoring it.*

Brooke quickly arrived at the scene that became our new EMDR target.

CLIENT: I am 10 years old. I just got home from school. I am all alone. Mom is at work; my sister is at soccer practice, and Dad doesn't live with us anymore. I am supposed to check blood sugar before I eat. I hate it. The phone rings. It's my dad calling to see if I am okay. I tell him I miss him and beg him to come home—to give Mom and us another chance. He gets mad and hangs up on me. I am home all alone and no one cares.

THERAPIST: *What picture represents the worst part of that memory?*

CLIENT: The anger in my dad's voice before he hung up on me.

THERAPIST: *What emotions do you feel?*

CLIENT: Sadness and frustration.

THERAPIST: *What do you notice in your body?*

CLIENT: I feel like a 100-pound weight is on my chest and I feel cold.

THERAPIST: *What do you believe about yourself?*

CLIENT: I am bad.

We began the EMDR processing of the childhood memory by turning on the pulsers. I observed closely as Brooke's breathing went from short and shallow to a long inhalation followed by a long exhalation. Brooke then opened her eyes, signaling me to stop the BLS.

THERAPIST: *What is happening now?*

CLIENT: I am shoving food in my face as fast as I can. I am mad at myself and telling myself that if I did not have diabetes, my parents wouldn't fight and they would still be married. I wouldn't be at home alone; I would be playing soccer or at a friend's house. I am so angry.

THERAPIST: *Go with that.* >>>>>>

Brooke had an entire network of childhood memories of benign neglect. Even though her parents provided for all of her basic needs, they were unable to give Brooke quality time and show her the love she needed to develop healthy, loving attachments. By bridging back to a childhood memory, we were able to get to the root of the trigger. In EMDR, when we clear the first or worst experience, it often generalizes up the neural network, clearing other traumatic events and linking in the developmental repair.

After a long set of BLS, Brooke opened her eyes to report.

CLIENT: This is ridiculous. How do they expect a kid to know how to take care of herself? And I don't mean just diabetes, I mean all of it. No wonder I feel so out of control and helpless.

THERAPIST: *Go with that.* >>>>>>

Brooke soon opened her eyes; she was tearful and agitated.

CLIENT: I feel so stuck.

I wanted to get located in time and place to see if the scene had moved at all, so I asked Brooke how old she was in the scene she was seeing. Brooke reported that she was still looping in the 10-year-old scene with her father hanging up on her. I used a Resource Interweave to get the child part out of distress and the processing back on track.

THERAPIST: *What does that little girl need?*

CLIENT: I need someone to be with me, help me, and explain to me what is happening.

THERAPIST: *Who can do that?*

CLIENT: My grandmother can.

THERAPIST: *Imagine that.* >>>>>>

Brooke began to narrate in a childlike voice as she processed with the BLS.

CLIENT: My grandmother comes and tells me that it is not my fault that my parents got divorced. She tells me that my parents still love me very much—they just don't love each other anymore. I am telling my grandmother that it is my fault because I have diabetes. My grandmother hugs me and says, "Benji, don't be silly, diabetes doesn't cause divorce. Sometimes grownups just can't live together anymore." She rubs the top of my head and offers to make me an after-school snack. Grandmother stays with me until my mother gets home and they make a plan so that I don't have to be alone after school anymore. Wow, now the nurse and the nanny are coming in to help my mom, too.

Brooke processed silently for a while longer and then opened her eyes.

CLIENT: Of course it wasn't my fault. I was just a kid.

THERAPIST: *Go with that.* >>>>>>

CLIENT: It is completely different now that I have my resources with me. I am fine. There is nothing left.

Brooke reported her level of distress between 0 and 1. When I asked her what she believed about herself now, Brooke replied, "I am in control, and I have an entire team who is available to help me . . . I just have to ask." This positive cognition was linked with the scene and then integrated further with BLS. When Brooke scanned her body, she reported that it felt warm, but calm and relaxed.

I then checked the scene at the refrigerator. Brooke said that it felt distant, and she no longer felt paralyzed. I asked Brooke if she could imagine a time in the future where she asked for what she needed. We added BLS as Brooke imagined talking with her nutritionist about how to better plan for dining out. Brooke was ecstatic and couldn't wait to try out this new plan.

When Brooke returned for the next session, she was excited to report that she had followed through with the nutritionist and made a plan for dining out. Still, she'd had two episodes of bingeing. Brooke identified that when she felt lonely or frustrated, she often felt the urge to binge.

"I'll go and just stand in front of the refrigerator, and then, the next thing I know, I have eaten everything in sight," she told me. "Then, of course, I manipulate my insulin so that I will be in a state of ketoacidosis. I see the pattern; why can't I break it?"

I hypothesized that the *urge* to binge, the *high* of withholding her insulin, and the *consequences* of the resulting DK from diabulimia were not linking up in her brain. I postulated that Brooke's continued bingeing was not denial, but rather a lack of integration. All Brooke seemed to remember after a binge was the pleasure associated with losing weight. I decided to utilize the Connecting the Consequences Protocol.

BLS links networks. Once the consequences get linked in, a natural aversion often develops.

THERAPIST: *Brooke, close your eyes and go inside. Play the movie from right before you are standing at the refrigerator; imagine the binge, the DK, the anticipated weight loss, and then move on to what comes next: the consequences of neuropathy, foot pain, macular degeneration, hospitalization and any other consequences you can think of. Play the movie forward, adding in the consequences of bingeing and diabulimia. Take your time adding in all of the parts.*

Brooke played the movie with continuous BLS.

CLIENT: This is unbelievable! As I was running the movie, my father comes in. Is that okay?
THERAPIST: *Would you like him there?*
CLIENT: YES! I am so tired of doing this all alone!

We continued playing the movie forward with BLS, linking the networks that were not previously linked.

CLIENT: He is taking me back to my diabulimia, showing me the symptoms of his diabetes that I have never noticed before. He shows me that when he was lying in bed so sick and vomiting, it was not the flu, it was ketoacidosis. He shows me that when he was too tired to walk, and it looked like he was walking on eggshells, that he couldn't walk because of his neuropathy. He shows me his binges and poor diabetes management and how it ultimately leads to his death.

THERAPIST: *What do you notice about that?*

CLIENT (CRYING): This is the first time that I can recognize the direct consequences of my own bingeing. Thank you, Dad.

I wanted to reinforce further the negative impact of diabulimia by linking the *urge* to binge and the *high* of the diabulimia with their *consequences*. I encouraged Brooke to continue playing the movie forward.

CLIENT: My dad is with me, lovingly showing me at each turn how my choices make my diabetes worse. He takes me to the moment I decide to withhold insulin, points out his own amputated toes and shows me my feet that I can hardly walk on. He calls me Benji, my childhood nickname, and says "Benji, you do not want to lose those lovely eyes." My dad tells me I am not alone—that he is with me, that death cannot stop him from helping me if I let him.

THERAPIST: *Scan the movie looking for any parts where you feel a charge.*

CLIENT: I feel so loved and taken care of. Like my dad is not only in the movie, but really here in the room with us. There is no charge; I feel relaxed.

THERAPIST: *Would you like to ask your father if there is anything else he would like you to know?*

Brooke closed her eyes and went inside.

CLIENT: He is telling me to let go.

THERAPIST: *Imagine letting go.* >>>>>>

CLIENT: He is telling me to let go of him and focus on myself. I am not sure if I can.

THERAPIST: *Would you like to try?*

CLIENT: Yes, if you will help me.

THERAPIST: *What do you imagine you might need to let go?*

CLIENT: Wait . . . I believe he is with me in death in a way he couldn't be in life. I can imagine letting go of the sick him and having the eternal him as one of my guardian angels.

THERAPIST: *Play the movie forward with this new information.* >>>>>>

CLIENT: I feel sick, but in a good way. Like I am actually getting it. My consequences are neuropathy, hospitalizations, and macular degeneration, and they are pretty crappy. But I feel hopeful because I do not have to die from this. My dad has shown that I will die if I keep this up, but that I have a choice. I do not have to die from this.

THERAPIST: *Brooke, I want you to imagine a huge split screen. On one side, have your father showing the negative consequences of diabulimia; and on the other, have your father showing you the positive consequences if you follow his advice to let him go and practice self-care.* >>>>>>

CLIENT: I can try to do that. One side I see myself exercising, eating better, and taking my insulin. My dad is supporting me when I follow his positive advice. On the other side I see myself losing my toes and eyesight if I continue down my current path.

THERAPIST: *Which do you choose?*

CLIENT: I want to choose the healthy path, but I feel some resistance.

I could have gone with the resistance, but I wanted to reinforce that the adult Brooke could ask for and receive the help she needed. Therefore, I opted to use a Resource Interweave.

THERAPIST: *Who can help you with the resistance?*

CLIENT: My father and my medical support team.

THERAPIST: *Play the movie forward with your medical support team and father helping you.* >>>>>>

CLIENT: My support team tells me that I can do this, and I do not have to do it alone. My father tells me he will watch over me and be my guide. I see myself exercising, eating better, and taking my insulin. It is odd; I actually feel good. I don't feel sick now. Like it is possible that I could have a life. I might not have to die an early death from this.

THERAPIST: *Okay, let's play the movie one more time from right before the binge. What do you notice?*

CLIENT: I get nothing. It feels like I am just a normal person looking in the refrigerator. I do not feel numb at all. I see all of the food, and I know that I can have most of what I want in moderation as long as I take my insulin as prescribed.

THERAPIST: *Would you like to imagine yourself in the future with this new information?*

CLIENT: I see myself going out socially, making better choices, taking my insulin, and participating in my life.

At our next session, I checked in with Brooke about her week. She reported that she had several moments when she thought about participating in diabulimia but was able to avoid it with the use of her resources. Brooke also indicated that every time she had thought about withholding her insulin, she had thought of her dad and that she did not have to die from diabetes. Brooke then reluctantly reported that though she was able to stave off the behavior of purging with diabulimia by withholding her insulin, she had still noticed the urge to purge. I pointed out to Brooke that she did not act on the urge, which is new. Brooke brought this new information fully into her awareness, and we tapped it in with BLS.

I then asked Brooke to bring up the urge to withhold insulin now, as strongly as she could. She reported the urge was significantly less since our last session, but that she feared it would come back. I asked her to rate the urge to use on a scale of 0 to 10, where 0 was no urge and 10 was the strongest urge possible. She reported it as a 3. I asked her what the 3 was about, and Brooke says that she needed to see the consequences on her own, without her father showing her.

I asked Brooke to run the movie without her dad in it, looking for any charge. Brooke added in the consequences unique to her situation and diabulimia, including her anorexic body and the sexual side effects. Brooke reported that she needed to have privacy from her father when linking in the consequences that have to do with her sexual self, and she could not link them in when her dad was present in the movie. I asked Brooke to rate the strength of her current urge to withhold insulin; it was a zero.

I then had Brooke run the movie of a positive future where she was completely free of diabulimia, adding in all of the positive consequences. Brooke saw herself able to walk without a cane, maintaining her eyesight, and with a future love interest. We tapped in the positive future self with BLS, letting it integrate more fully. Over the next several sessions, Brooke reported a marked decrease in symptoms. She was now able to identify the triggers that would start the cycle of diabulimia.

Identifying and developing a plan to cope with triggers is a wonderful relapse prevention tool. Once the primary triggers—loneliness and boredom—were identified, we were able to resource those triggers. Brooke gave a list of qualities including self-confidence, the ability to initiate contact with friends, patience, and self-awareness, and—perhaps the most important quality of all—the capacity to stay present in her body rather than "numb out." We went through each quality. I asked her to identify a time when she experienced the positive feelings or proficiency with the quality and to then tap it in.

Where Brooke was unable to come up with a personal experience, I asked her if she knew anyone who possessed the quality; then we connected with the quality and tapped it in. For example, we tapped in the decrease and near cessation of diabulimia, which was directly related to her ability to stay present and in her body. Brooke began to embody this newly found ability to identify and avert the loneliness without the life-threatening act of diabulimia.

Brooke was learning to manage her diabetes as an adult and stopped withholding her insulin. She quickly experienced many very positive consequences of improved diabetes management. Her health steadily improved, and soon she was able to walk without a cane. Brooke was able to stay out of the hospital and manage her symptoms with her team. Later that year, her endocrinologist wrote a medical release for Brooke to return to college out of state, where she completed her degree.

FOLLOW-UP SESSIONS

Brooke did not return back home after she finished her degree. Our follow-up sessions were conducted on school breaks and her visits home. Her diabulimia turned out to have many far-reaching effects on her health, including the inability to have biological children. We targeted and reprocessed the grief and sadness related to her illness and its impacts. Brooke continued to utilize Resource Tapping as a primary tool for self-regulation and calming.

At 6-month and 1-year follow-ups, Brooke reported no relapses with diabulimia. Our final session was spent reviewing the remarkable progress that Brooke had made during our work together. Lastly, Brooke tapped in self-compassion and acceptance related to the medical consequences that could not be reversed, the progress that she had made, and gratitude for her improved health.

Julie Probus-Schad, LCSW, is an EMDRIA-approved consultant as well as a facilitator and trainer for the Parnell Institute for EMDR. She has facilitated trainings with Laurel Parnell in the United States, Curaçao, Singapore and Malaysia. With 30 years of experience specializing in working with complex and single-incident trauma she uses Attachment-Focused EMDR and other trauma-informed therapies in her work. She has a private practice in Chesterfield, Missouri.

Concluding Thoughts

*Seek the wisdom that will untie your knot. Seek
the path that demands your whole being.*

—RUMI

Working with clients in recovery from addictions is challenging. It is, at times, frustrating—even heartbreaking. It is much easier to treat someone who is already in recovery or who is motivated to change than someone who is ambivalent and still caught up in their addiction. There is no one-size-fits-all solution. We try one thing; it doesn't work; and then we try another.

I've offered many resource tools here for you to add to your tool kit. Explore them. Discover what works best for your client. These resources aren't necessarily used in any sequence. I do think that for most people, beginning with strengthening through the four foundational resources is helpful. If vulnerability is your client's trigger for use, you may begin with the protector resources first. Other triggers suggest a different way in. It is essential that you get to know your client. What does this person need now to help them on their path?

Recovery is a bumpy, circuitous road. There are ups and downs, successes and failures, times of clarity and recovery, and times of relapse. The relationship you have with your clients is very important. You are working together with their healthy self to help them come home to their True Self.

Some people will need residential treatment. They need to experience more support than what can be provided in an outpatient setting. They may need to clean out their systems from the substances and get fully "reset" so that they can make use of what you have to offer them. That being said, all of the tools in this book can be used quite effectively in a residential setting. A good aftercare plan following residential treatment is important to maintain the changes. Many people need connections to a sober community to replace the one that they have relied on for their social contacts.

It is helpful to remember that we are working to rewire old patterns of thoughts, feelings, and behaviors. We want to reinforce new, healthy networks to change the brain and the old ways of living and behaving. This takes time, mindfulness, and compassion for the client and for yourself as the counselor or therapist.

If you would like information on EMDR training that is attachment-focused, as well as EMDR and Resource Tapping workshops, visit the Parnell Institute for EMDR website: www.parnellemdr.com.

I wish you all the best in your healing work.

—Laurel Parnell

Resource Tool Kit

Four Foundational Resources:
  Peaceful Place
  Nurturing Figures
  Protector Figures
  Wise Figures
Resources to Help with Anxiety
  Four Foundational Resources
  Ideal Mother
  Ideal Father
  Inner Sponsor/Mentor
  Inner Support Team
  Spiritual Figures
  Calm and Peaceful Resource Person
  Sacred Place
  Comfort Memories
  Food Memories
  Music and Sound
  Love Resources:
    Circle of Love,
    Memories of Loving and Being Loved,
    Loving-Kindness Meditation
  Images from Nature
  Memories of Being Peaceful
  Body Safe Place
Empowerment Resources
  Protector Figures
  Circle of Protection

Inner Strength
Courage
Music or Sound
Tapping without Imagery, with Encouraging, Supportive Words
Resources to Lift the Spirit
Gratitude
Experiences of Awe and Wonder
Beauty
Joy
Inspiration
Freedom and Expansion
Tools for Strengthening Motivation
Spiritual Resources
Higher Power
Spiritual Figures
Spiritual Experiences
Insights and Life Lessons
Spiritual Teachings
Connecting to Inner Strength
Memories of Inner Strength
Body Postures
Power Figures
Memories of Overcoming Obstacles
Example of Another Person Who Has Overcome Obstacles
Saying No, Setting Boundaries
Information from Various Sources About Maintaining Recovery
Tapping-in Coping Strategies for Recovery
Resources for Restoring a Sense of Inner Goodness
Love Resources
Loved Ones
Circle of Love
Loving-Kindness Meditation
Inner Child Loving-Kindness Meditation
More Resources for Enhancing Motivation
Linking in Resources to Accomplish Goals
Inner Sponsor
Sober, Healthy Self

Role Models
Recovery Support Dream Team
Memories of Being Successful
Strengthening Successes
Reasons for Recovery
Imagining Your Goals Actualized

Acknowledgments

There are many people to thank and acknowledge for the creation of this book. It is hard to tease out what I learned from whom, as we all learn from each other, and from those who came before us. My spiritual teachers, Lama Thubten Yeshe, Jean Klein, Suzanne Segal, the Dalai Lama, and Jack Kornfield taught me to delve deep inside, let go of all concepts and beliefs and discover for myself what is true. I learned that who we are is not defined by our actions, beliefs, or how we appear and that the power of imagination can be used to create change and facilitate healing.

Thank you to Daniel Siegel and Bessel van der Kolk for educating me about how our brains work and the potential for emotional healing. My deepest appreciation goes to Francine Shapiro for discovering the power of bilateral stimulation and the courage to bring the strange, paradigm-shifting EMDR therapy out into the world, and to Jamie Marich, A. J. Popky, and Robert Miller for their important contributions to EMDR and the treatment of addictions.

This book could never have been written without the clients with whom I have worked over the years in my practice as a psychologist. Through our therapy I was able to discover what helped and what didn't and was then able to share what I learned with others. I also want to thank the consultees who have presented their cases to me and tried out some of the things I suggested to them. Through them I was also able to more fully refine and develop many of the Resource Tapping protocols presented in this book. Special thanks to Mary McKenna and Rand Faulkner for the cases they so beautifully shared.

Big, big thank you to my dear friends, colleagues, and talented EMDR therapists Constance Kaplan, Elena Felder, and Julie Probus-Schad, all of whom provided excellent, innovative, clinically astute treatment to challenging clients with addictions. Their chapters helped bring to life the clinical techniques and protocols presented in the earlier part of the book. I am proud of them all. A special thank you to Elena Felder for a thorough editing of the manuscript. Her careful reading and perceptive comments helped me weave in material that I had missed, significantly improving the book.

Thank you to Melissa Block, my copyeditor for the first edition of the book, who understood what I was writing and why I was writing it, bringing her considerable skill to the undertaking.

Special appreciation goes to C. J. Hayden, whose keen intelligence, vast business experience, and broad contacts have provided me the support to develop the Parnell Institute for EMDR and connect me with the resources needed to complete this book. Thank you to my staff: Angela Ruggiero, online business manager, and Angee Robertson, virtual assistant, who are both proficient and delightful to work with.

I am deeply grateful to my husband, Pierre Antoine Blais, whose love sustains and nourishes me, to my sons, Catono Perez and Etienne Perez-Parnell, and delightful granddaughter, Katya Laurel Kudrya. Thank you.

Notes

1. Goodman, A. (2008). Neurobiology of addiction. An integrative review. *Biochem Pharmacol,75*(1), 266–322. Footnoted material on page 16 of article.

2. Goodman, A. (2008). Neurobiology of addiction. An integrative review. *Biochem Pharmacol, 75*(1), 266–322. Footnoted material on page 24 of article.

3. Goodman, A. (2008). Neurobiology of addiction. An integrative review. *Biochem Pharmacol, 75*(1), 266–322. See footnoted material on page 24 of article.

4. Parnell, L. (2013). *Attachment-Focused EMDR: Healing Relational Trauma.* New York: W.W. Norton.

5. Parnell, L. (2008). *Tapping In: A Step-By-Step Guide to Activating Your Healing Resources Through Bilateral Stimulation.* Boulder: Sounds True.

6. *Hebb, D.O. (1949). The Organization of Behavior. New York: Wiley & Sons.*

7. Kessler R.C., Berglund P., Demler O., Jin R., Merikangas K.R., Walters E.E. (2005). Lifetime prevalence and age-of-onset distributions of DSM-IV disorders in the National Comorbidity Survey Replication. *Archives of General Psychiatry, 62*(6), 593–602. doi: 10.1001/archpsyc.62.6.593.

   Kessler R., Sonnega A., Bromet E., Hughes M., Nelson C. (1995). Posttraumatic stress disorder in the National Comorbidity Survey. *Archives of General Psychiatry, 52*(12), 1048–1060. doi: 10.1001/archpsyc .1995.03950240066012.

   Pietrzak R.H., Goldstein R.B., Southwick S.M., Grant B.F. (2011). Prevalence and Axis I comorbidity of full and partial posttraumatic stress disorder in the United States: Results from Wave 2 of the National Epidemiologic Survey on Alcohol and Related Conditions. *Journal of Anxiety Disorders, 25*, 456–465. doi: 10.1016/j.janxdis.2010.11.010.

8. Hoge C.W., Castro C.A., Messer S.C., McGurk D., Cotting D.I., Koffman R.L. (2004). Combat duty in Iraq and Afghanistan, mental health problems,

and barriers to care. *New England Journal of Medicine, 351*(1), 13–22. doi: 10.1056/NEJMoa040603.

Petrakis I.L., Rosenheck R., Desai R. (2011). Substance use comorbidity among Veterans with posttraumatic stress disorder and other psychiatric illness. The American Journal on Addictions, 20,185–189. doi: 10.1111/j.1521-0391.2011.00126.x.

Centers for Disease Control Vietnam Experience Study. (1988). Health status of Vietnam veterans: I. Psychosocial characteristics. Journal of the American Medical Association, *259,* 2701–2707. doi: 10.1001/jama.1988.03720180027028.

9. Carter, A. C., Capone, C., & Short, E. E. (2011). Co-occurring Posttraumatic Stress Disorder and Alcohol Use Disorders in Veteran Populations. *Journal of dual diagnosis, 7*(4), 285–299. doi:10.1080/15504263.2011.620453

10. Wilsnack, S.C., Vogeltanz, N.D., Klassen, A.D., & Harris, T.R. (1997). Childhood sexual abuse and women's substance abuse: national survey findings. *Journal of Studies on Alcohol, 58*(3), 264–271

11. Khoury, L., Tang, Y. L., Bradley, B., Cubells, J. F., & Ressler, K. J. (2010). Substance use, childhood traumatic experience, and Posttraumatic Stress Disorder in an urban civilian population. *Depression and Anxiety, 27*(12), 1077–1086.

12. Huang, H., Gundapuneedi, T., & Rao, U. (2012). White matter disruptions in adolescents exposed to childhood maltreatment and vulnerability to psychopathology. *Neuropsychopharmacology, 37,* 2693–2701.

13. Scarinici, I. C., McDonald-Haile, J., Bradley, L. A., & Richter, J. E. (1994). Altered pain perception and psychosocial features among women with gastrointestinal disorders and history of abuse: A preliminary model. *American Journal of Medicine, 97*(8), 108–118.

14. McGovern, M. P., & Stecker, T. Co-occurring PTSD and substance use disorders. *Journal of Dual Diagnosis.* Published online on Nov. 10, 2011; available at http://www.tandfonline.com/toc/wjdd20/7/4.

15. Marich, J. (2010). Eye movement desensitization and reprocessing in addiction continuing care: A phenomenological study of women in recovery. *Psychology of Addictive Behavior, 24*(3), 498–507.

16. Covington, S. S. (2008). Women and addiction: A trauma-informed approach. *Journal of Psychoactive Drugs*, SARC Suppl. 5, 377–385.

17. Hase, M., Schallmayer, S., & Sack, M. (2008). EMDR reprocessing of the addiction memory: Pretreatment, posttreatment, and 1-month follow-up.

Journal of EMDR Practice and Research, 2(3), 179–179(10). Cited material on page 170 of article.

18. See https://overcomingpain.com.

19. See *Tapping In*, Parnell, 2008.

20. Watkins, J. G. (1971). The affect bridge: A hypnoanalytic technique. *International Journal of Clinical and Experimental Hypnosis, 19*(1), 21–27.

21. Parnell, L. (2007). *A Therapist's Guide to EMDR.* New York: W.W. Norton.

22. See *Attachment-Focused EMDR*, Parnell, 2013.

23. See *Attachment-Focused EMDR*, Parnell, 2013.

24. Stickgold, R. (2002). EMDR: A putative neurobiological mechanism of action. *Journal of Clinical Psychology*, 58, 61-75.

    Propper, R., Pierce, J.P., Geisler, M.W., Christman, S.D., & Bellorado, N. (2007). Effect of bilateral eye movements on frontal interhemispheric gamma EEG coherence: Implications for EMDR therapy. *Journal of Nervous and Mental Disease, 195*, 785–788.

    Amano, T., & Toichi, M. (2016). The Role of Alternating Bilateral Stimulation in Establishing Positive Cognition in EMDR Therapy: A Multi-Channel Near-Infrared Spectroscopy Study. *PloS one, 11*(10), e0162735. doi:10.1371/journal.pone.0162735

    Landin-Romero, R., Moreno-Alcazar, A., Pagani, M., & Amann, B. L. (2018). How does eye movement desensitization and reprocessing therapy work?: A systematic review on suggested mechanisms of action. *Frontiers in Psychology, 9*, 1395. doi:10.3389/fpsyg.2018.01395

    Renssen, M. (2002). Traumatherapie na verkeersongevallen. Eye Movement Desensitization and Reprocessing (EMDR) bij verkeersslachtoffers. Academisch proefschrift Vrije Universiteit Amsterdam.

25. See *Attachment-Focused EMDR*, Parnell, 2013.

26. From *Tapping In*, Parnell, 2008.

27. Parnell, 1999, 2007, 2008, 2013.

28. Grant, F., Stinson, F., & Dawson, D., et al. (2004). Prevalence and co-occurrence of substance use disorders and independent mood and anxiety disorders: Results from the National Epidemiologic Survey on Alcohol and Related Conditions. *Arch Gen Psychiatry, 61*(8), 807–816.

29. van Dam, D., Vedel, E., Ehring, T., & Emmelkamp, P. M. (2012). Psychological treatments for concurrent post-traumatic stress disorder and substance abuse disorder: A systematic review. *Clinical Psychology Review, 32*, 202–214.

30. Mahfoud, Y., Talih, F., Streem, D., & Budur, K. (2009). Sleep disorders in substance abusers: How common are they? *Psychiatry, 6*(9), 38–42.

31. See *Attachment-Focused EMDR,* Parnell, 2013.

32. From *Attachment-Focused EMDR,* Parnell, 2013.

33. Parnell, 2013.

34. Grant, F., Stinson, F., and Dawson, D., et al. (2004) Prevalence and co-occurrence of substance use disorders and independent mood and anxiety disorders: Results from the National Epidemiologic Survey on Alcohol and Related Conditions. *Arch Gen Psychiatry, 61*(8), 807–816.

35. Hendrickson, E., Schmal, M., & Ekleberry, S. (2004). *Treating co-occurring disorders: A handbook for mental health and substance abuse professionals.* Binghamton, NY: Haworth Press.

36. U.S. Department of Health & Human Services. National Epidemiologic Survey on Alcohol and Related Conditions (2006).

37. Cornelius, M. D., Lebow, H. A., & Day, N. L. (1997). Attitudes and knowledge about drinking: Relationships with drinking behavior among pregnant teenagers. *Journal of Drug Education, 27*(3), 231–243.

38. Emmons, R.A. (2007). *Thanks!: How practicing gratitude can make you happier.* New York: Houghton Mifflin Harcourt. Pg. 4.

39. Emmons, R. A., & McCullough, M. E. (2003). Counting blessings versus burdens: An experimental investigation of gratitude and subjective well-being in daily life. *Journal of Personality and Social Psychology, 84,* 377–389. doi: 10.1037/0022- 3514.84.2.377

40. Lyubomirsky, S., & Layous, K. (2013). How do simple positive activities increase well-being? *Current Directions in Psychological Science, 22,* 57–62. doi: 10.1177/0963721412469809

41. Parnell, 1999, 2007, 2008, 2013.

42. Klein, J. (1988).*Who am I?* Santa Barbara: Elements Books.

43. Here, we are not referring to clients with dissociative identity disorder (DID).

44. Popky, A. J. (2005). DeTUR, an urge reduction protocol for addictions and dysfunctional behaviors. In R. Shapiro (Ed.), *EMDR solutions: Pathways to healing* (pp. 167–188). New York: W. W. Norton.

45. Miller, R. (2012). Treatment of behavioral addictions using the feeling-state addiction protocol: A multiple baseline study. *Journal of EMDR Practice and Research, 6*(4), 159–169.

46. Watkins, J. G. (1971). The affect bridge: A hypnoanalytic technique. *International Journal of Clinical and Experimental Hypnosis, 19*(1), 21–27.

47. Parnell, 2007.

48. Parnell, 2013.
49. Diabetic Ketoacidosis Mayo Clinic. (n.d.). Retrieved from http://www
    .mayoclinic.org/diseases-conditions/diabetic-ketoacidosis/basics/define
50. Diabulimia | National Eating Disorders Association. (n.d.). Retrieved from
    https://www.nationaleatingdisorders.org/diabulimia-5

Index

About the Author

Laurel Parnell, Ph.D., is a clinical psychologist and director of the Parnell Institute for EMDR. One of the world's leading experts on Eye Movement Desensitization and Reprocessing (EMDR), she is the originator of the EMDR-related therapies, Attachment-Focused EMDR and Resource Tapping. An EMDR pioneer and innovator, Dr. Parnell has immersed herself in the practice and development of EMDR since 1991. Dr. Parnell brings a client-centered, attachment-focused approach to the work that emphasizes the importance of a compassionate, safe, therapeutic relationship and the adaptation of protocols and procedures according to the needs of the individual client. Dr. Parnell has served on the faculty of the California Institute for Integral Studies and John F. Kennedy University. She is the author of several books on EMDR, including *Attachment-Focused EMDR: Healing Relational Trauma, A Therapist's Guide to EMDR,* and *Tapping In.* Considered a master clinician, she has produced several videos of live EMDR sessions with clients that demonstrate her work as well as home study courses of her workshops on EMDR, Rewiring the Addicted Brain, and Attachment-Focused EMDR. Dr. Parnell keynotes conferences, trains clinicians in EMDR, and teaches workshops internationally on Resource Tapping, Attachment-Focused EMDR, and the treatment of addictions. Learn more about Laurel Parnell at www.parnellemdr.com.